D1248855

PHILOSOPHY IN AMERICA

PHILOSOPHY IN AMERICA

Essays

William P. Alston
Bruce Aune
S. F. Barker
Stanley Cavell
Thompson Clarke
Marshall Cohen
Joel Feinberg
Jerry A. Fodor
Charles D. Parsons
Alvin Plantinga
John Searle
Abner Shimony
Fred Sommers
Judith Jarvis Thomson

Edited by
MAX BLACK

CORNELL UNIVERSITY PRESS
ITHACA : NEW YORK

FIRST PUBLISHED IN THE UNITED STATES OF AMERICA, 1965
CORNELL UNIVERSITY PRESS

Second printing, 1967

Library of Congress Catalog Card Number 65–15046

PRINTED IN UNITED STATES OF AMERICA

PREFACE

In assembling the following specimens of work in progress, I have tried to exclude philosophers whose writings are well known on both sides of the Atlantic. The original papers here assembled are probably as representative in their styles, methods, and preoccupations, as could reasonably be expected. The various problems here discussed seem to me both important and unsolved: if others are stimulated to make further progress in solving them, the main purpose of this collection will have been achieved.

I am grateful to the many philosophers who supplied me with names of junior colleagues who might be eligible for inclusion (over 160 of them) and even more so to the writers who agreed to submit original work with no better than an even chance of ultimate acceptance.

Ithaca, New York
March 1964

MAX BLACK

CONTENTS

PHILOSOPHY IN AMERICA

I

EXPRESSING

by WILLIAM P. ALSTON

Professor of Philosophy, University of Michigan

The family of linguistic acts grouped under the term 'express'—expressing interest, conviction, sympathy, approval, intention, delight, enthusiasm, indignation, annoyance, disgust, appreciation, determination, belief, and so forth, has figured heavily in recent philosophical discussion. But most of these discussions have been seriously maimed through proceeding, explicitly or implicitly, on the basis of quite inadequate notions of what it is to express something in language. An examination of some of these inadequacies will point the way to a more adequate analysis.

I

Moral philosophers who are themselves 'emotivists', or who are discussing that position, will often make a sharp distinction between expressing a certain feeling or attitude, and asserting (stating, saying, telling someone) that one has a certain feeling or attitude. And it is said that if we maintain that moral judgements are *expressions* of attitudes or feelings we will get a very different ethical theory from the one we get if we maintain that moral judgements are *assertions* that one has certain attitudes or feelings. Consider the following passages from A. J. Ayer's *Language, Truth, and Logic.*[1]

For in saying that a certain type of action is right or wrong, I am not making any factual statement, not even a statement about my own state of mind. I am merely expressing certain moral sentiments. (107)

On our theory . . . in saying that tolerance was a virtue, I should not be making any statement about my own feelings or about

[1] Second edition, London 1946.

anything else. I should simply be evincing my feelings, which is not at all the same thing as saying that I have them. (109)

For whereas the subjectivist holds that ethical statements actually assert the existence of certain feelings, we hold that ethical statements are expressions and excitants of feeling which do not necessarily involve any assertions. (109)

At first glance this looks clear enough. But the stark lines of the contrast begin to soften when we ask what Ayer would take as a clear case of asserting that I have a certain feeling or attitude. I suppose that if I uttered any of the following sentences in normal circumstances, we would have clear cases of such assertions.

I am very enthusiastic about your plan.
That interests me very much.
I am disgusted.
You have my whole-hearted approval.
That annoys me no end.

And yet in all these cases it would be perfectly correct to report what went on by using 'express', that is, by saying that *S* (speaker) expressed his enthusiasm for *H*'s (hearer's) plan, that *S* expressed his interest in *X*, that *S* expressed his disgust with *X*. I can express my enthusiasm for your plan just as well by saying 'I'm very enthusiastic about your plan', as I can by saying 'What a tremendous plan!', 'Wonderful', or 'Great!' I can express disgust at *X* just as well by saying 'I'm disgusted', as by saying 'How revolting!', or 'Ugh'. I can express approval as well by saying 'I completely approve of what you are doing' as I can by saying 'Swell', or 'Good show'. And I can express annoyance as well by saying 'That annoys me no end' as by saying 'Damn'.

This shows that expressing and asserting are not mutually exclusive in the way commonly supposed. Of course we can have one without the other. For example, when we use interjections like 'Damn', 'Ugh', or 'Bully', we are expressing annoyance, disgust, or enthusiasm but not saying that we are annoyed, disgusted, or enthusiastic. But examples like those in the preceding paragraph show that in a large proportion of the cases in which one can be said to have asserted that one has a certain feeling, what went on can equally well be reported by saying that one expressed this feeling, and vice versa.

Why has this point been missed so consistently? I suspect that it is largely because philosophers have thought of expressing feelings and attitudes as something which is primarily done by cries, groans, squeals, writhings, looks, and tones of voice. It is these kinds of behaviour which are taken as paradigmatic. A linguistic performance could be regarded as expression only if it were very similar to them. The utterance of interjections but not the utterance of declarative sentences was thought to qualify on these grounds. It seems to me that this often unspoken but none the less influential conviction—that saying 'Ugh' is essentially the same thing as having a certain look on the face, while saying 'I'm disgusted' is something fundamentally different—constitutes the deepest root of the misconceptions we are seeking to remove. As against this conviction I wish to argue (1) that squeals, looks, and tones of voice do not express feelings in anything like the sense in which they are expressed by interjections;[1] (2) that it is in just the same sense of 'express' that a feeling is expressed by an interjection and by a declarative sentence in the first person present tense; (3) that there are only minor differences between expressing a feeling (linguistically) and asserting that one has it.

II

I say to you 'When I approached Jones on the matter, he expressed real enthusiasm for my plan'. You ask 'What did he say, exactly?', and I reply, 'Oh, he didn't say anything about it, but there was a definite glow in his eyes while I was talking'. It is clear that I misrepresented the situation when I said that Jones *expressed* enthusiasm for my plan. One does not express enthusiasm for something by throwing his hat in the air, dancing a jig, emitting squeals of delight, or 'lighting up' one's eyes. If the only reaction to a suggestion is of this character, one might be said to have shown, demonstrated, evinced,[2] or betrayed enthusiasm, but not to have *expressed* it. Again, if my only response to your helping me carry a heavy box was a gracious smile, I would not be said to have expressed appreciation for your help, though I might be said to

[1] This thesis is subject to a qualification which will be made explicit later. See p. 27.

[2] Note Ayer's implicit equation of evincing and expressing in the quotation on pages 15–16.

have shown that I appreciated it. In fact I might well be taken to task for not having expressed appreciation.

These examples suggest that there is a fundamental difference between *expressing* a feeling by saying something (interjectional or declarative), and showing, demonstrating, or manifesting a feeling by a 'facial expression'. To be sure, it would be an act of folly to place too much reliance on the word 'express' in this connection. We can, in cases of this sort, speak of facial expressions and the like as expressing something or other. Thus: 'Her face expressed great determination'; 'His every movement expressed his indignation at what was going on'. But note that in these cases we would not go from this to saying '*She* expressed great determination' and '*He* expressed his indignation at what was going on'. The presence of a certain facial expression or a certain demeanour is not a sufficient ground for saying that *the person* expressed determination or indignation, while having said something of an appropriate sort would be. If we are going to infer anything about what the person did from 'Her face expressed great determination', it will be that she showed, manifested, or displayed great determination.

Even if this is admitted, Ayer and those of like mind might take the position that there is a single sense of 'express' in which feelings are expressed both by looks and interjections—but not by declarative sentences in the first person singular present tense—even though this sense is not the one embodied in the ordinary use of phrases of the form 'He expressed his *F* for *X*'. The position would be that the distinctions marked by the use of this phrase are relatively superficial ones, and that underlying these distinctions is a much more fundamental identity. We are then faced with the question of whether any such sense can be specified.

Writers of this persuasion have done precious little to specify such a sense. Such suggestions as have been made take one or the other of two forms, both of which are adumbrated in the following passage from C. L. Stevenson's *Ethics and Language*.[1]

The emotive meaning of words can best be understood by comparing and contrasting it with the expressiveness of laughs, sighs, groans, and all similar manifestations of the emotions, whether by voice or gesture. It is obvious that these 'natural' expressions are direct behaviouristic symptoms of the emotions or feelings to

[1] New Haven, Conn. 1944.

which they testify. A laugh gives direct 'vent' to the amusement which it accompanies, and does so in such an intimate, inevitable way that if the laugh is checked, some degree of amusement is likely to be checked as well. In much the same way a sigh gives immediate release to sorrow; and a shrug of the shoulders integrally expresses its nonchalant carelessness. . . . Interjections . . . are *like* sighs, shrieks, groans, and the rest in that they can be used to 'give vent' to the emotions or attitudes in much the same way. The word 'hurrah', for instance, serves much the same purpose as any simple cry of enthusiasm, and releases the emotions with equal directness. (37–38)

The use of terms like 'release' and 'vent' suggests, in the absence of any further explanation, a sort of steam engine model, in which expressing is something like the opening of a relief valve. In expressing a feeling by an appropriate gasp, facial contortion, or interjection, one is working off steam, relieving the emotional tension involved in the feeling. But it does not seem that this is what always, or even typically, goes on when one expresses something by an interjection. It is simply not the case that one generally feels less disgust, enthusiasm, annoyance or indignation after expressing it than before. Of course, the above quotation also contains the opposite suggestion that expression serves to nourish or heighten the emotional state rather than to reduce it. But even if we construe expression as either a reduction or a heightening of emotional tension, it will not cover all cases of the verbal expression of feelings and attitudes by interjections. In general, when I express admiration, sympathy, approval, or satisfaction, there is no noticeable emotional tension involved. I am not thinking of insincerity, of expresssing feelings one does not have. The point is that in such cases one is not *expected* to be in a state of emotional tension. The steam engine model is much too crude to fit the facts.

A more promising suggestion might be extracted from the following sentence in the above quotation. 'It is obvious that these "natural" expressions are direct behaviouristic symptoms of the emotions or feelings to which they testify.' One might claim that what is common to all cases of 'expression' is that the agent is doing something which will provide an *indication* (to a properly trained observer) that he is in a certain psychological state. This position is hinted at more broadly in C. K. Ogden's and I. A. Richards' *The Meaning of Meaning*.[1]

> Besides symbolizing a reference, our words also are signs of emotions, attitudes, moods, the temper, interest or set of the mind in which the references occur. They are signs in this fashion because they are grouped with these attitudes and interests in certain looser and tighter contexts. Thus, in speaking a sentence we are giving rise to, as in hearing it we are confronted by, at least two sign-situations. One is interpreted from symbols to reference and so to referent; the other is interpreted from verbal signs to the attitude, mood, interest, purpose, desire, and so forth of the speaker, and thence to the situation, circumstances and conditions in which the utterance is made. (223)

This suggestion is reinforced by a consideration of the etymology of 'express': to press out. We can easily get from this to: to externalize, to exhibit to public view.

There is no doubt that such a concept could be employed. We could use 'express' for anything I do which would be a reliable indication of some feeling or attitude. But although this would give us a sense of 'express' which applies equally to grimaces and interjections, it applies just as clearly to declarative sentences like 'I'm disgusted'. It cannot be doubted that one way of providing someone with a reliable indication of my disgust is to tell him that I am disgusted. But no doubt the way in which saying 'I'm disgusted' is an indication of disgust is very different from the way in which a facial expression is an indication of disgust. Let us explore this difference, and try to determine on which side interjections fall.

III

To say that x is an indication of y is to say that from x one can (fairly safely) infer the existence of y. If this is what is common to all cases of indication, differences of kind will come from differences in the bases on which such inferences are made. Let us ask how one would support an inference from 'I'm disgusted', on the one hand, and from a facial expression on the other, to the person being

[1] New York 1923.

disgusted. To put the matter shortly, in the first case one would appeal to a general practice of *using* the sentence in a certain way, whereas in the second case nothing of the sort is involved; there we would appeal to a *de facto* correlation between a certain kind of facial expression and being disgusted. This latter exhibits basically the same structure as any case of taking one thing to be a natural sign of another, for example taking a certain noise in an engine to be an indication of an improperly seated valve. If it is the case that when people look a certain way they generally feel disgusted with something, then one can take that look as a sign of disgust, whether or not people are generally conscious of looking that way when they are disgusted and whether or not such looks are something which can be consciously controlled. The mere fact of the frequent correlation is sufficient. But in the other case the basis of the inference is not just that it is generally true that when a person says 'I'm disgusted' he is disgusted; although if this were not the case we would undoubtedly stop taking the utterance as a reliable indication of disgust. More fundamentally it is the fact that in the English language community there exists a practice of using the sentence in a certain way.[1] And to say that there exists such a practice is not to say that in fact the sentence is (often) used in that way; it is to say that there are rules in force in the community which assign the sentence to that use.

Within the limits of this paper I cannot give an adequate account of what it is for rules to be in force and what it is for a certain practice to exist. I can only say enough to bring out some crucial differences between a mere *de facto* regularity in behaviour and a rule governing behaviour. A clear case of the former would be my habit of waving my arms whenever I hear a Mozart piano concerto: a clear case of the latter would be the rule of tennis that the server must stand on the side of the court opposite to that into which he is serving. In both cases there is a by-and-large regularity; that there is something more in the latter case but not in the former is

[1] Thus one way of bringing out the difference is this. The fact that a certain look is an *expression* of disgust is constituted by the fact that it can be taken as a reliable indication of disgust. But with 'I'm disgusted' the dependence is in the opposite direction. One takes an utterance of 'I'm disgusted' as an indication of a feeling of disgust only because there exists a practice of using that sentence to express disgust. Hence the last use of 'express' cannot be explicated in terms of the notion of a reliable indication; on the contrary the reliability of the sentence as an indication presupposes its expressive function.

shown by what happens when an exception comes up. A case of my remaining immobile during a Mozart concerto has no particular significance, except as showing that the correlation is not invariable. But when a tennis player stands on the left side when serving into that forecourt, typical reactions ensue on the part of other players, umpires, and spectators. His serve will not be counted as valid, he may be upbraided, the necessity of standing in the proper position may be stressed to him, and so on. This is something more than a mere regularity; it is important for a certain area of social activity that this regularity hold as much as possible. Therefore, various social mechanisms are brought into play to train participants to exhibit the regularity, and deviations from it are met with various sorts of reactions designed to call attention to the deviation and to make it less likely that such deviations occur in the future. These are the hallmarks of the operation of a rule. Although *qua* regularity it may not be invariably true that tennis players *do* stand on the opposite side when serving, still one can say unqualifiedly that there is a rule of tennis which *requires* this in every instance.

It seems clear that the *utterance of 'I'm disgusted'—feeling of disgust* tie-up belongs on the rule side of this contrast. If in a particular case it turns out that the speaker did not in fact feel disgusted, we do not just take this as showing that the correlation is not invariable. We respond in ways which we have seen to be typical of the operation of rules. If the deviation issues from one who is learning the language—an infant or a foreigner—we do what we can to get it across to him that this sentence is not *to be uttered* unless the speaker feels disgusted. If the speaker can be presumed to have already mastered this stretch of the language, we take him to task, more or less sharply depending on the circumstances, for not having his mind on what he was saying, for insincerity, or for whatever else was responsible for the lapse. The way we treat the exceptional cases shows clearly that there is a rule in force in the English language community which stipulates that 'I'm disgusted' is not to be uttered, in certain sorts of situations,[1] unless the speaker feels disgusted.

[1] This qualification is necessary because of the fact that there are situations in which the sentence can be legitimately employed without this condition holding, for example, being ironical and giving examples (as I have just been doing). I am supposing that one can find marks for distinguishing those contexts in which this condition is required (that is, those contexts in which the sentence

It may not be equally clear that the *look on the face—feeling of disgust* connection is a mere regularity, but we shall be forced to that conclusion on reflection. The chief difficulty in separating this from rules lies in the fact that there are cases of deviation from this regularity in which we would upbraid the person for deception. 'Natural expressions' of feelings can be simulated; the art of drama depends on this possibility. And such simulation can be engaged in for purposes of deception. I can contrive to look disgusted when I am not, in order to get you to think that I am. But the possibility of deception does not itself mark a fundamental difference between rules and mere regularities. For I can deceive you into thinking that *x* is present, either by contriving to produce something which is in fact usually present only when *x* is present,[1] or by doing something which is tied by a rule to the presence of *x*. Therefore the possibility of deliberately looking a certain way in order to get you to think that I am disgusted does not itself settle the question as to what kind of connection this is. We have to determine whether any other indications of rules are present. It is evident that none are. Deception is the only sort of lapse from the regularity for which the indication-producer will be taken to task. There is no such thing here as instructing the novice in the proper use of a certain facial expression, or reproving someone for not having his mind sufficiently on what he is doing. Apart from the case of deception, a deviation from the regularity will simply be taken to show that the correlation is not an invariable one, and, perhaps, that we have not made fine enough discriminations between types of facial expression. Apart from the case of deception, when the inference does not work we do not blame the agent for having misused the indications; we 'blame' ourselves for placing too much reliance on a rough generalization. And the possibility of deception is, as we have seen, perfectly compatible with the supposition that it is a mere regularity which is involved.

Reflection on the possibility of deliberately deceptive facial expressions can lead us to a very simple way of showing the difference between our two cases. With facial expressions, deception (or the possibility of deception) comes in when one deliber-

can be legitimately used only in a straightforward way) from those contexts in which it can properly have derivative uses.

[1] This can be done with natural signs which are not themselves aspects of behaviour. I can put a room into disarray in order to get you to think that there has been a fight there.

ately sets about producing a certain look. We ordinarily take the look to be an indication of disgust because we suppose it to be a 'natural', spontaneous manifestation of being disgusted. As soon as we learn that someone is contriving to look that way, we properly suspect deception. Just the opposite is true of 'I'm disgusted'. Here we will take the utterance of the sentence to be a reliable indication of disgust only if we suppose it was done intentionally with the agent realizing what he was doing.[1] If we think the sentence was uttered in a fit of abstraction, its indicative value will be impaired if not altogether lost. We might well take this differential force of deliberateness on the reliability of the indication as a way of distinguishing signs, based on mere regularities, from 'symbols', the significance of which is based on rules.

In calling a facial expression a 'natural sign' of a feeling, we are not implying that it is natural or innate, as opposed to learned or acquired as a result of conditioning. It may well be that correlations between a certain look and a certain state of feeling differ from culture to culture; so that what in our culture would be a look of contempt would be a look of affection among the Kwakiutl. In that case it would seem obvious that the members of a society are somehow conditioned to 'express' their feelings by one facial configuration rather than another. What we are implying is that these regularities in behaviour were not set up through any explicit training, and, more importantly, that deviations from them are not corrected in the way in which deviations from rules are corrected. It is the distinction between the presence or absence of the operation of rules which is crucial, not the distinction between what is innate and what is acquired in the course of one's interaction with one's environment.

IV

We have seen that facial expressions of disgust and saying that one is disgusted are indications (or expressions) of disgust in radically different senses of these terms. It is the contention of philosophers like Ayer that what we do in expressing feelings by uttering inter-

[1] I hope it is not necessary at this hour of the day to point out that I am not using expressions like 'intentionally', 'realizing what he is doing', and 'with his mind on what he is doing' in such a way that they apply only if the overt activity is accompanied by a covert mental commentary or preceded by a conscious act of resolution.

jections is to be classed with the former rather than with the latter. But having come thus far we can see that this is not the case. An interjection like 'Ugh', 'Damn', or 'Bully' is an indication of disgust, annoyance, or approval, by virtue of certain rules holding, just as much as declarative sentences like 'I'm disgusted', 'That annoys me no end', or 'I fully approve of that'. Again we get a crucial test by seeing what happens when we encounter an exception to the regularity. When we discover that someone who said 'Bully!' really has no enthusiasm for what was under discussion, we will respond either by giving him further instruction in the language, reprimanding him for insincerity, or taking him to task for not having his mind on what he is saying, depending on the circumstances of the misuse, just as we do in the case of a deviant utterance of 'I am very enthusiastic about that', and just as we do not do with what we (incorrectly) take to be a look of enthusiasm.

Again, in expressing enthusiasm for your suggestion by saying 'Bully!' (but not in manifesting enthusiasm for your plan by the way I look), I am setting up relations of implication, presupposition, and incompatibility with other linguistic acts, or the products thereof, just as much as if I had said 'I'm very enthusiastic about your idea'. In saying 'Bully!' in those circumstances, I imply that I understood what you said, I presuppose that you have put forward something to which one might react either favourably or unfavourably, and I rule out the possibility that I consider your plan to be completely without merit. For if having said 'Bully!' in those circumstances I were to go on to say 'I didn't understand a word you were saying', or 'Your plan is completely without merit', then there would be something logically, and not just psychologically, odd about what I was doing. Adding these remarks would render my discourse unintelligible in just the same way as that in which it would become unintelligible, if I were to add to 'I'm trying to sell my car', something like 'I don't have a car' or 'My car has already been sold'. In both cases the additions would make it impossible to attach the usual sense to 'Bully' or 'I'm trying to sell my car', and we would be at a loss to understand what was being said. Thus an expression of enthusiasm by use of an interjection has at least some of the logical relations enjoyed by admitted cases of assertions. This is the other side of the coin exhibited in the last paragraph. It is because the use of interjections is made the sort of action it is by the operation of certain rules that the expression thus engendered can have logical relations.

It cannot be denied that there are some respects in which an utterance of 'Damn' is more like a frown than it is like an utterance of 'I am terribly annoyed by that'. In contrast with the latter the interjection is typically more spontaneous, less deliberate, more explosive; it more often carries with it an exhibition of annoyance. But these differences in degree cannot compare in importance with the common features we have just brought out. Interjection-utterances and declarative-sentence-utterances stand together as distinctively linguistic modes of activity. Thus the vernacular is justified in drawing a line between expressing a feeling on the one hand and evincing, betraying or manifesting a feeling on the other, and in drawing the line where it does. For this cut coincides with the distinction between behaviour which is an indication of feeling by being subject to certain rules, and behaviour which is an indication of feeling by virtue of mere regularities; and with the associated difference between indications which enter into logical relations and those which do not. And this is the most important line which can be drawn through this territory. This completes the defence of my first two theses, that feelings are expressed by interjections in just the same sense of the term in which they are expressed by declarative sentences, but in a different sense of the term from that in which they are expressed by facial expressions and demeanour.

The above discussion could be summed up by saying that to express one's F for x in language is to utter a sentence (or produce a sentence-surrogate) while recognizing that one's utterance is governed by a rule requiring that the speaker have F for x. It is the operation of such a rule which makes an utterance of any sort a case of expressing one's F for x. It is worthy of note that this account applies to expressions of intention, belief, and desire in just the same way as that in which it applies to expressions of annoyance or approval. What makes saying 'I am going to the meeting' an expression of intention is that one utters the sentence while recognizing that one's utterance is governed by a rule requiring that the speaker have an intention to go to the meeting in question. And what makes saying 'In all likelihood Jane has withdrawn' an expression of one's belief that Jane has withdrawn is the fact that one utters the sentence while recognizing that one's utterance is subject to a rule requiring that the speaker believe that Jane has withdrawn.[1] One of the merits of this account of expressing is that it reveals the basic identity between expressions of quite different sorts of items. This identity will be obscured by assimilation of linguistic expressions of feelings to grimaces and groans.

And now for the qualification which was promised on page 17. The distinction between expression which takes place via rules and expression which takes place via mere regularities does not quite coincide with the distinction between linguistic and non-linguistic expression. For it seems that there are pieces of non-linguistic behaviour which have the status of expressing feelings or attitudes by the operation of rules in just the way in which sentences do. Thus in a certain society it may be the case that a shrug of the shoulders in a certain kind of situation is assigned by rule to the expression of indifference, or a raising of the hand in a certain kind of situation is assigned by rule to the expression of approval. That is, it may be the case in some society that shrugging the shoulders in such a situation when one is not indifferent will be regarded as a misuse just as much as saying 'What difference does it make?' without really being indifferent. The question as to the extent to which such rule-governed non-linguistic communication exists in our society and in other societies is a largely unanswered question of considerable interest. But the bare possibility of this sort of thing is enough to inhibit us from construing our basic distinction as a distinction between linguistic and non-linguistic expression. It might be claimed that all such cases are derivative from linguistic expression in something like the way in which the Morse code and the notations of symbolic logic are derivative from saying things in language. In that case we could regard shrugs which have a rule-governed status as 'sentence-surrogates'. But it is not clear that they can all be so regarded.

In the preceding discussion we have repressed awareness of this phenomenon in order to concentrate on the difference between linguistic expression of feelings and the *manifestations* of feeling by looks and bearing, which are (normally) things one simply *has* rather than things which one does. We permitted ourselves this

[1] For an exposition and defence of this way of construing acts like expressing feelings, beliefs, and intentions, making requests, promises and predictions, and so forth, see W. P. Alston, 'Linguistic Acts', *American Philosophical Quarterly*, vol. 1 (1964).

emphasis partly because we were specifically interested in expressing as a linguistic act, and partly because linguistic expression is the clearest case of that kind of expressing which is constituted as such by the fact that rules are in operation. But having nailed down the difference between the extremes, we would be remiss if we did not explicitly recognize the existence of a large, unexplored intermediate area. This area *may* include things other than those just mentioned. For example, consider the case of a man who during a Catholic service deliberately stands up when others are sitting, leans back in a relaxed fashion when others are kneeling, and so forth. Here we might say that *he* expressed his contempt for the service by doing these things, as well as saying that he showed or displayed his contempt. Are these actions fitted to express contempt by virtue of a rule? It is difficult to say. Or again consider the statement 'In the Ninth Symphony Beethoven expressed his sense of triumph over his deafness'. Here it is clear that we want to say that he *expressed* his sense of triumph, rather than displayed, showed, or evinced his sense of triumph. But it seems equally clear that the Ninth Symphony does not have the status of an expression of such triumph by virtue of the operation of rules, in anything like the way in which a sentence would. We are unable to deal with such cases in this paper. But the fact that such problems are left dangling does not shake the conclusion that expressing a feeling by uttering a sentence (any sentence which is fitted for this job) is sharply distinguished from manifesting a feeling by something like a facial expression, in terms of the distinction between rules and regularities.[1]

V

Let us turn to our third thesis, that there is no *important* difference between expressing one's *F* for *x* and asserting that one has *F* for *x*. So far we have made explicit no basis for *any* distinction. The above account of expressing would seem to hold good of the corresponding assertions as well. To see this let us consider what it is, on this analysis, to make a certain assertion. To assert that one's car is stalled is to utter a sentence while recognizing that one's

[1] I am indebted to my colleagues, Frithjof Bergmann and Abraham Kaplan, both for forcing me to attend to these complexities and for furnishing me with useful examples.

utterance is governed by a rule requiring that the speaker's car be stalled (together with whatever is presupposed by this, for instance, that the speaker have a car). More generally, to assert that *P* is to utter a sentence while recognizing that one's utterance is governed by a rule requiring that *P*. But if this is so, then to assert that one has *F* for *x* is to utter a sentence while recognizing that one's utterance is governed by a rule requiring that one feel *F* for *x*. But it is the operation of just this kind of rule that makes an utterance a case of expressing one's *F* for *x*. Thus with respect to the rules which are operative—and this is what gives an utterance its content—the expression and the assertion are indistinguishable. It is this basic identity which brings it about that normal utterances of sentences like 'I am annoyed' can be characterized either as expressing one's annoyance or as asserting that one is annoyed.

Nevertheless there are cases of the one which are not also cases of the other. When we express a feeling by an interjection, we are not also asserting that we have the feeling. There are also, more rarely, cases of the assertion which are not cases of expression. Consider the following. You are trying to conceal your feelings, but I, for some reason, am determined to find out how you are reacting to the situation. I badger you until finally you very reluctantly say, in a flat tone of voice, 'Well, I am somewhat annoyed'. In this case you would not be said to be expressing annoyance. We have not fully understood expressing until we have brought out those features which distinguish it from asserting.

The latter difference is the easier to understand. The laboriously extracted report is not a case of expressing simply because we do not say that someone is *expressing* a feeling unless his performance is relatively spontaneous, unless the verbal utterance issues directly from the feeling and takes on a coloration therefrom. It is in this respect that there is a real continuity between facial expression and expressing as a linguistic act.

The attempt to say why one cannot assert that he is annoyed by using an interjection will get us into deeper water. First off we can see that one has not made an assertion unless one has uttered a sentence which could be used in a specification of the assertion in question. More precisely, one cannot be said to have asserted that *P* unless he has uttered a sentence which could replace '*P*' in 'He asserted that *P*'. This limits us to declarative sentences, for only declarative sentences fit into that slot. But if the only feature which attaches to asserting that one is annoyed, but not to expressing one's annoyance, is this restriction to a certain grammatical form of sentence, then the former is not a significantly richer concept. In that case this would be no more important a difference than that between expressing one's annoyance in English and expressing one's annoyance in Swahili. Surely the fact that, in a given linguistic community, a given kind of linguistic act can be performed by the utterance of some sentences and not others is a matter of convention in the most trivial sense. It seems clear that we could radically change the conventions assigning certain grammatical types of sentences to certain linguistic acts without thereby altering the role of those linguistic acts in thought and communication. But of course the matter would be altered if there were deeper differences behind this grammatical restriction.

One thing which would seem to give a declarative-sentence-utterance a fundamentally different status from any interjection-utterance is the way in which it invites certain responses. If I say 'I am enthusiastic about your plan', you could reply 'Oh, no you're not', 'I don't believe it', 'Why should I suppose that you really are?', 'Are you quite sure?', or 'But you haven't been acting that way'. Whereas none of these responses would be appropriate to 'Bully!', 'Capital!', or 'Swell!'. Thus in saying 'I'm enthusiastic about your plan', I am asserting a proposition, which can be said to be true or false, which can be contradicted, doubted, or denied, the grounds for which can be questioned, positive or negative evidence for which can be adduced; whereas in employing an interjection no proposition is being put forward, and so doubt, denial, contradiction, and the assembling of evidence are all out of place. It is because declarative sentences fit onto responses of this sort that the grammatical restriction is not trivial; what lies behind it is the notion of making a claim which can be evaluated as true or false, grounded or ungrounded, and which enters into logical relations, such as contradiction and implication, which go along with this status.

Before exploring this difference I must pause to take account of some recently prevalent doubts that even declarative-sentence-utterances of the sort we have been considering constitute real assertions. It has been suggested[1] that utterances like 'I am annoyed' differ in crucial respects from clear cases of assertion, for

[1] See, for example, G. Ryle, *The Concept of Mind*, London 1949, p. 102.

instance, in not admitting the responses 'How do you know?', or 'Surely you are mistaken'. It is claimed that it makes no sense to think of the speaker being mistaken in these cases, that requests for grounds of his 'statement' are out of place, and that one can reject what he says only if one doubts his truthfulness. Now it is not clear to me that a person cannot be mistaken in saying how he feels about something. Perhaps those who hold that it makes no sense to say that he is mistaken are overlooking the human capacity for self-deception. Granted that one can't make a mistake here in some of the ways he can in other matters, for example through not having gathered enough data or through not being able to get a close enough look, still one might make a mistake through not being willing to admit to oneself what one's real feelings on the matter are. But even if it is an *a priori* truth that mistake is impossible in these matters, there is still enough continuity with admitted assertions to give ample ground for so classifying these cases. Even if the speaker cannot be mistaken, another can reject or contradict his statement, doubt whether it is so, and look for supporting evidence, and this would seem to be enough to make what he is saying an assertion, though the philosophical use of 'assertion' is too loose to permit a definitive decision.

As John Austin has pointed out,[1] we should take the traditional distinction between assertions and other linguistic acts with more than a grain of salt. Whenever I say anything, my utterance carries certain claims which can be evaluated as true or false, founded or unfounded. If I ask you to unlock my car, what I say carries the claims that I have a car and that it is locked; if I advise you to accept an offer from Stanford, my act of advising carries the claims that you have received an offer from Stanford and that you are in a position to accept it; if I congratulate you on your presidential address, I am committing myself to the proposition that you have delivered a presidential address. And all of these claims are subject to the same evaluations, the same reactions, as any assertion. No doubt in all these cases there is a real point to distinguishing the linguistic performance involved from making an assertion; this stems from the fact that asking, advising, and congratulating involve something more than committing oneself to the propositions mentioned. To *ask* you to unlock my car goes beyond asserting that I have a car, that it is unlocked, that you are capable of unlock-

[1] *How To Do Things With Words*, London 1962, esp. Section XI.

ing it, and so forth; just as advising you to accept an offer from Stanford goes beyond asserting that you have received an offer from Stanford, that you are in a position to accept it, and so on. (Unfortunately the limits of this paper do not allow us to go into what the additional feature is in these cases.) Since we focus our attention on the respects in which linguistic performances of these sorts go beyond making assertions, we would say that the propositions mentioned in each case are presupposed rather than explicitly asserted. But as a corrective to the traditional assumption that assertions differ from other linguistic actions by virtue of possessing something very important which the others lack, it is worth while emphasizing the point that assertions are poorer, not richer, than their relations. The defining features of assertion-making pervade linguistic performances throughout; linguistic actions which are not assertions are those which go beyond these.

To return to our problem, there is much less reason to distinguish expressing one's enthusiasm (by an interjection) from asserting that one is enthusiastic than there is for distinguishing asking you to open my car from asserting the propositions we saw to be involved in that request. For here the extra dimension is lacking. This can be seen by the following considerations. To the request to unlock my car one *can* respond by 'But it isn't locked', 'What makes you think it's locked?', or 'It was unlocked two minutes ago'. That is, one *can* respond in any way which is appropriate to the assertion, 'My car is locked'. And so for the other propositions involved in the request. But over and above these there are responses like 'No, I won't,' 'All right', 'Why should I?', 'I'm too busy', and so forth. And it is these responses which are distinctive of requests and other 'imperative' actions. The existence of such responses shows that there is an extra dimension to the request, over and above the presupposed assertions. But we will search in vain for a class of responses which would distinguish the interjectional expression from its assertive correlate. The interjectional expression of enthusiasm, as much as the assertion that one is enthusiastic, can give rise to such reactions as denials or doubts that one is really enthusiastic, and the citing of positive or negative evidence. It is true that they will have to take a different verbal form.[1] If the utterance is 'Splendid!' the retort will have to be

[1] Presumably it is this which leads people to take the position that they cannot give rise to the same reactions.

'You're not really enthusiastic' rather than 'No, you're not', 'But you haven't been acting enthusiastic' rather than 'You haven't been acting as if you are', or 'It's not true that you are enthusiastic' rather than 'That's not true'. That is, the claim is spelled out in the declarative sentence, 'I'm very enthusiastic about your plan' in such a way as to allow for more elliptical responses than are possible to 'Splendid!' But this can hardly be supposed to affect the substance of the responses. There are many factors which force us to spell something out more explicitly on one occasion than on another. It is still the case that anything which can be appropriately said in response to 'I'm terribly enthusiastic abour your plan', can be said in response to 'Splendid!', and vice versa. The triviality of the difference in grammatical requirements for the responses nicely mirrors the triviality of the difference in grammatical requirements for the original utterance.

Thus it is a mistake to think that the concept of asserting that one has *F* for *x* is significantly richer than the concept of expressing one's *F* for *x*. The restriction to declarative sentences for the asserting turns out to be trivial. It carries with it no associated difference in logical status, no difference in the force of what is being said. It is a carry-over from other areas, like the assertion-request distinction, where the difference in grammatical form does mirror significant differences in the role of the utterances in communication. The only difference which is at all noteworthy is the one, mentioned briefly above, that 'express', unlike 'assert', is restricted to those cases in which the utterance is relatively spontaneous and in which the feeling is exhibited in the way one's words are uttered. (The latter part of this requirement applies only to expressions of feelings and, perhaps, attitudes. It is nonsense to speak of a belief or an intention being exhibited in the way one utters one's words.) And this difference carries with it no difference in the logical or epistemological status of what one is saying.

VI

One thing shown by this discussion is that several widely held views about the difference between asserting and expressing are totally without foundation.

(1) Assertion is 'cognitive', expression 'non-cognitive'.

(2) Assertions stand in logical relations, expressions only in causal relations.

(3) Assertions present propositions which can be evaluated as true or false, expressions do not.

The sooner it is realized that such contrasts are spurious the sooner we can get down to the job of giving an adequate account of the relation of expressions of feelings and attitudes to moral judgements, value judgements, factual generalizations, and affirmations of religious faith.

II
ON THE COMPLEXITY OF AVOWALS

by BRUCE AUNE

Assistant Professor of Philosophy, University of Pittsburgh

It has been said that when we are tempted to speak of different senses of a word that is clearly not equivocal, we may infer that we are in fact pretty much in the dark about the character of the concept it expresses. This appears to be true, oddly enough, of such simple words as 'pain'. They are clearly not equivocal, yet philosophers have persistently been tempted to accord them significantly different meanings when they appear, respectively, in first- and third-person discourse. This temptation, which is quite as alive today as it was when solipsism seemed irrefutable, indicates that even relentless discussion has not achieved the clarification that such ubiquitous little words as 'pain' need and deserve. A contribution to this clarification will accordingly be attempted here.

I

The temptation in point appears to owe its life to two main considerations. First, one's mastery of first- and third-person uses of these words is apparently measured by entirely different criteria. In order to learn their application to other persons one must evidently learn something about behaviour: in the case of 'pain', for instance, one must come to recognize the characteristic symptoms of personal distress. Yet familiarity with behavioural patterns has apparently nothing whatever to do with one's ability to apply those words correctly to oneself. Secondly, one's basis for saying 'I am in pain' is radically different from any basis one could possibly have for saying 'He is in pain', and the chances of going wrong in these two cases are profoundly different as well—indeed, the idea of going wrong in the first case seems thoroughly unintelligible.

Given these considerations, it is hard to avoid the conclusion that words like 'pain' cannot be taken to refer to the same thing in first- and third-person (present tense) uses. For, in the light of learning as well as verification, it appears that in contexts like 'He is in pain' these words must refer to something rooted in behaviour; while in such contexts as 'I am in pain' these words are either used to refer to something private, not involving the uncertainties of overt behaviour (the allegedly dangerous idea of traditional philosophy) or else they are not strictly used to *refer* to anything at all: their use here is perhaps merely expressive, having the sort of significance of a wince or groan. This latter alternative, occasionally defended today, would at least account for the peculiar immunity to error that these first-person uses seem to possess.

As indicated earlier, the temptation to drive a wedge between these two uses is pretty clearly a symptom of some kind of confusion. After all, it can hardly be a matter of doubt that when a person answers the question 'How do you feel?' by saying 'I am in pain' he is not just exhibiting behaviour but is in fact saying something about himself which he knows, usually, to be true—and is in fact saying the very same thing about himself as another would be saying who, referring to him, used the words 'He is in pain'. Still, the considerations that lead one to defend the split-personality view of psychological words (as I shall call it) are not entirely without substance. Indeed, anyone who rejects this view will have to master a thicket of thorny puzzles, not the least of which is how, if pain *is* essentially rooted in behaviour, a person's claim that he is in pain can be made without reference to his own behaviour and yet enjoy the peculiar infallibility that it is said to have.

Since it is the split-personality view that is out of line with what one would naturally think—with, in fact, what dictionary writers normally say—it is perhaps best to begin by considering its basis more carefully. How, for instance, are the facts of language-learning supposed to support this view? Well, consider the familiar picture once sketched by Professor Malcolm:

[As a child] grows older and begins to talk it will normally come about that often when his behaviour and circumstances are those of a person in pain he will say the words 'It hurts', or some synonymous ones; and hardly ever will he say them when either his behaviour or circumstances do not satisfy the original criterion of pain. This development fulfills our criterion of his *understanding* those words.[1]

Presumably something analogous could be said to hold in the case of the other-person uses. Supposing that a child's training has reached the point where he can say 'He is in pain' on appropriate occasions—when, that is, either someone else is, or gives strong indications of being, in pain—it might appear that the criteria for his understanding the words that he utters have been satisfied. If so, it would be quite possible for a child to understand the full force of saying 'I am in pain' and yet be entirely ignorant of the meaning of 'He is in pain' and vice-versa. The child could, that is to say, utter 'I am in pain' at just the right times but vary in the wildest way with 'He is in pain', and the other way around. If this is possible, it is then reasonable to think that 'pain' has two quite distinct senses, which could be thoroughly mastered independently of one another.

It is not difficult, however, to see that this picture of language-learning is excessively simplified and entirely misleading. Consider, for instance, the first-person case. Notice that if a child in pain merely satisfied the criteria that Malcolm mentioned above—if he could say nothing other than 'It hurts' or 'I am in pain'; if he had absolutely no idea of the effects his words were likely to have on those around him; if he were completely unable to recognize a denial or misinterpretation of his words; if indeed he could follow none of the usual talk concerned with pains, including words of advice and warning—then his linguistic sophistication would in no way exceed that of a Skinnerian parrot that had been carefully conditioned to squawk out the sounds *ai am in pein* when and only when a painful stimulus was applied. And surely this is not sufficient to constitute an understanding of *words in a language*.

To understand the conventional significance of a group of words is at least to understand what one can use these words to say or do. And this points to the fundamental inadequacy of the above picture. For merely to exercise a habit of responding with special noises in certain circumstances is not, by itself, to *use* language at all. One typically *uses* something for a purpose or end. And so with a sentence: one uses it, because it has a certain conventional significance, to inform, to amuse, to deceive, and so on. That one

[1] Norman Malcolm, *Dreaming*, London 1959, p. 15.

uses a sentence *for some purpose* does not of course mean that one always has an end in mind before one utters the words, or that one always knows exactly what one wants to say or do before one finds a means of saying or doing it.[1] But in order to use a sentence to make an assertion, tell a lie, or relate a joke, one must at least utter it in a certain *frame of mind*, that is, in a certain state of intellectual readiness to re-express or attempt to clarify what one has said, to follow it up with further remarks, to handle objections, appreciate comments, and the like. Indeed, it is largely this frame of mind, which is so far beyond the powers of a parrot to attain, that often determines which action one performs when one utters a string of very familiar noises.

Important as these considerations are for any adequate discussion of language-learning, it is not necessary to dwell on them here, since the simplified picture presented by Malcolm fails for a very trivial reason. It is this. In order to understand the sentence 'I am in pain' you must understand it whenever and wherever it is properly used—and this means understanding it when it is uttered by another person. But this understanding is not given by the trained disposition on *your* part to utter the words (sounds) 'I am in pain' when you are in pain. Hence, if you can understand the *sentence* 'I am in pain' you must not only understand another person who uses it as saying that *he* is in pain, but you must have some idea of what counts for and against the truth of what he says—which is to say that you must be aware of principles that connect 'I am in pain' with other sentences of English, those sentences, namely, that might naturally be used to express these confirming and disconfirming facts. But because these facts, being about him, no doubt concern his behaviour, it follows that if you can understand the *sentence* 'I am in pain' you must not only know something about behaviour but you must know that the word 'pain' can apply to another person as well as to yourself.

Actually, once it is noticed that understanding a sentence is a matter of understanding it whenever and wherever it is properly used, it becomes apparent, virtually on grammatical grounds, that 'I am in pain' and 'He is in pain' are so related that a full understanding of either requires an understanding of the other. To see this, recall that when another person uses 'I am in pain' he uses it to talk about himself, not about me; and if I did not know some-

[1] Cf. R. G. Collingwood, *The Principles of Art*, Oxford 1938, Ch. 6.

thing about the logic of pronouns, I could not possibly appreciate this. This logic turns, moreover, on a fundamental contrast between 'I' and 'he': anyone calling himself an 'I' is a *he* (or *she*) to others; when they talk about *me*, when they endorse or quarrel with my remarks, they use 'he' or 'you' in reference to me, and I must accordingly know something about these words in order to know how my remarks about myself are taken. Similarly, when I react to their first-person utterances, I can show my understanding of what each of them says only if, for the most part, I am able to endorse or in some way quarrel with their remarks; and I can do this, generally, only by using 'he' or 'you' in reference to them. Hence the grammars of 'I' and 'he' are intimately related, and to understand the force of one, you must understand the force of the other. Since the meaningfulness of saying 'We are in pain' implies that 'pain' has the very same meaning in 'I am in pain' that it has in 'He is in pain' it follows, almost as a matter of grammar, that a person can fully understand the former only if he can understand the latter.[1]

II

Having thus seen that our criteria for appraising the success of language-learning actually refute rather than support the split-personality view of psychological terms, we are now in a position to consider the other argument that seems to count in its favour. This argument may be introduced as follows. 'When you honestly say of yourself that you are in pain, what you say is presumably infallible—and it is not based on an observation of your own behaviour. Yet if the truth of what you say must wait on behaviour —if, that is to say, a failure to behave in the appropriate way shows that you are not in pain—then it is hard to see how your avowals could have this infallibility, for your future behaviour at any time

[1] Actually, this is an oversimplification, holding only for those who understand no other language comparable to English. Obviously a Frenchman could understand 'I am in pain' if its French translation, and only this, were made available to him. He could do this, however, only because the French 'je' plays the role of a first-person pronoun, having an essential contrast with 'il' and 'vous'. Hence, my point here is more accurately stated thus: to understand the full force of 'I' one must appreciate *the linguistic role* that is played by a third-person pronoun of some language or other. On the significance of such linguistic roles, see Wilfrid Sellars, 'Abstract Entities', *Review of Metaphysics*, vol. 17 (1963), pp. 627–671.

is always slightly uncertain. Besides, it apparently makes no sense to speak of your verifying that you are in pain; but another person *can* verify this, and what he verifies is not intrinsically certain. Does this not show that what you say of yourself, when you say "I am in pain", is quite different from what he says of you, when he says "He is in pain"? After all, if the same thing were said, if the same statement were made, in both of these cases, we should have something that is both verifiable and non-verifiable, infallible and only practically certain. But surely this is impossible if anything is.'

Though extremely confused, this argument brings us to the very heart of the perplexities engendered by avowals. But assuming that honest assertions of 'I am in pain' *are* in some way infallible (an assumption that I shall examine later), the question about how the same assertion can be both verifiable and non-verifiable is easily answered; that is, it can readily be shown to rest on confusion. For if, as Wittgenstein, Malcolm, and many others have held, saying 'I am in pain' can become—as it is, for sophisticated speakers—a criterion of being in pain, then what one asserts or states in uttering this sentence can be verified by one's mere act of uttering it. That is, in uttering 'I am in pain' (in a certain frame of mind, in certain circumstances) one asserts something or makes a certain statement. This assertion or statement, which is not only different from the noises one emits but which can also be made by someone else using different words, has the peculiarity, however, that its truth may be verified by reference to the words or sounds that one utters. One's utterance of 'I am in pain' thus performs two functions: (*a*) it serves to make a statement and (*b*) it serves as an indicator or criterion of what one feels. And while, if one has the mentality of a mere parrot, one's utterance may perform the second function without performing the first, a fully conscious use of the sentence 'I am in pain' involves both—in which case the truth of what one says is to be verified with reference to the words one utters (among other things). We do not therefore have a statement that is both verifiable and non-verifiable; for the statement, as opposed to the noises, is verifiable *tout court*—both for the one who makes it, who verifies it (establishes its truth) in the very act of uttering certain noises, and for the one to whom it is addressed, who may verify it by attending to these noises, as well as other things, and interpreting their significance.

There is still, however, the problem of infallibility or incorrigibility: how are we to understand the alleged incorrigibility of utterances of 'I am in pain'? Malcolm, who unlike most philosophers has gone to the trouble of discussing this question at some length,[1] seems to provide two rather different interpretations of this infallibility. According to one interpretation, a person's words about his present sensations have the same logical status as his cries and facial expressions, so that a mistaken use of 'I am in pain' is just as peculiar as a mistaken groan:

A man cannot be in *error* as to whether he is in pain; he cannot say, 'My leg hurts', by mistake, any more than he can groan by mistake. It is senseless to suppose that he has wrongly identified a tickle as pain. . . . True, he may be undecided as to whether it is best described as an 'ache' or a 'pain' . . ., but his very indecision *shows* us what his sensation is, *i.e.*, something between an ache and a pain.[2]

The idea here is that after suitable training, saying 'I am in pain' becomes learned pain-behaviour. As such, it attains the expressive function of crying or groaning, and it is therefore 'incorrigible'.

Although this argument is highly suggestive, it is, I think, far from sufficient to fulfil Malcolm's (or Wittgenstein's) purpose. For one thing, it is clear that an utterance of 'I am in pain' is normally a use of language in a way that groans and the like are not. Malcolm, of course, recognizes this difficulty,[3] but his manner of avoiding it is unsatisfactory. For his remark that groans may be *used* to inform others of how one feels suggests that one might even groan by mistake. Groans are, after all, under our voluntary control much of the time; and although a man may have agreed to answer a certain signal of his dishonest bridge-partner by uttering a short cough, he might momentarily forget this at a crucial point in the game and respond with a groan instead. If we assume that the man is just as anxious to cheat as his scheming partner, he might actually curse himself for making this mistake—and it would be a mistake, because he deliberately made a noise that he

[1] Norman Malcolm, 'Review of Wittgenstein's *Philosophical Investigations*', *Philosophical Review*, vol. 63 (1954), pp. 542 ff.

[2] *Ibid.*

[3] He registers an inclination to object: 'The natural expressions . . . are not used to inform others; they are not "used" at all; they have no purpose, no function, they escape from me'. *Ibid., p.* 541

immediately recognized as inappropriate for the purpose at hand.

This objection may appear too contrived, but actually it grips the very nerve of Malcolm's argument. For when it makes no sense to speak of a groan's being mistaken, there will be no question of a person's groaning for a purpose. When a person just groans—when the groan just escapes him—there is never any question of his making a mistake; for he is not trying to do anything. Similarly with linguistic behaviour: if a man merely emits certain noises—no matter what they are, so long as they merely escape from his lips—there is again no question of his making a mistake. But such an emission of noises does not count as an identification or a description of anything either. To identify in words the feelings that you have, it is not sufficient that the words just escape from your lips; for while others might know from this expression what your feeling is (as they might know what a parrot feels from the sound of its squawk), your utterance does not count as a verbal indentification of anything, or even as a move in a language game, unless, among other things, you produce those words in a suitable frame of mind (compare above, p. 38).

The point is, we do sometimes identify our feelings in words: our words do not always just escape from our lips. And if Malcolm's incorrigibility thesis extends to our words when they represent an honest, self-conscious attempt to communicate with others, then his thesis is not established by the above argument. For to the extent that our utterances are just expressions of feeling (as moaning *in order* to gain attention is not), to that extent they are not *uses* of language: more is involved, after all, in saying that you feel pain, in making this assertion, than is involved in uttering a few noises—no matter how much training in producing them you have had. On the other hand, of course, even the most sustained and careful training never removes the possibility of a wrong response. And if making a mistake about one's feelings *were* just a matter of uttering the wrong noises, then there would be little justification for arguing that there is something 'senseless' about the idea of such a mistake. Malcolm's contention that indecision whether to say (= utter after training) 'It hurts' or 'It itches' *shows* that the feeling one has is 'an indefinite, ambiguous' one is thus slightly inaccurate;[1] for another possibility has to be ruled out,

[1] *Philosophical Review*, vol. 63 (1954), pp. 542 ff.

namely the possibility that the response, or the wavering between responses, is simply irregular—something that should not happen given one's previous training. Of course, assuming that the training is sufficient to set up a strong verbal habit, we are usually justified in rejecting the latter possibility. But a rejection on this basis is insufficient to warrant our saying that the question of mistake is in any way senseless.

As I remarked earlier, Malcolm provides an additional interpretation of the incorrigibility of first-person utterances. According to this interpretation, inappropriate utterances of 'I am in pain' do not count as assertive utterances; to say, honestly and affirmatively, 'I am in pain' when one is not in pain is to show that one has not mastered the use of the words one utters. The point can be put this way, although this is not the way that Malcolm puts it: the conditions under which one makes a true statement in uttering the words 'I am in pain' are precisely those conditions under which one exhibits one's understanding of the words one utters. Thus, if a person who is not in pain utters the words 'I am in pain' with no intent to deceive, make a joke, or anything of the sort, he shows, by the mere fact that he utters these words in these circumstances, that he does not possess a complete mastery of the words he is using, and that, although he utters these words, he is not actually making the assertion he seems to be making—and is not, *a fortiori*, making the false assertion he seems to be making. Hence, any genuine, honest assertion that one is in pain is 'incorrigible': for its truth conditions are identical with its being the *bona fide* assertion that it seems to be.[1]

Plausible as this argument may sound, I think it can be shown to rest on a subtle misconception, a misconception that makes it natural to suppose that our criteria for having the concept of pain are so terribly strict that no matter how much a person may know about the causes and occasions of pain, if he lacks the ability to make spontaneous avowals of being in pain he is thereby incapable

[1] This argument seems to be borne out by Malcolm's quotation from Wittgenstein: 'If anyone said "I do not know if what I have got is a pain or something else", we should think something like, he does not know what the English word "pain" means, and we should explain it to him. . . . If he now said, for example: "Oh, I know what 'pain' means; what I don't know is whether *this*, that I have now, is 'pain'"—we should merely shake our heads and be forced to regard his words as a queer reaction which we have no idea what to do with (228).' *Philosophical Review*, vol. 63 (1954), p. 555.

of making any legitimate, assertive use of the sentence 'I am in pain'. I shall try to expose this misconception at a later stage of my argument, when several crucial distinctions are conveniently at hand. For the moment, I want to point out that even if Malcolm's argument here is sound, it does nothing to show that first-person *utterances* are infallible or incorrigible, or that whenever a person utters the words 'I am in pain' with no intent to deceive or amuse he says something that is true.

That a person's utterances are not incorrigible is perhaps obvious, since utterances are not statements, the sort of thing to which the technical expressions 'corrigible' and 'incorrigible' intelligibly apply. But perhaps it is not so obvious that, given the soundness of Malcolm's criteriological argument for incorrigibility, one could meaningfully be said to utter the words in an honest, earnest, assertive frame of mind and yet fail to say something that is true. This point follows, however, from the consideration that if a man's hold on his language is slipping, as often happens, for example, with persons having schizoid tendencies, then his utterance might not qualify as an assertion. The contradictory of 'saying something true' is, after all, 'not saying something true'; and if inadequate training, incipient schizophrenia, too much drink, or countless other things, indicate even a momentary conceptual confusion or incoherence, then, whether a person realizes it or not, he may well fail to say something true when in all honesty he says 'I am in pain'—for according to the criteria we are alleged to have, he might not really be asserting anything, let alone something true.

III

In order to come to the very bottom of these difficulties concerning the infallibility of avowals, something must obviously be said about the concept of awareness. For even if, like Malcolm and others, one throws aside the traditional idea that awareness is what confers infallibility on a man's honest avowals, it remains true that awareness is not an entirely empty notion: it surely has *something* to do with the making of avowals. The question is, 'Just what is this something?'

In his book *Dreaming*, Professor Malcolm made a very tantalizing remark about awareness. He said: 'it makes no sense to speak of *finding out* that one is in pain, where this would imply that one was previously in pain but not aware of it.'[1] This remark is tantalizing because in the light of his well-known critique of introspection,[2] it seems very unlikely that he would hold the *esse est percipi* doctrine of pain. Yet if he does not hold this doctrine, what could he mean by the above remark? What, indeed, could he mean by the expression 'being *aware* of one's pain'?

Well, the answer to this question is not clear—and anyway, this essay is not the place for exegesis. But notice that the senselessness of speaking of finding out in connection with one's pains can scarcely be defended by resorting to the traditional idea that feeling pain is a 'mode of awareness' and that 'being aware of one's pain' just means 'feeling one's pain'. For if feeling is to count as awareness, the connection between being aware and finding out is then left entirely obscure. After all, what one finds out is always the truth of some proposition; yet what one feels, and what one is thus aware of in this traditional sense, is not a proposition at all. But if the thing felt is quite different from the thing found out—as a feeling is different from a proposition—just why should the two be inseparable? Why should it be impossible to feel pain and yet not know, and so later come to find out, *that* pain is what one feels?

One reason for this opinion arises from the historical tendency to run together two quite different kinds of awareness. One of these is the kind already mentioned, of which feeling is a determinate form. (Whether this sense of 'awareness' is a philosopher's invention, I shall not say.) The other differs from the first in having a very obvious connection with the matter of finding out. For here one is aware *that* such and such is the case, which is to say that what one is aware of here is *the same* as what one might find out, namely the truth of some proposition. It is easy to see that once these distinct kinds of awareness are confused, it becomes natural to assume that finding out could not possibly occur in connection with what is felt; for one can find out that *p* only if one was previously unaware that *p*, and this would be impossible in the case of feeling pain, *if* feeling were just a determinate form of being aware that. . . .

There is, however, another, more recent line of argument pur-

[1] *Dreaming*, p. 10.
[2] Cf. his 'Knowledge of Other Minds', *Journal of Philosophy*, vol. 40 (1958), pp. 969–978.

porting to show that it makes no sense to speak of finding out in connection with one's own feelings. This argument, which springs from the later Wittgenstein,[1] begins by emphasizing that 'finding out that *p*' implies 'knowing that *p*', and then goes on to argue that 'He knows that he is in pain' is actually senseless. If the latter contention were true, then of course 'He found out that he is in pain' would have to be senseless as well.

Though this argument is, to my mind, extremely weak, it is so commonly accepted, and has such important consequences, that it deserves rather careful consideration. Essentially, it is based on the following line of thought. It is only sensible to speak of knowing where there is room for doubt, where there is a meaningful contrast between 'He knows that *p*' and 'He merely thinks, or doubts, that *p*'. But one cannot merely think, or doubt, that one is in pain. To doubt or merely think something is to exercise some concept; hence to doubt or merely think that one is in pain is to employ the concept of pain. A criterion of having this concept, however, is that one has gained the tendency to say 'I am in pain' confidently on the appropriate occasions, to say it, namely, when one is indeed in pain. If, on a given occasion, one hesitates to say 'I am in pain' for fear of saying the wrong thing, this shows not that one really doubts whether one is in pain but only that one is none too clear about what pain is. But if doubting requires concepts, and if having the concept of pain demands confidence about one's feelings—demands in fact that one is never really wrong about being in pain—it then follows that doubting and merely thinking that one is in pain are impossibilities, and hence that 'knowing' has no place here.

One of the first things to notice about this argument is that it hinges on the *undefended* contention that 'He knows that *p*' makes sense only if 'He doubts, or merely thinks, that *p*' makes sense. But this contention is dubious on at least two counts. First, if every meaningful sentence must have an intelligible contrast, a contrast for 'He knows that *p*' can be supplied by its contradictory, 'He does not know that *p*'; and when its contradictory, rather than its mere contrary, is used as contrast, then 'He knows that he is in pain' *is* meaningful by the contrast test; for while a suitably trained person may be presumed incapable of being mis-

[1] Ludwig Wittgenstein, *Philosophical Investigations*, tr. Anscombe, Oxford 1953, sec. 246.

taken about being in pain, it is always possible that he either lacks this training or has lost his grips on the concept of pain—in which case he would not know the answer to the question 'Are you in pain?' and hence would not know that he is in pain (he would simply have no idea of what pain is). Secondly, the universal applicability of the contrast between knowing and doubting is also dubious on the ground that if there were such a thing as *a priori* knowledge, knowledge resting entirely on the analysis of concepts, then it would be natural to suppose that there would be *many cases* in which the criteria for knowing and understanding coincide—where, that is to say, the criteria for understanding a statement are the same as those for recognizing its truth. Thus, to take a trivial example, if a person did not know that one plus one equals two, it would probably be held that he did not know what addition is, or that he did not know what is meant by 'one', 'two', or 'equals'. Under these conditions it could be argued that a person could not possibly doubt whether one plus one equals two, since to doubt this would require him to exercise these primitive arithmetical concepts. If it were true, however, that knowing always implies the possibility of doubt, we would then have to conclude that 'one plus one equals two' states something that could not be said to be known—which is extremely doubtful considering the normal usage of the word 'know'.

There is, nevertheless, another kind of argument that might be used against me here. It is this. Although I have elucidated a 'use' for the sentence 'He knows that he is in pain' by contrasting it with 'He does not know, or he is ignorant of the fact, that he is in pain', I have done nothing to show that 'I know that I am in pain' is significant. Yet if this latter sentence has no intelligible use, or at any rate has no use that differs from that of 'I *am* in pain', then it is still senseless to insist that one might, oneself, know that one is in pain, and so be capable of finding out that pain is what one feels. That is, while 'knowing' and 'finding out' may well be applied to other persons in this connection, one could not in this way apply them to oneself.

This sort of objection is unfortunately very weak. For if 'He knows that he is in pain' is meaningful, and capable of being used to make true statements, then others might use it to make true statements about *me*, to say that I, Bruce Aune, know that I am in pain. (Note that this last sentence implies, if it is meaningful, that

'I know that I am in pain' may constitute a perfectly meaningful part of another sentence, which it could not do if it really were a meaningless string of words.) There might, of course, be something peculiar about *my* using the words 'I know that I am in pain' by themselves—something pragmatically peculiar, perhaps—but it would not follow that they *could not* be used to make a statement, the statement, namely, that others might make by uttering the words 'He knows that he is in pain'.

This trivial answer actually brings us face to face with Wittgenstein's well-known challenge: What is 'I know that I am in pain' supposed to mean, except perhaps that I *am* in pain?[1] Fortunately, an answer to this challenge is not hard to find. For 'I know that I am in pain', unlike the mere 'I am in pain', says that I have knowledge of a particular matter of fact, the fact, namely, that I am in pain. The objection that is generally raised against this obvious kind of answer, namely 'Is there any real difference between the statement that I know this fact about myself and the less pretentious statement that I just *am* in pain?', simply rests on a subtle confusion concerning the various senses in which something may be communicated, or 'said', when one uses a particular sentence. This confusion becomes obvious when one considers that if there is to be any real temptation to equate the force of saying 'I am in pain' with that of the remark involving the word 'know', an utterance of 'I am in pain' must be understood to convey in some way at least part of the information that an utterance of 'I know that I am in pain' was traditionally thought to convey, in particular the information that the speaker is entirely confident, indeed knows full well, that pain is what he feels. But while one who utters 'I am in pain' undoubtedly does convey this information, it is essential to see that this 'conveying' is not *asserting*. Strictly, in saying 'I am in pain' he says nothing whatever about being confident or about having knowledge, nor does the statement he makes *imply* that he has confidence, knowledge, or indeed even concepts. There is nothing odd or contradictory about my saying this, for the *statement* the man makes is after all no different from the statement that others might make by using the words 'He is in pain'—and this statement, which could be true of a child, dog, or moron as well as a sophisticated adult, plainly does not imply anything about the cognitive

[1] Ludwig Wittgenstein, *Philosophical Investigations*, tr. Anscombe, Oxford 1953, sec. 246.

abilities of the subject. True enough, when a man utters the words '*I* am in pain' *he* conveys this information about himself. But he does this not because he is saying anything *about* his cognitive abilities but because he could not say what he does say unless he had these abilities—unless he had a language, had concepts, and thus knew full well what he felt when he uttered the words 'I am in pain'. To put all of this in another way: it is the fact that a man makes the one statement about his feelings which implies (contextually) that the other statements about his cognitive abilities are true; the implication, that is to say, holds between a description of his speech-act, not his statement, and for instance the statement, which he does not make, that he *knows* a particular fact about himself. The temptation to think that he would be saying the same thing by uttering 'I know that I am in pain' as he would by uttering 'I am in pain' thus trades on a confusion about the sense in which something is said: for he would not be making the same *assertion* in both cases, though the total implications of his two speech-acts might indeed be the same.[1]

So far I have been arguing that because 'He knows that he is in pain' may be contrasted with 'He does not know, or he is ignorant of the fact, that he is in pain', the former is a perfectly legitimate, entirely meaningful sentence, which could, moreover, be often used to make a true statement. My grounds for this contrast were not, of course, novel; in fact they were simply an application of the Kantian idea that factual knowledge—that is, knowledge of what's what, as opposed to know-how knowledge—always presupposes some conceptual scheme. Since a man's mastery of a certain conceptual scheme is at best a contingent fact about him, there is thus nothing absurd in saying that he might lack the concept of pain, and all similar concepts, and so not know that he is in pain when pain is what he feels. To insist that it is *senseless* to deny such a man knowledge of his own pains—and hence senseless, rather than perhaps mistaken, to credit him with such knowledge—is just to coast on the momentum of the old idea that knowing, in at least one of its forms, is *not* sharply distinguishable from feeling, from experiencing something that is 'given'.

[1] The distinction that I am insisting upon here is not trivial, since a failure to observe it could land one in a nest of contradictions. An example of how this might happen can be developed from the fact that while 'X knows that *p*' entails that-*p*, *we* generally imply that-*p* when we *say* 'X does *not* know that *p*'.

As this allusion to Kant indicates, my purpose in defending the propriety of such locutions as 'He knows that he is in pain' was not just the grammatical one of correcting what I take to be an unjustifiable restriction of the possible contexts in which the little word 'know' can reasonably appear. On the contrary, apart from wanting to expose the shakiness of several well-known arguments, I was mainly concerned to *reverse* the current idea that there is something philosophically dangerous about such locutions, that their use is likely to involve one in serious philosophical errors. For the fact is, to think that there is something dangerous about these locutions is to overlook the immense difference that exists between actually knowing something and merely having a certain feeling. Indeed, even to deny that it can ever be illuminating to use the word 'know' in relation to a man's awareness of his feelings is to give the erroneous impression that this difference hardly exists at all.

This last point brings out another of my concerns in the previous argument. By emphasizing the legitimacy of saying that a man may know that he feels pain, that he may be fully aware of the truth of this proposition, I wanted to take at least a small step towards elucidating a persistently neglected sense of 'awareness', a sense that involves the possession of concepts, of some sort of language. This sense needs elucidation because it is only too easily confused with the traditional sense which, although lacking any obvious connection with 'thinking' and 'finding out', has historically been taken to describe the true *basis* for first-person reports or avowals. When this confusion is made by contemporary philosophers, who are struck by the uselessness of trying to treat a feeling, taken as a 'mode of awareness', as a basis that guarantees the truth of first-person reports, they are very naturally tempted to junk the idea of awareness altogether.

To yield to this temptation is, of course, to make a mistake. For while one may indeed cast aside the sense of 'awareness' that counts feeling as one of its determinate forms without flying in the face of reason, one cannot do this with every sense of the term. After all, it makes perfectly good sense to speak of a man's being consciously aware of his aches and pains; and as the word 'consciously' implies, this kind of awareness is a *cognitive* one, which resists being lumped together with brute feeling. To be aware of an ache or pain in this sense—to be aware of it as only a language-user can be aware of it—is not, that is to say, just a matter of having or feeling it; it is rather a matter of being able to recognize it for what it is: of being able to describe it, to think about it, to worry about it, and, perhaps, to appreciate its significance in at least the ethical life of man. All this plainly cannot be done naturally, pre-conceptually, without any learning whatever.

But if there is then an important sense of 'awareness'—call it 'conceptual awareness'—that applies only to the experience of a concept-possessing animal, can we say that it is this awareness that serves as the true basis for a man's honest avowals? To raise this question is unfortunately to flounder in a fog, for the idea of a basis in this connection is utterly unclear. If it is supposed to be a basis of inference, though, the answer is a straightforward 'No'. For to be aware that one is in pain is just to be in pain and to be ready to describe it, to classify it, to scout ways of alleviating it, and the like. And this kind of readiness, which Ryle has called 'a frame of mind', is not something that has implications; it is not, any more than a feeling is, a peculiar kind of premise, from which we may draw inferences. Of course, in feeling pain a suitably trained person is in a position to make statements about it—but these statements are not founded, in any quasi-logical sense, either on the feeling or on one's awareness. On the contrary, the mere fact that one *has* a certain feeling disposes one to make any number of linguistic moves of a certain sort: no such basis is required. What justifies the linguistic moves one makes here is the fact, emphasized by Wittgenstein, Malcolm, and many others, that one has been trained in such a way that the words one utters have a *prima facie* claim to truth.

An avowal, as opposed to a typical grunt or groan, is, then, the product of consciousness. But consciousness cannot be conceived in the traditional way: it is not, for instance, a bundle of feelings and thoughts, nor is it a sort of generalized experience. In fact it is not even a ghost in the machine. To be conscious in the sense described, to be 'humanly conscious', is to be prepared to make moves, largely linguistic, that are appropriate to one's condition and circumstances. If one is prepared to do this, if one's wiring diagram has been properly shaped by training and experience, one is then a conscious agent, a creature capable of making self-conscious avowals, of making moves in the normative activity of reasoning and speaking.

V

In emphasizing the complex variety of linguistic abilities involved in an awareness that one has a certain feeling, I have overlooked a very old, persistent line of objection. It may be put as follows. 'If, as you say, one must have a battery of mainly linguistic abilities in order to be (conceptually) aware of even the simplest datum of experience, it would then follow, assuming what you have said about the interrelations of these abilities, that all such awareness and all such knowledge is patently impossible. For you have claimed that the ability to understand such locutions as 'I am in pain' requires the ability to understand such related locutions as 'He is in pain' and *vice-versa*; yet this implies that an understanding of either locution, and hence a grasp of the concept of pain, could never possibly be attained, since its attainment would then involve the hopeless task of trying to understand a sentence before one understood it.'

This objection, fortunately, is not difficult to meet. In order to see why I am not committed to such a circularity, it is only necessary to consider what understanding a sentence (and therefore having a concept and so being capable of an awareness-that) amounts to. For as I have implicitly suggested already, this understanding is simply a matter of having a particular set of abilities—to utter certain words when one has certain feelings, to respond to questions with appropriate words, to act appropriately when particular sounds are heard, and so on. One of course gains these *abilities* piecemeal: as one grows up, one is gradually trained to make responses of the appropriate sort, and this training normally extends over a period of many years. But no one of these abilities, such as that of uttering the words 'I am in pain' when and only when one is in pain, is itself sufficient to constitute an understanding of the words in question. To say, therefore, that one does not fully understand one sentence until one understands another and vice-versa is only to say that the verbal and other abilities the having of which constitutes an understanding of one sentence are so wide-ranging and various that one could not have them without thereby satisfying the criteria for understanding the other sentence as well. There is thus no circularity in my account of understanding: a whole battery of abilities is gradually acquired as one grows older, and when it is sufficiently complex so that one satisfies the criteria for understanding one sentence, it is *ipso facto* complex enough so that one satisfies the criteria for understanding other, related sentences. (There are, needless to say, degrees of understanding, since one's grasp of a sentence may be more or less adequate.)

This talk of the mutual interrelations of 'I am in pain' and 'He is in pain' prompts a venerable old question which I have so far been neglecting: Would a person who had never felt pain really understand the meaning of the word 'pain'? Would he, in fact, understand the force of either 'I am in pain' or 'He is in pain'? To both of these questions I should say 'Yes, to a very large degree'. It is true, of course, that anyone who had never felt pain would presumably lack the ability to recognize such a feeling in the normal way; that is, his pain-reporting mechanism would evidently not be developed. But if his other training in the use of English had been of the usual kind, he would still be able to tell when others are in pain: he would know the sort of question to which 'I am in pain' is an appropriate answer; he would know how to act, what to say, if another cried 'I am in pain', and so on. In fact it does not appear unreasonable to say that he could possess *most* of those abilities (to speak, to act, to infer) in which full understanding of 'I am in pain' consists. True, he could not imagine, at least very well, what it is like to feel pain, though if he had experienced a wide range of tickles, itches, pangs, etc. he would perhaps not be entirely in the dark. But he would surely know enough so that if he were to be in pain for the first time he would be able to give an accurate description of his condition by attending to his own behaviour—by treating himself as another person, as it were. All this, I should say, would count for a very high degree of understanding.

The temptation to reject this view out of hand, to argue that without having had the feeling an understanding of the word 'pain' is obviously impossible, can be nothing other than an echo of the traditional, matrimonial theory of mentalistic words: the theory that such words have meaning because, and only because, they are married to certain feelings. This theory, fortunately, is not widely held today; for apart from the objections that Wittgenstein and his followers have made, it is easy to see that even if words could be married to feelings, their union would not produce the peculiar syntax that is characteristic of mentalistic words in common use. Thus, even though the ability to make spontaneous and truthful avowals of being in pain is admittedly necessary for a completely thorough or entirely unqualified mastery of the word 'pain', the role of this word is so complex, so highly caught up in the intricate web of language, that one who lacks this ability does not *thereby* lack all understanding of the word whatever. Indeed, one who had never felt pain but who knew the language well would have an incomparably greater understanding of even the sentence 'I am in pain' than any parrot would, no matter how often tortured and how well trained it was, or than the child would, who had merely satisfied Malcolm's conditions for understanding it, that is, who had only been trained to the point where saying 'I am in pain' had become spontaneous pain-behaviour. For the man would at least know something about the role of this sentence in the language-game called English; and this is something, a very important something, of which both the bird and the boy would be ignorant.

The idea that someone who had never felt pain could understand the use of 'I am in pain'—and could, indeed, use this sentence with understanding, though perhaps only in a lie—is, however, contrary to the view of Malcolm, according to which an utterance of this sentence can be a use of language only if a connection has been established between being in pain and uttering the sounds *ai am in pein.*[1] It is also, obviously, contrary to the Wittgenstein–Malcolm contention that a condition of having the concept of pain is that one be able to recognize one's pains for what they are without hesitation. The present issue makes it necessary, therefore, to reconsider the 'criteriological' argument for the incorrigibility of first-person psychological utterances.

If we reflect on the Wittgensteinian argument supporting the view that a person who could not say whether he is in pain or not would thereby exhibit his ignorance of what 'pain' means,[2] it becomes clear that the force of this argument rests on the tacit assumption that if a person could not tell when he is in pain, he

[1] 'His saying "I am in pain" can be a use of language only because a connection has been established between the words and the outward phenomena that are the original criterion of pain', *Dreaming*, p. 16.

[2] *Vide* footnote to p. 43 above.

could not tell when others are in pain either—that is, in lacking the ability to identify his own condition, he would lack the relevant 'third-person' abilities, too. Why is this? Because even if his acquired ability to respond correctly without thinking became disorganized, he could still rely on his own behaviour, thus mobilizing the linguistic abilities normally concerned with the case of the other person. Consequently if a person in pain really did not know how to describe his own condition, he would presumably not understand the significance of his own behaviour—which shows not only that his pain-reporting mechanism has broken down (or has not been developed) but that he has lost (or never gained) the ability to interpret the significance of pain-behaviour generally.

Malcolm, of course, has gone on record as saying that one cannot use 'I am in pain' to state a conclusion,[1] but this assertion strikes me as either a false account of what we can do, given our present conventions, or as an unnecessary and misleading act of legislation about what we ought to do. It is, of course, true that 'I am in pain' is normally used in spontaneous avowals; and it is true that anyone who understands the sentence must know what this normal use is. But this does not imply that the person who finds it necessary to conclude that he is in pain is misusing language or doing something that is linguistically illegitimate. For one thing, if he were misusing language it would be appropriate to correct him; yet I can think of few reprimands more absurd than the solemn injunction: Never conclude that you are in pain: always avow it! For another thing, unusual uses of language are by no means always illegitimate, especially when the unusual feature of their use concerns only the manner in which the words are produced, not the content of what is said. Whether one concludes that one is in pain or simply avows it, one is, after all, saying the same thing about one's condition—and is, therefore, in an important sense, using the sentence 'I am in pain' in the normal way. Finally, the fact that a person is unable to use 'I am in pain' in making spontaneous avowals does not show that he does not know what avowals are or that he does not understand what the normal, avowal use of 'I am in pain' is. He understands this, presumably, if he can make sense of the avowals of others.

It is important to see in this connection that being able to avow or say without reflection that one is in pain is not, strictly speaking,

[1] 'Knowledge of Other Minds', p. 977.

a matter of know-how; the sentence 'He knows how to avow that he is in pain' is, that is to say, extremely misleading.[1] For, gaining the ability to say 'I am in pain' at the appropriate times is not actually a process of coming to understand something that one could not understand by attending to the linguistic behaviour of other people. True, one must *learn* to make avowals; but this only means that one's ability to say certain words, spontaneously and reliably, results from training, from verbal conditioning. One gains an ability, to be sure; but this ability does not alone bring with it a special kind of understanding. The only kind of understanding peculiarly connected with avowals is an understanding of their conventional significance—and this can be gained by attending to the behaviour of others. We must not suppose, after all, that we begin our lives with a wholly natural, preconceptual understanding of what pain is, and then, after linguistic training, we come to understand that *this* and *that* are to be called 'pain', that the time to say 'I am in pain' is when I have *this*. To suppose such a thing is obviously to trail clouds of empiricist error, to signal one's allegiance to the Myth of the Given.

All this is not to deny, however, that a person who has to conclude that he is in pain lacks a very important ability that people normally have. But if such a person's other linguistic abilities are sufficiently varied and complicated, there is surely a strong basis for crediting him with some understanding of what he says when he concludes that he must be feeling pain. To assume that he necessarily gibbers or misuses language is tantamount to saying that Helen Keller gibbered or misused language when she wrote and spoke of the perceptible world around her.

It is clear, then, that the Wittgenstein-Malcolm 'criteriological' argument for the infallibility of first-ever psychological utterances requires considerable revision—indeed, like the 'pain-behaviour' argument, it clearly fails to show that there is anything intrinsically incorrigible about such utterances. For if we allow that a person who had never felt pain, or whose pain-avowing mechanism is not fully developed, may still have a high degree of understanding of the sentence 'I am in pain' if he has most of the abilities in which a

[1] This sentence is constantly, though perhaps inadvertently, used by philosophers sympathetic to the later Wittgenstein. See, e.g., Malcolm's *Dreaming*, where he asks such questions as: 'How can one verify that another person understands *how to use* this sentence to describe his own state?' (p. 9; my italics).

completely unqualified understanding of the sentence consists, then it would be possible for him honestly to assert that he is in pain and yet be wrong: for in relying, as he must, on behaviour that is accessible to all, his statement faces the same risks as the statements that other people might make about him, or as the statements that he might make about the feelings of others. A person in his position is, of course, rare, for man's lot is not a numb one; and it is natural, therefore, to assume that a living person in his position is unlikely to be found. But the possibility of such a man is still relevant to the philosophical task of testing the bounds of our concepts, for it shows that our criteria for an assertion that one is in pain are *not* so strict or definite that a mistake about being in pain is a conceptual impossibility, something it is 'senseless' to talk about.

Summary. I have tried in this paper to bring out the considerable complexity that lurks, apparently unnoticed by many philosophers even today, in simple avowals of being in pain. I tried to show, more specifically, that there is nothing about the criteria for understanding such words as 'pain', and nothing about the criteria for using them to make assertions, that supports the perennial temptation to regard these words as being somehow equivocal, involving different 'senses' in first- and other-person uses. On the contrary, I tried to show, in what was perhaps tedious detail, that the facts generally advanced in favour of this view are importantly misunderstood, and that when these facts are clarified, they can be seen to support, rather than refute, the less paradoxical view of common sense, namely, that these words, taken literally, are harmlessly univocal in both first- and other-person uses.

III

MUST EVERY INFERENCE BE EITHER DEDUCTIVE OR INDUCTIVE?

by S. F. BARKER

Professor of Philosophy, The Johns Hopkins University

Philosophical problems often take the form of questions about how we can know certain kinds of things which we do appear to know, yet our knowledge of which seems difficult to account for. How can we know the truth of statements about what the world outside our minds is like? How can we know the truth of statements about what is in the minds of others? How can we know the truth of statements about what is morally right? How can we know the truth of statements about whether a work of art is aesthetically good? How, if at all, can we know the truth of religious statements? Questions like these are perplexing because the statements that we want to justify do not appear to follow either deductively or inductively from the kind of evidence available to us. In dealing with questions like these, philosophers of an earlier generation often tried to answer by appealing to some special mode of knowing. They often held that we attain our knowledge of these matters either noninferentially through synthetic *a priori* insight into the truth of the statements concerned, or inferentially by deducing those statements from other more general statements whose truth is apprehended through synthetic *a priori* insight. Nowadays the synthetic *a priori*, that traditional asylum of ignorance, is no longer in favour; the postulating of special modes of knowing is no longer regarded as an adequate way of answering philosophical questions like these. In place of that approach, one of the newer ways of treating such philosophical problems is by appeal to special forms of inference, special modes of reasoning. We hear talk nowadays of special modes of reasoning about moral questions, about legal questions, about questions of aesthetic criticism, even about religious questions. According to this sort of view, certain kinds of conclusions, even though they do not follow either deductively or inductively from the attainable evidence, can nevertheless be reached by logically legitimate reasoning: but the reasoning itself is of some hitherto unrecognized kind that is neither deduction nor induction.

To many ears, however, the suggestion that there could be logically legitimate modes of inference that are neither deductive nor inductive sounds paradoxical, or even self-contradictory. The suggestion clashes with the idea that deduction and induction are the sole modes of inference; and this idea has become widespread and well entrenched not only in the writings of philosophers but also in elementary textbooks of logic. According to this widespread view, any inference that reaches its conclusion in a logically legitimate manner must be either deductive or inductive. If an inference is deductive, then deductive standards of rigour are to be used in judging its validity, while if it is inductive, less stringent inductive standards of rigour should be used in judging whether it is logically legitimate. But an inference that measured up neither to deductive standards nor to inductive ones would be no legitimate inference at all; it would necessarily be a logically unjustified way of arriving at a conclusion.

In this essay I want to examine the conflict between these two points of view: on the one hand, the view that there are logically legitimate modes of inference that are neither deductive nor inductive, and, on the other, the view that every logically legitimate inference must be either deductive or inductive. I do not propose to say anything about the specific new modes of inference that may or may not be found in specific fields of inquiry, nor do I propose to consider the question whether induction does or does not deserve to be regarded as a mode of inference essentially distinct from deduction. I wish to discuss here only the abstract general question whether there can be inferences that are neither deductive nor inductive.

What conception of deduction and what conception of induction are involved in this current view that regards them as the sole two modes of reasoning? As for deduction, categorical syllogisms are usually cited as simple paradigm instances of deductive inference. Thus if someone argues, 'All vegetarians are teetotallers, no Frenchmen are teetotallers, therefore no Frenchmen are vegetarians', this is a clear-cut case of deduction. Deduction is thought of as having the following combination of traits. First of all, a valid deductive inference is *demonstrative*, in the sense that the premises if one knew beyond question that they were true would provide one with unsurpassably complete justification for believing the conclusion.[1] Moreover, in a valid deduction the conclusion is ***not more general*** than are the premises from which it is derived. This feature of deduction was often stressed as important by traditional philosophers of logic, though the notion of generality involved here was more commonly emphasized than explained. Suffice it to say that, roughly speaking, to call the conclusion of an inference more general than the premises is to say that there are two classes c and c', concerning whose interrelation the premises entail merely that part at least of c is included in (or excluded from) c', while the conclusion by itself entails that all, or at any rate a more inclusive part, of c is included in (or excluded from) c'. The point then is that a logically legitimate deduction has the negative feature that its conclusion is not more general than are its premises. Furthermore, as a third feature, a valid deduction is *explicative*, in the sense that the conclusion cannot have empirical content going beyond that of the premises; in other words, any empirical observation or discovery that would count against the conclusion would have to count against the premises to an at least equal degree.[2]

Induction is thought of as the kind of reasoning that is basic to the scientific method; the kind of reasoning by which, ultimately, all inferential claims about matters of fact must be justified. A simple, clear-cut example of the sort of reasoning that is thought of as inductive would be: 'Each of the vegetarians with whom I've been acquainted was a teetotaller; therefore, probably all vegetarians are teetotallers.' (I shall not consider whether this is good or bad inductive reasoning; it serves merely as an example of reasoning that is clearly inductive.) Induction is thought of as having a combination of traits that contrast with the traits of deduction. An inductive argument is never demonstrative, but at its best is only ***problematic;*** that is, the premises confirm or support the conclusion, they make it reasonable to believe the conclusion but do not entail it.[3] Moreover, in induction the conclusion ***can be***

[1] The terms 'demonstrative' and 'problematic' are borrowed from W. E. Johnson, *Logic*, Part I, Cambridge 1919, p. 19.

[2] The term 'explicative' is borrowed from C. S. Peirce, *Collected Papers*, Cambridge (Mass.) 1932, vol. II, sections 680, 709.

[3] The terms 'demonstrative' and 'problematic' are borrowed from W. E. Johnson, *op. cit.*, p. 19.

more general than are the premises, or data, upon which it is based. Furthermore, an inductive argument can be *ampliative;* that is, its conclusion can have empirical content not present in the premises —which is to say that there can be empirical discoveries that could count against the conclusion without counting to an at least equal extent against the premises.[1]

In discussing the question whether every logically legitimate inference must necessarily be either deductive or inductive, we must consider just how we are to understand the terms 'deduction' and 'induction'. The traits that are commonly attributed to deductive inferences have been mentioned, as have the contrasting traits that are commonly attributed to inductive inferences. But if we are to make headway with the question whether the categories of deduction and induction exhaust the field of logically legitimate inferences, we must be more specific about how deduction and induction are to be defined. Does every deduction have by definition all three of the traits that were mentioned, and is every inference having them a deduction? Does every induction have by definition all three of the contrasting traits that were mentioned, and is every inference having them an induction? We must look further at the definitions of these two modes of reasoning.

With regard to deduction, it seems safe to say that practically all philosophical writers who use the term nowadays use it in such a way that valid deductions must exhibit all three of the traits that were mentioned. If we regard its being demonstrative as the essential trait of any valid deduction, then we can see that any such inference must possess also the trait of not having a conclusion that is more general than the premises—since any inference whose conclusion was more general than its premises could not be demonstrative, as knowing the truth of the premises could not absolutely justify one's believing the conclusion. Moreover, any demonstrative inference must possess also the trait of being explicative—since an inference whose conclusion had any sort of empirical content going beyond that of its premises would be an inference in which knowing that the premises were true could not absolutely justify one's believing the conclusion. One qualification is called for, however. It would be misleading simply to define

[1] The term 'ampliative' is borrowed from C. S. Peirce, *op. cit.*, sections 680, 709.

deductive inference as inference that is demonstrative, for according to that usage, there could be no such thing as a fallacious deductive inference; yet it is customary to speak of logically bad deductions as well as of logically good ones. We can set this matter right if we define deduction by saying that an inference is deductive if and only if either its premises do strictly guarantee its conclusion, or else at any rate the speaker advances those premises with the claim that they do so.

This way of defining deduction makes reference to the speaker's claim, yet it would be unfair to suppose that this introduces an improperly psychological element into logic. Our definition of deduction must refer to what the speaker is claiming, if it is to allow us to distinguish between invalid deductions and nondeductions. Suppose someone argues, 'All vegetarians are teetotallers, and he's a teetotaller, so I think he's a vegetarian.' Is this inference a definitely illegitimate deduction, or is it an induction which may possibly be logically legitimate? We cannot decide without considering whether the speaker is claiming that his conclusion is strictly guaranteed by the premises (in which case, the inference is a fallacious deduction) or whether he is merely claiming that the premises supply real reason for believing the conclusion (in which case, the inference is an induction which in an appropriate context might be legitimate).

So much for the definition of deduction. The term 'induction' is comparatively more troublesome, for there is less general agreement about the manner in which it is to be defined. Aristotle employs the word 'epagoge' as a technical term, and the word 'induction' was coined as an English translation for it.[1] Aristotle conceived of induction as the process of establishing a universal fact not by deduction from a wider principle, but rather by appeal to the particular cases in which its truth is shown. He seems mainly to have regarded it as a process of deriving a conclusion to the effect that all members of a genus possess a certain property from premises to the effect that for each of the several species falling under that genus, all members of the species possess this property. In discussing our contemporary problem we cannot rest content with Aristotle's usage, however. He does not explain very clearly what sense he intends his term to have, so that it is hardly possible for us to say, regarding new inferences that we meet, whether they

[1] H. W. B. Joseph, *An Introduction to Logic*, Oxford 1916, p. 378.

are or are not forms of induction in Aristotle's sense. Moreover in so far as we can grasp what it is, we can see that Aristotle's notion of induction differs distinctly from current notions of it, for Aristotle seems not to conceive of induction as either problematic or ampliative. Uses of the term 'induction' in earlier modern philosophy also differ distinctly from our current use; when Bacon and Newton speak of induction they seem to mean a method for making scientific discoveries, rather than a mode of inference capable of justifying conclusions.

Due in considerable measure to the influence of J. S. Mill, along with Whewell and others, the term 'induction' has now come to be commonly used by philosophers to refer to a mode of inference, or proof, as well as to a way of forming hypotheses or making discoveries. Here we begin to find a sense of the term 'induction' that is relevant to our question whether every inference must be either deductive or inductive. Harking back to Aristotle, Mill defines induction as the inferring of a proposition from other propositions less general; and this he contrasts with Ratiocination, or Syllogism, which he defines as the inferring of a proposition from propositions equally or more general.[1] Many subsequent writers have followed in Mill's footsteps, identifying induction with generalization. For example, W. E. Jevons adopted a definition of induction almost identical to Mill's,[2] as did W. E. Johnson.[3] This sort of usage has been embraced also by various more recent writers. Thus, for instance, Cohen and Nagel identified induction with generalization[4]; John Dewey defined induction as a kind of generalization[5]; so does Max Black, who declares that 'induction is a process of reasoning in which a proposition of the form *all P are Q* is asserted on the basis of a number of propositions having the form *this P is Q* . . .'[6]; Braithwaite defines induction as 'the inference of an empirical generalization from its instances' (though he adds the awkward amplification, 'or of a scientific hypothesis from empirical evidence for it')[7]; and J. P. Day[8] and Henry

[1] John Stuart Mill, *A System of Logic*, New York 1870, p. 182.
[2] W. S. Jevons, *Elementary Lessons in Logic*, London 1898, p. 211.
[3] W. E. Johnson, *Logic*, Part III, Cambridge 1924, p. 47.
[4] Morris R. Cohen and Ernest Nagel, *An Introduction to Logic and Scientific Method*, New York 1934, p. 14.
[5] John Dewey, *Logic: The Theory of Inquiry*, New York 1938, pp. 422, 426.
[6] Max Black, *Critical Thinking*, New York 1946, p. 276.
[7] R. B. Braithwaite, *Scientific Explanation*, Cambridge 1953, p. 257.
[8] John Patrick Day, *Inductive Probability*, London 1961, p. 1.

Kyburg[1] both follow this same line, identifying induction with generalization.

Not all contemporary writers define induction as generalization, however. A second line of definition identifies inductive inferences with problematic inferences. Thus Strawson holds that 'reasoning from non-necessary statements to a non-necessary conclusion in which the first does not entail the second . . . is generally called induction.'[2] Presumably Strawson would want to distinguish between induction and fallacious deduction, so we should understand his definition to mean that induction is reasoning in which the premises do not entail the conclusion, and the speaker does not intend to claim that they do so. Thus, induction is being defined as nondeductive inference that is claimed to be problematic only. This conception is echoed by the authors of some widely used elementary textbooks in logic. For example, Copi presents as the essential feature of inductive arguments that the reasoning does not claim to be conclusive.[3] Beardsley introduces the notion of induction in the same way, explaining as its essential feature that 'the inductive argument makes a claim that the evidence is sufficient to make the conclusion, at the very least, more likely to be true than false.'[4] This conception of inductive inference as nondeductive inference that claims only to be problematic is now rather widespread.

There is also a third line of definition of the term 'induction' which deserves consideration, even though it has been less widely advocated. Mill, when he comes in his discussion of reasoning to his section entitled 'The true type, what', gives us his view that the kind of reasoning upon which all our knowledge ultimately rests is reasoning from observed particulars to observed particulars; and it is the ampliative rather than the problematic character of such reasoning that Mill stresses.[5] Mill himself did not apply the term 'induction' to this type of reasoning, but if we are impressed by the importance of its ampliative character, we might go on to define inductive reasoning simply as nondeductive reasoning that

[1] Henry E. Kyburg, Jr., *Probability and the Logic of Rational Belief*, Middletown 1961, p. 270.

[2] P. F. Strawson, *Introduction to Logical Theory*, London 1952, p. 237.

[3] Irving M. Copi, *Introduction to Logic* (second edition), New York 1961, p. 9.

[4] Monroe C. Beardsley, *Practical Logic*, New York 1950, p. 201.

[5] John Stuart Mill, *A System of Logic*, Bk. II, ch. III.

is ampliative. One of von Wright's definitions of induction in effect amounts to this.[1]

So far, we have noticed three different contemporary conceptions of how induction is to be defined: the conception of induction as generalization, the conception of induction as nondeductive inference that claims only to be problematic, and the conception of induction as nondeductive ampliative inference. Someone may ask, why all this scholastic niggling? What does it matter whether

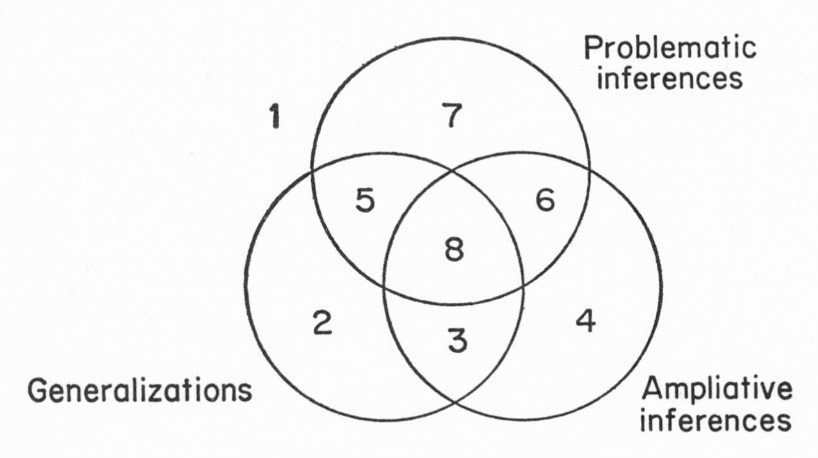

FIG. 1. Logically Legitimate Inferences

we define induction as generalization, whether we define it as problematic reasoning, or whether we define it as ampliative reasoning? There isn't any significant difference between these conceptions, is there? It all comes to the same thing, doesn't it? This is what we must look into. Let us consider the interrelations of these three traits, as they pertain to inferences that are logically legitimate (that is, which commit no fallacy). The matter can be represented in a Venn diagram (Fig. 1).

Region 1 of this diagram represents inferences that are nonproblematic (that is, demonstrative), nonampliative (that is, explicative), and whose conclusions are not more general than their premises. Such inferences, and these alone, are logically legitimate deductions.

[1] G. H. von Wright, *A Treatise on Induction and Probability*, New York 1951, p. 13.

Region 8 of the diagram represents inferences that are ampliative, whose conclusions are more general than their premises, and that are problematic (here we take this last to mean that the premises support the conclusion but do not guarantee it, and that the speaker claims no more than this). Such inferences are clear-cut instances of induction; they count as inductions according to each of the current definitions of induction. Thus, regions 1 and 8 contain the clear-cut cases of deduction and induction. The way in which the nature of induction is explained by many philosophers and by many elementary textbooks in logic tends to give the impression that all the remaining regions of the diagram must be empty. Whether they are empty is what we now need to consider.

Regions 2, 3, and 4, at any rate, do have to be empty. Regions 2 and 3 would represent logically legitimate nonproblematic inferences whose conclusions were more general than their premises; but it is clear that there can be no such inferences, for having a conclusion more general than its premises precludes the possibility of being nonproblematic. Such an inference can at best be problematic, since the truth of the premises would not be sufficient absolutely to guarantee the truth of the conclusion. Similarly, region 4 must be empty, for being ampliative likewise precludes being nonproblematic.

The three remaining regions, 5, 6, and 7, are not so easily disposed of. With regard to each, there are controversial ramifications which cannot be fully treated in a brief essay such as this; but we can at least examine prospective examples of inferences which appear to fit into each region. Let us consider these regions in turn.

Region 5 represents problematic inferences that are generalizations (that is, that have conclusions more general than their premises), yet that are not ampliative. Are there any such explicative problematic generalizations? Consider the following example. Noticing that calculations made concerning various particular sizes of right triangles show in each case that the square of the hypothenuse equals the sum of the squares of the other two sides, a novice at geometry might generalize that therefore this may well be true of all right triangles. Here the form of the reasoning is like that of more normal cases of inductive generalization: noticing that a number of known cases bear out a generalization and that no known case conflicts with it, one infers that the generalization holds. The example differs from normal cases of induction in that the conclusion is not an empirical statement, nor are the premises. Now, of course, this procedure is not something to rest content with in mathematics, where rigorously deductive proofs are desired. Surely, however, it would not be right to say that this inference is bound to be logically fallacious. It is an inference, and not a logically fallacious or contemptible one, provided that the speaker does not claim too much: he is entitled to claim that he has found a genuine reason for believing the conclusion, though of course he is not entitled to claim that he has found demonstrative proof of it. For someone ignorant of the deductive proof of the Pythagorean theorem, this problematic explicative generalization provides some modest but genuine ground for believing the conclusion. Therefore we must regard region 5 of the diagram as not empty.

Next let us consider region 6 of the diagram. This region represents ampliative problematic inferences that are not generalizations. Are there any logically legitimate inferences of this type? What seems to be a paradigm example of this sort is offered by Wisdom: the jays are now chattering in just that excited way they've so often done in the past when the fox proved near at hand; so we may expect soon to have a view of our quarry this morning.[1] Here the inference is based upon observations of past cases, but instead of reaching a generalization as the conclusion, a conclusion relating to a single further case is inferred. The reasoning is problematic, for it provides good but not conclusive grounds for our believing the conclusion. And it is ampliative, in that the conclusion goes beyond the empirical content of the premises. The example seems to show that region 6 is not vacant.

However, some philosophers would insist that the sort of reasoning 'from particulars to particulars' involved in this example really must implicitly include generalization; and if that were so, the example would not belong to region 6. Such philosophers presumably would hold that an example like this one about the fox and jays must be analysed as involving two steps, first an inductive generalization and then a deductive syllogism in which the generalization is applied to the particular case at hand. According to this proposal the reasoning would take the form:

In various past cases when the jays chattered thus, the fox soon appeared.

[1] John Wisdom, *Other Minds*, Oxford 1952, p. 74.

Probably, therefore (by inductive generalization), whenever the jays chatter thus the fox soon appears.
Today the jays are chattering thus.
Therefore (by a deductive syllogism), today the fox will soon appear.

But now, if this were the correct analysis of the reasoning, it would mean that the conclusion about today's hunt cannot be more probable than is the generalization from which it is deduced (since a logical chain of this sort can be no stronger than its weakest link). Yet that is incorrect. The conclusion about today's hunt may very well be much more probable than is any generalization from which it can be deduced. Thus the proposed analysis is unacceptable; we should not regard the reasoning as involving generalization in this way. This brings us back to the view that the example is an ampliative problematic inference that is not a generalization; and this means that region 6 of the diagram is not empty.

There remains one further region of the diagram which requires consideration; it is region 7, the region representing nonampliative problematic inferences that are not generalizations. Are there any logically legitimate inferences of this type? In reflecting on this, let us begin by considering a specimen of reasoning occurring in Hume's *Dialogues Concerning Natural Religion*, which may be paraphrased as follows.

To Cleanthes, who thinks that the argument 'Watches have elaborately organized parts and they have makers, so the world, which has elaborately organized parts, must have a maker too' is cogent, Philo replies: Absurd! You might as well say that the argument 'There's blood in men and it circulates, and there's sap in plants, so it must circulate too' is cogent. (*A*)

Philo's argument here is an argument about an argument; Philo is disputing the logical cogency of Cleanthes' reasoning. In trying to show that Cleanthes' inference is of poor quality, Philo offers an analogy: he compares Cleanthes' inference with another which is very clearly of poor quality. Cleanthes' argument in favour of God's existence, the argument which Philo is discussing, is a piece of ampliative problematic reasoning that is not a generalization (like the example of the fox and jays, it belongs to region 6 of our diagram). But what is the character of Philo's argument about Cleanthes' argument?

To begin with, Philo's argument is explicative, not ampliative. To maintain that Philo's argument was ampliative would be to maintain that Philo's conclusion expresses an empirical conjecture going beyond what his premises say. But this is not so. When Philo asserts that Cleanthes' reasoning is bad, Philo is not making any sort of empirical prediction; Philo's conclusion embodies no conjecture about what the future course of sense experience is going to bring forth. Philo's conclusion is that Cleanthes' thinking is illogical, and this conclusion relates to a matter of logic, it does not express any empirical conjecture at all, therefore *a fortiori* none which goes beyond the premises. Thus we must regard Philo's inference as explicative, not as ampliative.

Now for the more vexing question: is Philo's a demonstrative inference, or is it a problematic one? That is, does his argument purport to establish its conclusion conclusively, or does it purport only to give some support to its conclusion? Let us examine what ensues if we try to classify Philo's argument as demonstrative. If we try to suppose that Philo is here making a demonstrative inference, then we shall have to say that his reasoning is enthymematic, that he is employing an unstated premise. We shall have to suppose that Philo is really saying something like this: that all arguments by analogy which involve a certain feature *F* are bad, that Cleanthes' reasoning is an argument by analogy involving feature *F*, and that Cleanthes' reasoning is therefore bad. What might this feature *F* be? What feature is the essential one that makes Cleanthes' argument logically unsatisfactory? If we try to enunciate what this feature is, we can say only something quite vague. We can say only that the requisite feature *F* has to do with there being an insufficient similarity between the items with regard to which the analogy is being drawn. Then we shall have to interpret Philo's meta-argument as follows:

All arguments by analogy that involve an insufficient similarity between the items with regard to which the analogy is being drawn are logically bad arguments;

Cleanthes' argument is an argument involving insufficient simi-

larity between the items (watches and the world) with regard to which the analogy is being drawn;
therefore, Cleanthes' argument is logically bad. (*B*)

This is how we must interpret Philo's reasoning, if we are to view his reasoning as demonstrative. But is this an acceptable way of interpreting Philo's argument?

Suppose that an argument is of such a kind that nobody would feel dubious about its conclusion without feeling at least equally dubious about one or another of its premises. Such an argument can never really accomplish anything towards demonstrating the truth of its conclusion to someone who had been dubious of the conclusion; it can never fulfil the function of proving its conclusion to someone. An argument like that is said to commit the fallacy of *petitio principii*, or begging the question. Now, when we try to supply the supposedly suppressed premise and thus transform Philo's reasoning *A* into syllogism *B*, the result inevitably is that we trivialize Philo's argument by turning it into a *petitio principii*. Philo's original argument *A* is not a *petitio principii*. On the contrary, it is an argument which might very well succeed in proving its point to someone like Cleanthes; it might very well show a person who had doubted the conclusion (about the lack of cogency in Cleanthes' reasoning) that this conclusion is right. Argument *B* is an empty, contemptible piece of reasoning, however. No one who had any serious doubt about the conclusion of argument *B* would fail to have at least equally serious doubt about its minor premise. Anyone who is inclined to believe that Cleanthes' argument is good will be at least equally inclined to believe that there is a sufficient similarity between watches and the world. Because of this difference between *B* and *A*, argument *B* cannot be regarded as an acceptable translation of *A*. Hence, we must conclude that Philo's original argument *A* cannot be regarded as demonstrative. It is an example of a problematic explicative inference that is not a generalization, and so it serves to show that region 7 of our diagram is not vacant.

This example drawn from Hume is clearly an explicative inference, since its conclusion is not an empirical statement at all, and therefore of course has no empirical content going beyond that of the premises. Might we also have inferences belonging to region 7 that have empirical statements as their conclusions? Consider the following case. Suppose that there are people who have seen dogs, cows, fish, porpoises, and all such animals. They have observed a great deal about the appearance, behaviour, and physiology of these creatures. Yet they have not yet reached agreement about whether the porpoise is a fish or a mammal. One of them might reason: 'Though it lives in the sea like a fish, what's more important, in the light of all that we've observed, is that the porpoise breathes air and suckles its young as the dog and cow do; so it's a mammal and not a fish.'

Here we have a disagreement between opposing parties, but the disagreement is not about what future experience is going to bring to light; we are supposing that these people are very familiar with the creatures both of land and sea, and that the difference between the opposing parties is not one about what they expect to learn from future experience. Let us assume that none of these persons expects anything observable to happen with regard to porpoises which others of them do not expect. Still, though they do not disagree in their predictions about what observable things will happen, these people do disagree about whether the porpoise is a fish. Their disagreement is not of a hopeless kind, however, for reasoning may perhaps enable them to reach agreement: reasons may be given to show that porpoises are not fish. The reasoning employed here will not be ampliative, since the conclusion that porpoises are not fish does not embody any empirical conjecture going beyond the assumptions already agreed to. These people who disagree about whether porpoises are fish are not disagreeing about what will happen next, what they are disagreeing about is the pattern of what is already known. Even though there is no particular observation or prediction about creatures of land or sea that one person accepts and the other does not, still there is a pattern in these particular facts which one of them has seen, while the other has not detected it. The one who has seen this pattern of fundamental similarities between porpoises and dogs, cows, and pigs may be able to help the other person to see it too. The reasoning by which he does this will proceed by analogy, tracing the similarities and differences among the creatures involved.

Moreover, the reasoning here is not demonstrative but is only problematic; a reason, but not an absolutely conclusive reason, is being offered for believing that porpoises are mammals. The reasoning here is not of the demonstrative form, 'All creatures that suckle their young are mammals, the porpoise does so, so it's a mammal'; in that syllogism the major premise is more dubious even than the conclusion, so the syllogism would be valueless for convincing our doubter of the mammalhood of porpoises. In contrast, this nonampliative reasoning by analogy might intellectually convince him. Here then is a second example of reasoning of the kind that belongs in region 7 of our diagram, and this example differs from the previous example in that 'Porpoises are mammals' is an empirical conclusion. This conclusion is an empirical statement and does need to be supported by observation (that is, we are

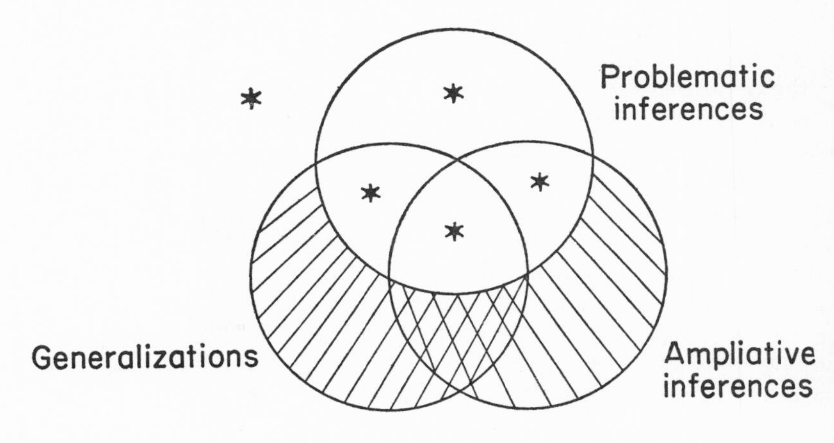

FIG. 2

understanding the sentence as empirical; of course someone else might think of it as true by definition). But in this specific discussion the reasoning used to establish this conclusion is explicative, since the conclusion does not have empirical content going beyond the assumptions accepted by both parties to this discussion.[1]

We can now enter on our diagram the various results we have arrived at (Fig. 2). What does the diagram now show regarding the question whether every inference must be either deductive or inductive? It shows that if by induction we mean nondeductive inferences that claim merely to be problematic, then of course every inference must be either deductive or inductive. However,

[1] Many examples of inferences of this type are discussed by Wisdom, for example in his *Philosophy and Psycho-Analysis*, Oxford 1953, pp. 156–58.

if we adopt that definition of induction we must remember that there will be inductive inferences of certain often overlooked kinds. We shall have to recognize inductions that are not generalizations and we shall have to recognize inductions that are explicative rather than ampliative. On the other hand, if we define induction as generalization, then we must recognize that there are inferences which are neither deductive nor inductive; some of these will be ampliative and some will not. Finally, if we choose to define induction as nondeductive inference that is ampliative (and this is the definition perhaps least likely to mislead), we must then recognize the existence of inferences neither deductive nor inductive, and these will be problematic explicative nongeneralizations. But whatever definition of induction we choose, we should not allow ourselves to be misled into supposing that only regions 1 and 8 of our diagram are open possibilities. That widespread but incorrect notion does not do justice to the diversity of inferences.

IV

AESTHETIC PROBLEMS OF MODERN PHILOSOPHY

by STANLEY CAVELL

Associate Professor of Philosophy, Harvard University

The Spirit of the Age is not easy to place, ontologically or empirically; and it is idle to suggest that creative effort must express its age, either because that cannot fail to happen, or because a new effort can create a new age. Still, one knows what it means when an art historian says, thinking of the succession of plastic styles, 'not everything is possible in every period'.[1] And that is equally true for every person and every philosophy. But then one is never sure what is possible until it happens; and when it happens it may produce a sense of revolution, of the past escaped and our problems solved—even when we also know that one man's solution is another man's problem.

Wittgenstein expressed his sense both of the revolutionary break his later methods descry in philosophy, and of their relation to methods in aesthetics and ethics.[2] I have tried, in what follows, to suggest ways in which such feelings or claims can be understood, believing them to be essential in understanding Wittgenstein's later philosophy as a whole. The opening section outlines two problems in aesthetics each of which seems to yield to the possibilities of Wittgensteinian procedures, and in turn to illuminate them. The concluding section suggests resemblances between one kind of judgment recognizable as aesthetic and the characteristic claim of Wittgenstein—and of ordinary language philosophers generally—to voice 'what we should ordinarily say'.

What I have written, and I suppose the way I have written, grows from a sense that philosophy is in one of its periodic crises of method, heightened by a worry I am sure is not mine alone, that

[1] Heinrich Wolfflin, *Principles of Art History*, foreword to the 7th German edition. Quoted by E. H. Gombrich, *Art and Illusion*, New York 1960, p. 4.

[2] Reported by G. E. Moore, 'Wittgenstein's Lectures in 1930–33', reprinted in Moore's *Philosophical Papers*, London 1959, p. 315.

method dictates to content; that, for example, an intellectual commitment to analytical philosophy trains concern away from the wider, traditional problems of human culture which may have brought one to philosophy in the first place. Yet one can find oneself unable to relinquish either the method or the alien concern.

A free eclecticism of method is one obvious solution to such a problem. Another solution may be to discover further freedoms or possibilities within the method one finds closest to oneself. I lean here towards the latter of these alternatives, hoping to make philosophy yet another kind of problem for itself; in particular, to make the medium of philosophy—that is, of Wittgensteinian and, more generally, of ordinary language philosophy—a significant problem for aesthetics.

TWO PROBLEMS OF AESTHETICS[1]

Let us begin with a sheer matter of words—the controversy about whether a poem, or more modestly, a metaphor, can be paraphrased. Cleanth Brooks, in his *Well Wrought Urn*,[2] provided a convenient title for it in the expression 'The Heresy of Paraphrase', the heresy, namely, of supposing that a 'poem constitutes a "statement" of some sort' (p. 179); a heresy in which 'most of our difficulties in criticism are rooted'. (p. 184)

The truth of the matter is that all such formulations [of what a poem says] lead away from the centre of the poem—not toward it; that the 'prose sense' of the poem is not a rack on which the stuff of the poem is hung; that it does not represent the 'inner' structure or the 'essential' structure or the 'real' structure of the poem. (p. 182) We can very properly use paraphrases as pointers and as short-hand references provided that we know what we are doing. But it is highly important that we know what we are doing and that we see plainly that the paraphrase is not the real core of meaning which constitutes the essence of the poem. (p. 180)

[1] Most of the material in this section was presented to a meeting of the American Society for Aesthetics at Harvard University in October 1962.

[2] *The Well Wrought Urn*, New York 1947. All page references to Brooks are to this edition. 'The Heresy of Paraphrase' is the title of the concluding chapter.

We may have some trouble in seeing plainly that the paraphrase is *not* the real core, or essence, or essential structure or inner or real structure of a poem; the same trouble we should have in understanding what *is* any or all of these things, since it takes so much philosophy just to state them. It is hard to imagine that someone has just flatly given it out that the essence, core, structure, and the rest, of a poem is its paraphrase. Probably somebody has been saying that poetry uses ornaments of style, or requires special poetic words; or has been saying what a poem means, or what it ought to mean—doing something that makes someone else, in a fit of philosophy, say that this is distorting a poem's essence. Now the person who is accused in Brooks' writ is probably going to deny guilt, feel that words are being put into his mouth, and answer that he knows perfectly well that a 'paraphrase, of course, is not the equivalent of a poem; a poem is more than its paraphrasable content'. Those are the words of Yvor Winters, whose work Professor Brooks uses as '[furnishing] perhaps the most respectable example of the paraphrastic heresy' (p. 183).[1] And so the argument goes, and goes. It has the gait of a false issue—by which I do not mean that it will be easy to straighten out.

One clear symptom of this is Brooks' recurrent concessions that, of course, a paraphrase is all right—if you know what you're doing. Which is about like saying that of course criticism is all right, in its place; which is true enough. But how, in particular, are we to assess a critic's reading the opening stanza of Wordsworth's 'Intimations' Ode and writing: '. . . the poet begins by saying that he has lost something' (Brooks, p. 116). We can ransack that stanza and never find the expression 'lost something' in it. Then the critic will be offended—rightly—and he may reply: Well, it does not actually say this, but it means it, it implies it; do you suggest that it does not mean that? And of course we do not. But then the critic has a *theory* about what he is doing when he says what a poem means, and so he will have to add some appendices to his readings of the poetry explaining that when he says what a poem means he does not say exactly quite just what the poem means; that is, he only points to its meaning, or rather

[1] For Winters' position, I have relied solely on his central essay, 'The Experimental School in American Poetry' from *Primitivism and Decadence*, itself republished, together with earlier of his critical works, under the title *In Defense of Reason.*

'points to the area in which the meaning lies'. But even this last does not seem to him humility enough, and he may be moved to a footnote in which he says that his own analyses are 'at best crude approximations of the poem'. (p. 189) By this time someone is likely to burst out with: But *of course* a paraphrase says what the poem says, and an *approximate* paraphrase is merely a bad paraphrase; with greater effort or sensibility you could have got it exactly right. To which one response would be: 'Oh, I can tell you exactly what the Ode means', and then read the Ode aloud.

Is there no real way out of this air of self-defeat, no way to get *satisfying* answers? Can we discover what, in such an exchange, is causing that uneasy sense that the speakers are talking past one another? Surely each knows exactly what the other means; neither is pointing to the smallest fact that the other fails to see.

For one suggestion, look again at Brooks' temptation to say that his readings *approximate* to (the meaning of) the poem. He is not there confessing his personal ineptitude; he means that any paraphrase, the best, will be only an approximation. So he is not saying, what he was accused of saying, that his own paraphrase was, in some more or less definite way, inexact or faulty: he denies the ordinary contrast between 'approximate' and 'exact'. And can he not do that if he wants to? Well, if I am right, he *did* do it. Although it is not clear that he *wanted* to. Perhaps he was *led* to it; and did he realize that, and would his realizing it make any difference? It may help to say: In speaking of the paraphrase as approximating to the poem (the meaning of the poem?) he himself furthers the suggestion that paraphrase and poem operate, as it were, at the same level, are the same kind of thing. (One shade of colour approximates to another shade, it does not approximate, nor does it fail to approximate, to the object of which it is the colour. An arrow pointing approximately north is exactly pointing somewhere. One paraphrase may be approximately the same, have approximately the same meaning, as another paraphrase.) And then he has to do everything at his philosophical disposal to keep paraphrase and poem from coinciding; in particular, speak of cores and essences and structures of the poem that are not reached by the paraphrase. It is as if someone got it into his head that really pointing to an object would require actually touching it, and then, realizing that this would make life very inconvenient, reconciled himself to common sense by saying: of course we *can* point to objects, but we must realize what we are doing, and that most of the time this is only approximately pointing to them.

This is the sort of thing that happens with astonishing frequency in philosophy. We impose a demand for absoluteness (typically of some simple physical kind) upon a concept, and then, finding that our ordinary use of this concept does not meet our demand, we accommodate this discrepancy as nearly as possible Take these familiar patterns: we do not really see material objects, but only see them indirectly; we cannot be certain of any empirical proposition, but only practically certain; we cannot really know what another person is feeling, but only infer it. One of Wittgenstein's greatest services, to my mind, is to show how constant a feature of philosophy this pattern is: this is something that his diagnoses are meant to explain ('We have a certain picture of how something must be'; 'Language is idling; not doing work; being used apart from its ordinary language games'). Whether his diagnoses are themselves satisfying is another question. It is not very likely, because if the phenomenon is as common as he seems to have shown, its explanation will evidently have to be very much clearer and more complete than his sketches provide.

This much, however, is true: If you put such phrases as 'giving the meaning', 'giving a paraphrase', 'saying exactly what something means (or what somebody said)', and so on, into the ordinary contexts (the 'language games') in which they are used, you will not find that you are worried that you have not really *done* these things. We could say: *That* is what doing them really is. Only that serenity will last just so long as someone does not start philosophizing about it. Not that I want to stop him; only I want to know what it is he is then doing, and why he follows just those particular tracks.

We owe it to Winters to make it clear that he does not say any of the philosophical things Brooks attributes to him. His thesis, having expressed his total acquiescence to the fact that paraphrases are not poems, is that *some* poems cannot be paraphrased—in particular, poems of the chief poetic talent of the United States during the second and third decades of the twentieth century; that poems which are unparaphrasable are, in that specific way, defective; and that therefore this poetic talent was led in regrettable directions. The merit of this argument for us, whether we agree with its animus or not, and trying to keep special theories about poetic discourse at arm's length, is its recognition that paraphrasability is one definite characteristic of uses of language, a characteristic that some expressions have and some do not have. It suggests itself that uses of language can be distinguished according to whether or not they possess this characteristic, and further distinguished by the kind of paraphrase they demand. Let us pursue this suggestion with a few examples, following Wittgenstein's idea that we can find out what kind of object anything (grammatically) is (for example, a meaning) by investigating expressions which show the kind of thing said about it (for example, 'explaining the meaning').

It is worth saying that the clearest case of a use of language having no paraphrase is its literal use. If I tell you, 'Juliet [the girl next door] is not yet fourteen years old' and you ask me what I mean, I might do many things—ask you what *you* mean, or perhaps try to teach you the meaning of some expression you cannot yet use (which, as Wittgenstein goes to extraordinary lengths to show, is not the same thing as *telling* you what it means). Or again, if I say, 'Sufficient unto the day is the evil thereof', which I take to be the literal truth, then if I need to explain my meaning to you I shall need to do other things: I shall perhaps not be surprised that you do not get my meaning and so I shall hardly ask you, in my former spirit, what you mean in asking me for it; nor shall I, unless my disappointment pricks me into offense, offer to teach you the meaning of an English expression. What I might do is to try to *put my thought another way*, and perhaps refer you, depending upon who you are, to a range of similar or identical thoughts expressed by others. What I cannot (logically) do in either the first or the second case is to *paraphrase* what I said.

Now suppose I am asked what someone means who says, 'Juliet is the sun'. Again my options are different, and specific. Again I am not, not in the same way, surprised that you ask; but I shall *not* try to put the thought another way—which seems to be the whole truth in the view that metaphors are unparaphrasable, that their meaning is bound up in the very words they employ. (The addition adds nothing: where else is it imagined, in that context, that meanings are bound, or found?) I may say something like: Romeo means that Juliet is the warmth of his world; that his day begins with her; that only in her nourishment can he grow. And his declaration suggests that the moon, which other lovers use as emblems of their love, is merely her reflected light, and dead in comparison;

and so on. In a word, I paraphrase it. Moreover, if I could not provide an explanation of this form, then that is a very good reason, a perfect reason, for supposing that I do not know what it means. Metaphors are paraphrasable. (And if that is true, it is tautologous.) When Croce denied the possibility of paraphrase, he at least had the grace to assert that there were no metaphors.

Two points now emerge: (1) The 'and so on' which ends my example of paraphrase is significant. It registers what William Empson calls the 'pregnancy' of metaphors, the burgeoning of meaning in them. Call it what you like; in this feature metaphors differ from some, but perhaps not all, literal discourse. And differ from the similar device of simile: the inclusion of 'like' in an expression changes the rhetoric. If you say 'Juliet is like the sun', two alterations at least seem obvious: the drive of it leads me to expect you to continue by saying in what definite respects they are like (similes are just a little bit pregnant); and, in complement, I *wait* for you to tell me what you mean, to deliver your meaning, so to speak. It is not up to me to find as much as I can in your words. The over-reading of metaphors so often complained of, no doubt justly, is a hazard they must run for their high interest. (2) To give the paraphrase, to understand the metaphor, I must understand the ordinary or dictionary meaning of the words it contains, *and* understand that they are not there being used in their ordinary way, that the meanings they invite are not to be found opposite them in a dictionary. In this respect the words in metaphors function as they do in idioms. But idioms are, again, specifically different. 'I fell flat on my face' seems an appropriate case. To explain its meaning is simply to *tell* it—one might say you don't *explain* it at all; either you know what it means or you don't; there is no richer and poorer among its explanations; you need imagine nothing special in the mind of the person using it. And you will find it in a dictionary, though in special locations; which suggests that, unlike metaphors, the number of idioms in a language is finite.[1]

One final remark about the difference between idioms and metaphors. Any theory concerned to account for peculiarities of

[1] In some, though not all, of these respects the procedure of 'giving the meaning' of an idiom is like that in translating: one might think of it as translating from a given language into itself. Then how is it different from defining, or giving a synonym?

metaphor of the sort I have listed will wonder over the literal meaning its words, in that combination, have. This is a response, I take it, to the fact that a metaphorical expression (in the '*A* is *B*' form at least) sounds like an ordinary assertion, though perhaps not made by an ordinary mind. Theory aside, I want to look at the suggestion, often made, that what metaphors literally say is *false*. (This is a response to the well-marked characteristic of 'psychic tension' set up in metaphors. The mark is used by Empson; I do not know the patent.) But to say that Juliet is the sun is not to say something false; it is, at best, wildly false, and that is not being just false. This is part of the fact that if we are to suggest that what the metaphor says is true, we shall have to say it is wildly true—mythically or magically or primitively true. (Romeo just may be young enough, or crazed or heretic enough, to have meant his words literally.) About some idioms, however, it is fair to say that their words literally say something that is quite false; something, that is, which could easily, though maybe comically, imagined to be true. Someone might actually fall flat on his face, have a thorn in his side, a bee in his bonnet, a bug in his ear, or a fly in his ointment —even all at once. Then what are we to say about the literal meaning of a metaphor? That it has none? And that what it literally says is not false, *and* not true? And that it is not an assertion? But it sounds like one: and people do think it is true and people do think it is false. I am suggesting that it is such facts that will need investigating if we are to satisfy ourselves about metaphors; that we are going to keep getting philosophical theories about metaphor until such facts are investigated; and that this is not an occasion for adjudication, for the only thing we could offer now in that line would be: all the theories are right in what they say. And that seems to imply that all are wrong as well.

At this point we might be able to give more content to the idea that some modes of figurative language are such that in them what an expression means cannot be said at all, at least not in any of the more or less familiar, conventionalized ways so far noticed. Not because these modes are flatly literal—there is, as it were, room for an explanation, but we cannot enter it. About such an expression it may be right to say: I know what it means but I can't say what it means. And this would no longer suggest, as it would if said about a metaphor, that you really do not know what it means —or: it might suggest it, but you couldn't be sure.

Examples of such uses of language would, I think, characteristically occur in specific kinds of poetry, for example Symbolist, Surrealist or Imagist. Such a use seems to me present in a line like Hart Crane's 'The mind is brushed by sparrow wings' [cited, among others, in the Winters essay], and in Wallace Stevens' 'as a calm darkens among water-lights', from *Sunday Morning*. Paraphrasing the lines, or explaining their meaning, or telling it, or putting the thought another way—all these are out of the question. One may be able to say nothing except that a feeling has been voiced by a kindred spirit and that if someone does not get it he is not in one's world, or not of one's flesh. The lines may, that is, be left as touchstones of intimacy. Or one might try *describing* more or less elaborately a particular day or evening, a certain place and mood and gesture, in whose presence the line in question comes to seem a natural expression, the only expression.

This seems to be what Winters, who profitably distinguishes several varieties of such uses of language, distrusts and dislikes in his defence of reason, as he also seems prepared for the reply that this is not a *failing* of language but a feature of a specific approach of language. At least I think it is a reply of this sort, which I believe to be right, that he wishes to repudiate by appealing to 'the fallacy of expressive (or imitative) form', instanced by him at one point as 'Whitman trying to express a loose America by writing loose poetry', or 'Mr Joyce [endeavouring] to express disintegration by breaking down his form'. It is useful to have a name for this fallacy, which no doubt some people commit. But his remarks seem a bit quick in their notation of what Whitman and Joyce were trying to express, and in their explanation of why they had to express themselves as they did; too sure that a break with the past of the order represented in modern art was not itself necessary in order to defend reason; too sure that convention can still be attacked in conventional ways. And they suggest scorn for the position that a high task of art has become, in our bombardment of sound, to create silence. (*Being* silent for that purpose might be a good example of the fallacy of imitative form. But that would depend on the context.) The fact is that I feel I would have to forgo too much of modern art were I to take his view of it.

Before we leave him, we owe it to Brooks to acknowledge a feature of Winters' position which may be causing his antipathy to it. Having wished to save Winters from a misconstruction of paraphrase, we gave back to that notion a specificity which, it now emerges, opens him to further objection. For his claim that poems that cannot be paraphrased—or, as he also puts it, do not 'rest on a formulable logic'—are therefore defective now means or implies that all poems not made essentially of metaphorical language (and/or similes, idioms, literal statements) are defective. It is certainly to be hoped that all *criticism* be rational, to be demanded that it form coherent propositions about its art. But to suppose that this requires all poetry to be 'formulable', in the sense that it must, whatever its form and pressure, yield to paraphrase, the way single metaphors specifically do, is not only unreasonable past defence but incurs what we might call the fallacy of expressive criticism.

In summary: Brooks is wrong to say that poems cannot in principle be fully paraphrased, but right to be worried about the relation between paraphrase and poem; Winters is right in his perception that some poetry is 'formulable' and some not, but wrong in the assurance he draws from that fact; both respond to, but fail to follow, the relation between criticism and its object. And now, I think, we can be brought more unprotectedly to face the whole question that motivates such a conflict, namely what it is we are doing when we describe or explain a work of art; what function criticism serves; whether different arts, or forms of art, require different forms of criticism; what we may expect to learn from criticism, both about a particular piece of art and about the nature of art generally.

The second problem in aesthetics must be sketched even more swiftly and crudely.

Is such music as is called 'atonal' (not distinguishing that, for our purposes now, from the term 'twelve-tone') really without tonality? (The little I will say could be paralleled, I think, in discussing the nature of the painting or sculpture called abstract or non-objective.) The arguments are bitter and, to my knowledge, without issue; and many musicians have felt within themselves both an affirmative and a negative answer.[1] Against the idea that this music lacks tonality are (1) the theory that we are so trained to our perception of musical organization that we cannot help hearing it in a tonal frame of reference; and (2) the fact that one *can*, often, *say* what key a so-called 'atonal' piece is in. In favour of the idea that it lacks

[1] I am told, by Professor David Lewin, that this was true of Anton Webern, who was in doubt about his own music in this regard.

tonality are (1) a theory of composition which says that it does, and whose point was just to escape that limitation, while yet maintaining coherence; and (2) the fact that it simply sounds so different. Without our now even glancing at the theories, let us look at the fact we recorded as 'being able to say, often, what key a piece is in'. Does that have the weight it seems to have? An instance which once convinced me of its decisiveness was this: in listening to a song of Schoenberg's, I had a clear sense that I could, at three points, hear it cadence (I almost said, try to resolve) in F♯ minor. Then surely it is *in* F♯ minor? Well, the Chopin *Barcarolle* is in the key of F♯ major. How do I know that? Because I can hear it try to cadence in F♯ major? Three or more times? And after that I am convinced it is, feel slightly relieved and even triumphant that I have been able to hear some F♯ major? But that is absurd. I *know* the key; everyone knows it; everyone knows it from the opening measure—well, at least before the bass figure that begins on the pitch of F♯: it does not take a brick wall to fall on us. I would not even know how to go about doubting its key or *trying* to hear it in its key. And I know it because I know that now it has moved to the subdominant of the key, and now the dominant of the key is being extended, and now it is modulating, and now it is modulating to a more distant key. And to know all this is to know the grammar of the expression 'musical key'. Sometimes, to be sure, a solidly tonal composer will, especially in 'development sections', obliterate the sense of placement in a key; but this is here a special effect, and depends upon an undoubted establishment of key. So if I insist upon saying that atonal music is really tonal (and to be said it has to be insisted upon) I have, so far as my ear goes, to forgo the grammar of the expression 'tonality' or 'musical key'—or almost all of it: I can retain 'almost cadences in' and 'sounds like the dominant of' but not 'related key', 'distant key', 'modulation' etc. And then I am in danger of not knowing what I am saying. Wittgenstein says that 'the speaking of language is part of an activity, or of a form of life' (*Investigations*, par. 23), and also 'To imagine a language means to imagine a form of life' (*ibid.*, par. 19). The language of tonality is part of a particular form of life, one containing the music we are most familiar with; associated with, or consisting of, particular ways of being trained to perform it and to listen to it; involving particular ways of being corrected, particular ways of responding to mistakes, to nuance, above all to recurrence and to variation and modification. No wonder we want to preserve the idea of tonality: to give all *that* up seems like giving up the idea of music altogether. I think it *is—like* it.

I shall not try to say why it is not fully that. I shall only mention that it cannot be enough to point to the obvious fact that musical instruments, with their familiar or unfamiliar powers, are employed—because *that* fact does not prevent us from asking, But is it music? Nor enough to appeal to the fact that we can point to pitches, intervals, lines and rhythm—because we probably do not for the most part know what we are pointing to with these terms. I mean we do not know *which* lines are significant (try to play the 'melody' or 'bass' of a piece of Webern's) and which intervals to hear as organizing. More important, I think, is the fact that we may see an undoubted musician speak about such things and behave toward them in ways similar (not, I think, more than similar) to the ways he behaves toward, say, Beethoven, and then we may sense that, though similar, it is a new world and that to understand a new world it is imperative to concentrate upon its inhabitants. (Of course there will be the usual consequences of mimicry and pretension.) Moreover, but still perhaps even more rarely, we may find ourselves *within* the experience of such compositions, following them; and then the question whether this is music and the problem of its tonal sense, will be . . . not answered or solved, but rather they will disappear, seem irrelevant.

That is, of course, Wittgenstein's sense of the way philosophical problems end. It is true that for him, in the *Investigations* at any rate, this happens when we have gone through a process of bringing ourselves back into our natural forms of life, putting our souls back into our bodies; whereas I had to describe the accommodation of the new music as one of naturalizing ourselves to a new form of life, a new world. That a resolution of this sort is described as the solution of a philosophical problem, and as the goal of its particular mode of criticism, represents for me the most original contribution Wittgenstein offers philosophy. I can think of no closer title for it, in an established philosophical vocabulary, than Hegel's use of the term *Aufhebung*. We cannot translate the term: 'cancelling', 'negating', 'fulfilling' etc. are all partial, and 'sublate' transfers the problem. It seems to me to capture that sense of *satisfaction* in our representation of rival positions which I was asking for when I rehearsed the problems of Brooks and Winters.

Of course we are no longer very apt to suppose, with Hegel, that History will make us a present of it: we are too aware of its brilliant ironies and its aborted revolutions for that. But as an ideal of (one kind of) philosophical criticism—a criticism in which it is pointless for one side to refute the other, because its cause and topic is the self getting in its own way—it seems about right.

In the *Tractatus* Wittgenstein says: 'The solution of the problem of life is seen in the vanishing of the problem' (6.521); and in the *Investigations* he says: '. . . the clarity that we are aiming at is indeed *complete* clarity. But this simply means that the philosophical problems should *completely* disappear' (par. 133). Yet he calls these problems *solved* (*Investigations*, *ibid.*); and he says that when 'there are . . . no questions left . . . this itself is the *answer*' (Tractatus; 6.25, my emphasis). In the central concept of his later work, this would seem to mean that the problems of life and the problems of philosophy have related grammars, because solutions to them both have the same form: their problems are solved only when they disappear, and answers are arrived at only when there are no longer questions—when, as it were, our accounts have cancelled them.

But in the *Investigations* this turns out to be more of an answer than, left this way, it seems to be; for it more explicitly dictates and displays the ways philosophy is to proceed in investigating problems, ways leading to what he calls 'perspicuous representation' (*übersichtliche Darstellung*). It is my impression that many philosophers do not like Wittgenstein's comparing what he calls his 'methods' to therapies (par. 133); but for me part of what he means by this comparison is brought out in thinking of the progress of psychoanalytic therapy. The more one learns, so to speak, the hang of oneself, and mounts one's problems, the less one is able to *say* what one has learned; not because you have *forgotten* what it was, but because nothing you said would seem like an answer or a solution: there is no longer any question or problem which your words would match. You have reached conviction, but not about a proposition; and consistency, but not in a theory. You are different, what you recognize as problems are different, your world is different. ('The world of the happy man is a different one from that of the unhappy man' (*Tractatus*, 6.43).) And this is the sense, the only sense, in which what a work of art means cannot be *said*. Believing it is seeing it.

When Wittgenstein says that 'the concept of a perspicuous representation . . . earmarks the form of account we give' (par. 122), I take him to be making a grammatical remark about what he calls a 'grammatical investigation', which is what his *Investigations* consist in (par. 90): no other form of resolution will count as philosophical. He says of his 'form of account' that it is 'the way we look at things'; and he then asks, parenthetically, 'Is this a "Weltanschauung"?' (par. 122). The answer to that question is, I take it, not No. Not, perhaps, Yes; because it is not a *special*, or competing, way of looking at things. But not No; because its mark of success is that the world seem—be—different. As usual, the claim to severe philosophical advance entails a reconception of the subject, a specific sense of revolution.

AESTHETIC JUDGMENT AND A PHILOSOPHICAL CLAIM

Another good cause for stumbling over the procedures of ordinary language philosophy lies in its characteristic appeal to what 'we' say and mean, or cannot or must say or mean. A good cause, since it is a very particular, not to say peculiar appeal, and one would expect philosophers dependent upon it themselves to be concerned for its investigation. I will suggest that the aesthetic judgment models the sort of claim entered by these philosophers, and that the familiar lack of conclusiveness in aesthetic argument, rather than showing up an irrationality, shows the kind of rationality it has, and needs.

Hume is always a respectable place to begin. Near the middle of his essay 'Of the Standard of Taste', he has recourse to a story from *Don Quixote* which is to illustrate that 'delicacy' of taste said to be essential to those critics who are to form our standard of it.

It is with good reason, says Sancho to the squire with the great nose, that I pretend to have a judgment in wine: This is a quality hereditary in our family. Two of my kinsmen were once called in to give their opinion of a hogshead, which was supposed to be excellent, being old and of a good vintage. One of them tastes it; considers it; and after mature reflection pronounces the wine to be good, were it not for a small taste of leather, which he perceived in it. The other, after using the same precautions, gives also his verdict in favour of the wine; but with the reserve of a taste of iron, which he could easily distinguish. You cannot imagine how much they were both ridiculed for their judgment. But who laughed in the end? On emptying the hogshead, there was found at the bottom, an old key with a leathern thong tied to it.

First of all, the fine drama of this gesture is greater than its factual decisiveness—a bit quixotic, so to say: for the taste may have been present and the object not, or the object present and the taste not. Second, and more important, the gesture misrepresents the efforts of the critic and the sort of vindication to which he aspires. It dissociates the exercise of taste from the discipline of accounting for it: but *all* that makes the critic's expression of taste worth more than another man's is his ability to produce for himself the thong and key of his response; and his vindication comes not from his pointing out that it is, or was, in the barrel, but in getting us to taste it there. Sancho's ancestors, he tells us, in each case after the precautions of reflection, both pronounced in favour of the wine; but he does not tell us what those reflections were, nor whether they were vindicated in their favourable verdict. Hume's essay, I take it, undertakes to explore just such questions, but in his understandable difficulty in directing us to the genuine critic and distinguishing him from the pretender, he says about him just what he, or anyone, says about art itself: that he is valuable, that we may disagree about his merits in a particular case, and that some, in the long run, 'will be acknowledged by universal sentiment to have a preference above others'. But this seems to put the critic's worth at the mercy of the history of taste; whereas his value to us is that he is able to make that history a part of his data, knowing that in itself, as it stands, it proves nothing—except popularity. His value to art and culture is not that he agrees with its taste—which would make him useful for guiding one's investments in the art market—but that he sets the terms in which our tastes, whatever they happen to be, may be protected or overcome. Sancho's descendants would, by the eighteenth century, have risen to gentlemen, exercising distinction in a world which knew what was right, and not needing to make their tastes their own. But it is Quixote who is the patron saint of the critic, desperate to preserve the best of his culture against itself, and surviving any failure but that of his honesty and his expression of it.

The idea of the agreement or 'reconciliation' of taste controls

Hume's argument; it is agreement that the standard of taste is to provide, so far as that is attainable. Hume's descendants, catching the assumption that agreement provides the vindication of judgement, but no longer able to hope for either, have found that aesthetic (and moral and political) judgements lack something: the arguments that support them are not conclusive the way arguments in logic are, nor rational the way arguments in science are. Indeed they are not, and if they were there would be no such subject as art (or morality) and no such art as criticism. It does not follow, however, that such judgements are not conclusive and rational.

Let us turn to Kant on the subject, who is, here as elsewhere, deeper and obscurer. Universal agreement, or as he also calls it, the 'harmony of sentiment' or 'a common sense of mankind', makes its appearance in the *Critique of Judgment* not as an empirical problem—which is scarcely surprising about Kant's procedure—but as an *a priori* requirement setting the (transcendental) conditions under which such judgements as we call aesthetic could be made *überhaupt*. Kant begins by saying that aesthetic judgement is not 'theoretical', not 'logical', not 'objective', but one 'whose determining ground can be *no other than subjective*'.[1] Today, or anyway the day before yesterday, and largely under his influence, we would have said it is not cognitive; which says so little that it *might* have been harmless enough. Kant goes on immediately to distinguish two kinds of 'aesthetical judgments', or, as he also calls them, judgements of taste; and here, unfortunately, his influence trickled out. The first kind he calls the taste of sense, the second the taste of reflection; the former concerns merely what we find pleasant, the latter must—logically must, some of us would say—concern and claim more than that. And it is only the second whose topic is the beautiful, whose role, that is, would be aesthetic in its more familiar sense. The something more these judgements must do is to 'demand' or 'impute' or 'claim' general validity, universal agreement with it; and when we make such judgements we go on claiming this agreement even though we know from experience that they will not receive it. (Are we, then, just wilful or stupid in going on making them?) Kant also describes our feeling or belief when we make such judgements—judgements in which we demand 'the assent of everyone', although we cannot 'postulate' this assent

[1] All quotations from Kant are from sections 7 and 8 of the *Critique of Judgment*.

as we could in making an ordinary empirical judgment—as one of '[speaking] with a universal voice'. That is the sort of thing that we are likely nowadays to call a piece of psychology, which is no doubt right enough. But we would take that to mean that it marks an accidental accompaniment of such judgments; whereas Kant says about this claim to universal validity, this voice, that it 'so essentially belongs to a judgment by which we describe anything as *beautiful* that, if this were not thought in it, it would never come into our thoughts to use the expression at all, but everything which pleases without a concept would be counted as pleasant'.[1] The possibility of stupidity here is not one of continuing to demand agreement in the face of the fact that we won't attain it; but the stupidity of going on making aesthetic judgements at all (or moral or political ones) in the face of what they cost us, the difficulties of finding them for ourselves and the risk of explicit isolation.

Kant seems to be saying that apart from a certain spirit in which we make judgements we could have no concepts of the sort we think of as aesthetic.[2] What can the basis for such a claim be? Let us look at the examples he gives of his two kinds of aesthetic judgements.

> . . . [someone] is quite contented that if he says, 'Canary wine is pleasant', another man may correct his expression and remind him that he ought to say, 'It is pleasant *to me*'. And this is the case not only as regards the taste of the tongue, the palate, and the throat, but for whatever is pleasant to anyone's eyes and ears. . . . To strive here with the design of reproving as incorrect another man's

[1] One might compare with this Wittgenstein's question: 'What gives us *so much as the idea* that living beings, things, can feel?' *Investigations*, par. 283.

[2] Another way of describing this assumption or demand, this thing of speaking with a universal voice, of judging 'not merely for himself, but for all men', Kant also describes as '(speaking) of beauty as if it were a property of things'. Only 'as if' because it cannot be an ordinary property of things: its presence or absence cannot be established in the way ordinary properties are; that is, they cannot be established publicly, and we don't know (there aren't any) causal conditions, or usable rules, for producing, or altering, or erasing, or increasing this 'property'. Then why not just say it *isn't* a property of an object? I suppose there would be no reason not to say this, if we could find another way of recording our conviction that it is one, anyway that what we are pointing to is *there*, in the object; and our knowledge that men make objects that create this response in us, and make them exactly with the idea that they will create it; and the fact that, while we know not everyone will agree with us when we say it is present, we think they are *missing something* if they don't.

judgement which is different from our own, as if the judgements were logically opposed, would be folly. . . .

The case is quite different with the beautiful. It would (on the contrary) be laughable if a man who imagined anything to his own taste thought to justify himself by saying: 'This object (the house we see, the coat that person wears, the concert we hear, the poem submitted to our judgement) is beautiful *for me*.' For he must not call it *beautiful* if it merely pleases him. . . .

What are these examples supposed to show? That using a form of expression in one context is all right, and using it in another is not all right. But what I wish to focus upon is the kind of rightness and wrongness invoked: it is not a matter of factual rectitude, nor of formal indiscretion but of saying something laughable, or which would be folly. It is such consequences that are taken to display a difference in the kind of judgement in question, in the nature of the concepts employed, and even in the nature of the reality the concepts capture. One hardly knows whether to call this a metaphysical or a logical difference. Kant called it a transcendental difference; Wittgenstein would call it a grammatical difference. And how can psychological differences like finding something laughable or foolish (which perhaps not *every* person would) be thought to betray such potent, or anyway different, differences?

Here we hit upon what is, to my mind, the most sensitive index of misunderstanding and bitterness between the positivist and the post-positivist components of analytical philosophy: the positivist grits his teeth when he hears an analysis given out as a logical one which is so painfully remote from formality, so obviously a question of how you happen to feel at the moment, so psychological; the philosopher who proceeds from everyday language stares back helplessly, asking, 'Don't you feel the difference? Listen: you *must* see it.' Surely, both know what the other knows, and each thinks the other is perverse, or irrelevant, or worse. (Here I must appeal to the experience of anyone who has been engaged in such encounters.) Any explanation of this is going to be hard to acquire. I offer the following guess, not because it can command much attention in itself, but as a way of suggesting the level I would expect a satisfying explanation to reach, a way of indicating why we lack as yet the concepts, even the facts, which must form a serious accommodation.

We know of the efforts of such philosophers as Frege and Husserl to undo the 'psychologizing' of logic (like Kant's undoing Hume's psychologizing of knowledge): now, the shortest way I might describe such a book as the *Philosophical Investigations* is to say that it attempts to undo the psychologizing of psychology, to show the necessity controlling our application of psychological and behavioural categories; even, one could say, show the necessities in human action and passion themselves.[1] And at the same time it seems to turn all of philosophy into psychology—matters of what we call things, how we treat them, what their role is in our lives.

For one last glance, let us adapt Kant's examples to a form which is more fashionable, and think of the sort of reasons we offer for such judgements:

1. *A*: Canary wine is pleasant.
   B: How can you say that? It tastes like canary droppings.
   A: Well, I like it.
2. *A:* He plays beautifully doesn't he?
   B1: Yes; too beautifully. Beethoven is not Chopin.

Or he may answer:

> *B2*: How can you say that? There was no line, no structure, no idea what the music was about. He's simply an impressive colourist.

Now, how will *A* reply? Can he now say: 'Well, I liked it'? Of course he *can*; but don't we feel that here that would be a feeble rejoinder, a *retreat* to personal taste? Because *B*'s reasons are obviously relevant to the evaluation of performance, and because they are *arguable*, in ways that anyone who knows about such things will know how to pursue. *A doesn't have* to pursue them; but if he doesn't, there is a price he will have to pay in our estimate of him. Is that enough to show it is a different kind of judgement? We are still in the realm of the psychological. But I wish to say

[1] Consider, for example, the question: 'Could someone have a feeling of ardent love or hope for the space of one second—*no matter what* preceded or followed this second?'; *Investigations*, par. 583. We shall not wish to say that this is logically impossible, or that it can in no way be imagined. But we might say: given our world this cannot happen; it is not, in our language, what 'love' or 'hope' mean; necessary in our world that this is not what love and hope are. I take it that our most common philosophical understanding of such notions as necessity, contingency, synthetic and analytic statements will not know what to make of our saying such things.

that the price is necessary, and specific to the sorts of judgements we call aesthetic.

Go back to my saying 'he doesn't have to pursue' the discussion, and compare the following case:

A: There is a goldfinch in the garden.
B: How do you know?
A: From the colour of its head.
B: But goldcrests also have heads that colour.
A: Well, *I* think it's a goldfinch (it's a goldfinch to me).

This is no longer a feeble rejoinder, a retreat to personal opinion: and the price that would be paid here is not, as it would be in the former case, that he is not very articulate, or not discriminating, or has perverse tastes: the price here is that he is either mad, or doesn't know what the word 'know' means, or is in some other way unintelligible to us. That is, *we rule him out* as a competent interlocutor in matters of knowledge (about birds?): whatever is going on, he *doesn't* know there is a goldfinch in the garden, whatever (else) he thinks he 'knows'. But we do not, at least not with the same flatness and good conscience, and not with the same consequences, rule out the person who liked the performance of the Beethoven: he still has a claim upon us, however attenuated; he *may* even have reasons for his judgement, or counters to your objections, which for some reason he can't give (perhaps because you've brow-beaten him into amnesia).

Leaving these descriptions so cruelly incomplete, I think one can now imagine the familiar response: 'But you admit that arguments in the aesthetic case may go on, may perhaps never end, and that they needn't go on, perhaps can't go on in some cases, and that they may have different "prices" (whatever they may mean), presumably depending on where they stop. How do you get logic out of that? What you cannot claim is that either party to the dispute, whether in the case Kant calls the taste of sense or the case he calls the taste of reflection, can *prove* his judgement. And would he want to even if he could? Isn't that, indeed, what all your talk about criticism was about: The person accounts for his own feelings, and then, at best "proves" them *to* another, shows them to whomever he wants to know them, the best way he can, the most effective way. That's scarcely logic; and how can you deny that it is psychology?'

It may help to reply to this: You call it psychology just because it so obviously is not logic, and it must be one or the other.[1] Contrariwise, I should admit that I call it 'logic' mostly because it so obviously is not 'psychology' in the way I think you mean it. I do not really think it is either of those activities, in the senses we attach to them now; but I cannot describe to anyone's satisfaction *what* it is. Wittgenstein called it 'grammar'; others might call it 'phenomenology'.

Those of us who keep finding ourselves wanting to call such differences 'logical' are, I think, responding to a sense of necessity we feel in them, together with a sense that necessity is, partly, a matter of the *ways* a judgement is supported, the ways in which conviction in it is produced: it is only by virtue of these recurrent patterns of support that a remark will count as—will be—aesthetic, or a mere matter of taste, or moral, propagandistic, religious, magical, scientific, philosophical. . . . It is essential to making an aesthetic judgement that at some point we be prepared to say in its support: don't you see, don't you hear, don't you dig? The best critic will know the best points. Because if you do not see *something*, without explanation, then there is nothing further to discuss. Which does not mean that the critic has no recourse: he can start training and instructing you and preaching at you—a direction in which criticism invariably will start to veer. (A critic like Ruskin may be a calamity, but he is no accident.) At some point, the critic will have to say: this is what I see. Reasons—at definite points, for definite reasons, in different circumstances—come to an end. (*Cf. Investigations*, par. 217.)

Those who refuse the term 'logic' are responding to a sense of arbitrariness in these differences, together with a sense that 'logic' is a matter of arriving at conviction in such a way that anyone who can follow the argument must, unless he finds something definitely wrong with it, *accept the conclusion*, agree with it. I do not know what the gains or disadvantages would be of unfastening the term 'logic' from that constant pattern of support or justification whose peculiarity is that it leads those competent at it to this kind of agreement, and extending it to patterns of justification having

[1] I do think that is the *entire* content of 'psychology' in such objections. Such a person knows what he means by logic: how to do it, how to recognize it when he sees it done, what he can expect from it, etc. But who knows any of this about the 'psychology' in question?

other purposes and peculiarities. All I am arguing for is that *pattern* and *agreement* are distinct features of the notion of logic.

If we say that the *hope* of agreement motivates our engaging in these various patterns of support, then we must also say, what I take Kant to have seen, that even were agreement in fact to emerge, our judgements, so far as aesthetic, would remain as essentially subjective, in his sense, as they ever were. Otherwise, art and the criticism of art would not have their special importance nor elicit their own forms of distrust and of gratitude. The problem of the critic, as of the artist, is not to discount his subjectivity, but to include it; not to overcome it in agreement, but to master it in exemplary ways. Then his work outlasts the fashions and arguments of a particular age. That is the beauty of it.

Kant's 'universal voice' is, with perhaps a slight shift of accent, what we hear recorded in the philosopher's claims about 'what we say': such claims are at least as close to what Kant calls aesthetical judgements as they are to ordinary empirical hypotheses. Though the philosopher seems to claim, or depend upon, severer agreement than is carried by the aesthetic analogue, I wish to suggest that it is a claim or dependence of the same kind.

We should immediately notice an obvious failure in the analogy between aesthetic judgements and the philosophical claim to voice what we say. The philosophical claim seems clearly open to refutation by an empirical collection of data about what people in fact say, whereas it makes no obvious sense to confirm or disconfirm such a judgment as 'The Hammerklavier Sonata is a perverse work' by collecting data to find out whether the Sonata is in fact perverse. It is out of the question to enter into this difficult range of problems now. But I cannot forbear mentioning several points which I have tried elsewhere to suggest, with, to judge from results, evident unsuccess.[1]

(1) I take it to be a phenomenological fact about philosophizing from everyday language that one feels empirical evidence about one's language to be irrelevant to one's claims. If such philosophizing is to be understood, then that fact about it must be understood. I am not saying that evidence about how (other) people speak can never make an ordinary language philosopher withdraw

[1] See J. Fodor and J. Katz, 'The Availability of What We Say', in the *Philosophical Review*, January 1963, an attack, primarily, on my paper 'Must We Mean What We Say?' which appeared in *Inquiry* in 1958 (vol. I, no. 3).

his typical claims; but I find it important that the most characteristic pressure against him is applied by producing or deepening an example which shows him that *he* would not say what he says 'we' say.

(2) The appeal to 'what we should say if . . .' requires that we imagine an example or story, sometimes one more or less similar to events which may happen any day, sometimes one unlike anything we have known. Whatever the difficulties will be in trying to characterize this procedure fully and clearly, this much can be said at once: if we find we disagree about what we should say, it would make no obvious sense to attempt to confirm or disconfirm one or other of our responses by collecting data to show which of us is in fact right. What we should do is either (*a*) to try to determine why we disagree (perhaps we are imagining the story differently)—just as, if we agree in response we will, when we start philosophizing about this fact, want to know why we agree, what it shows about our concepts; or (*b*) we will, if the disagreement cannot be explained, either find some explanation for *that*, or else discard the example. Disagreement is not disconfirming: it is as much a datum for philosophizing as agreement is. At this stage philosophizing has, hopefully, not yet begun.

(3) Such facts perhaps only amount to saying that the philosophy of ordinary language is not about language, anyway not in any sense in which it is not also about the world. Ordinary language philosophy is about whatever ordinary language is about.

The philosopher appealing to everyday language turns to the reader not to convince him without proof but to get him to prove something, test something, against himself. He is saying: look and find out whether you can see what I see, wish to say what I wish to say. Of course he often seems to answer or beg his own question by posing it in plural form: 'We say . . . ; We want to say . . . ; We can imagine . . . ; We feel as if we had to penetrate phenomena, repair a spider's web; We are under the illusion . . . ; We are dazzled . . . the idea now absorbs us. . . . we are dissatisfied. . . .' But this plural is still first person: it does not, to use Kant's word, 'postulate' that 'we', you and I and he, say and want and imagine and feel and suffer together. If we do not, then the philosopher's remarks are irrelevant to us. Of course he doesn't think they are irrelevant, but the implication is that philosophy, like art, is, and should be, powerless to *prove* its relevance; and that says something about the kind of relevance it wishes to have. All the philosopher, this kind of philosopher, can do is to express, as fully as he can, his world, and attract our undivided attention to our own.

Kant's attention to the 'universal voice' expressed in aesthetic judgement seems to me, finally, to afford some explanation of that air of dogmatism which claims about what 'we' say seem to carry for critics of ordinary language procedures, and which they find repugnant and intolerant. I think that air of dogmatism is indeed present in such claims; but if that is intolerant, that is because tolerance could only mean, as in liberals it often does, that the kind of claim in question is not taken seriously. It is, after all, a claim about *our lives*; it is differences, or oppositions, of these that tolerance, if it is to be achieved, must be directed toward. About what we should say when, we do not expect to have to tolerate much difference, believing that if we could articulate it fully we would have spoken for all men, found the necessities common to us all. Philosophy has always hoped for that; so, perhaps, has science. But philosophy concerns those necessities we cannot, being human, fail to know. Except that nothing is more human than to deny them.

V

SEEING SURFACES AND PHYSICAL OBJECTS

by THOMPSON CLARKE

Assistant Professor of Philosophy, University of California at Berkeley

More than one philosopher of impressive intelligence has taken the fact that normally we can see no more of a physical object than part of its surface to have paradoxical implications, that is, to signify that the 'common-sense' belief that we can see physical objects and on this basis know that there are such objects must either be flatly rejected or importantly qualified.[1] The critical response to this view has typically been that, on the contrary, to see a physical object just is (trivially) to see a part of its surface. According to critics,[2] some philosophers have been overly impressed by a trivial fact because they have assumed that it is part of the meaning of 'see' that 'see' is true of *A* only if 'see' is true of every bit of *A*.

Are these critics right? Is it because they have made this assumption that philosophers have been led to think that the fact

[1] For example: C. D. Broad, *The Mind and Its Place in Nature*, New York 1937, esp. pp. 148–151; G. E. Moore, *Some Main Problems of Philosophy*, London 1953, esp. pp. 33–34.

This would also be the position reached in the following argument which Descartes gives in the 2nd Meditation if this argument were carried to its logical conclusion:

'From this I should conclude that I knew the wax by means of vision and not simply by the intuition of the mind; unless by chance I remember that, when looking from a window and saying I see men who pass in the street, I really do not see them, but infer that what I see is men, . . . And yet what do I see from the window but hats and cloaks which may cover automatic machines? Yet I judge these to be men.'

[2] These views are so widely held that few philosophers bother to put them in print. But see, for example: Martin Lean, *Sense Perception and Matter*, New York 1953, esp. pp. 68–69.

In his recent book Chisholm, too, has maintained that the philosopher reaches his position owing to the mentioned 'assumption'.

Roderick M. Chisholm, *Perceiving: A Philosophical Study*, Ithaca, New York 1957. esp. pp. 153–156.

that normally we can see no more of a physical object than part of its surface (which I shall refer to for the sake of brevity as 'the *HM* fact', '*HM*' being an abbreviation for 'How Much') is not trivial but has important and surprising epistemological significance? Indeed, is the alleged *HM* fact really trivial?

I

How do philosophers who hold that the *HM* fact is not trivial support this conclusion? It is interesting that they present no argument on its behalf. On the contrary, they talk as if all we need do is *note* that we can't see the far side and inside but only part of the surface of the object before us and then we shall *see immediately* that we are not as well off as Common Sense supposed. They talk as if reaching their conclusion is like suddenly noticing a knock in the engine which hadn't registered on us before, and thus immediately being shaken out of our false complacency. But we can hardly resist dismissing this suggestion without a second thought, for can anything be more absurd than the supposition that generations of plain men have failed to notice that normally we can see no more of a physical object than part of its surface? Therefore it is difficult to refrain from thinking that some unexpressed premiss(es) must have led the philosopher to think that the *HM* fact has paradoxical implications.

Nevertheless we shall never do justice to the philosopher's position if dismissing his own account of how he arrives at his paradoxical conclusions we begin searching for assumptions which we suppose he *must* have made. It would have been obvious that there is important truth in his own account if the philosopher had presented his case as *P* does here:

Consider a situation in which another person *X* is looking at a physical object, say a tomato, in normal conditions (represented by diagram *ST*; '*ST*' is an abbreviation for 'Seeing the Tomato'). Perhaps he is seated at his desk in his study and the tomato is in front of him on the desk. Now this is the sort of situation in which we'd say that another person, *X*, can see a tomato.

But how much of the tomato can *X* see? He can't see any of the far side or inside. Let's mark this fact in the diagram, the cross-marks indicating the amount of the physical object which *X* can't see. (Ideally, say in a lecture using a blackboard, we would begin with *ST*, and subsequently mark these facts in *ST*. Here, though, we must mark them in a separate diagram, *STm*, which is the same as *ST* except for the marking. The letter '*m*' in '*STm*' is an abbreviation for 'marked'. The cross marks in the half of the tomato towards *X* indicate that all of this half except the surface hemisphere towards *X* is not seen by *X*.) All he can actually see of the physical object is a portion of the surface towards him. Let's indicate this fact more explicitly in the diagram by marking black the portion of the surface that he can see.

How do things look now that we have marked these facts in the

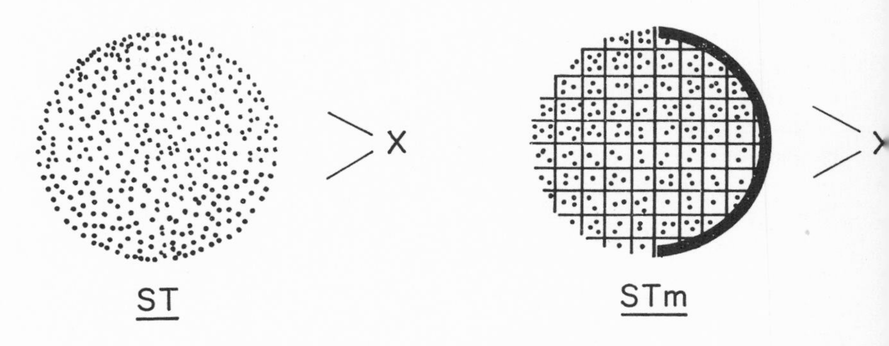

diagram? (Now, of course, we are considering *STm*.) We said that this was the sort of situation in which we'd say that *X* could see the tomato. But can he? No, he can't. Obviously all he can *really* see is that portion of the surface towards him indicated by the black line. So we now see that we were wrong to suppose that *X* could really see the physical object itself.

P's presentation of his case reveals how philosophers could have come to think that once we (merely) note the *HM* fact we see that we are not as well off perceptually as we had imagined. When we pass from *ST* to *STm* we *seem*, as *P* says, simply to have noted or marked the fact that *X* can't see any more of the physical object than part of its surface. Yet when we pass to *STm X*'s position suddenly does *seem* worse. The puzzle is not how *P* could possibly have supposed that once he (merely) noted the *HM* fact he saw that *X*'s position was worse than he and we, as plain men, would have supposed—for this is exactly what does *seem* to happen—but rather how it could be that this is *not* what really happens. If there is a sleight of mind here, what is it?

II

Although I think it may be obvious enough that *X*'s perceptual position does look worse when we pass to *STm*, I shall try in a moment to make this plainer still, or, rather, to establish a stronger claim about the workings of *P*'s presentation. For to say that *X*'s perceptual position in *STm* seems, but perhaps *only* seems, worse than the position we commonly suppose he can be in in a situation like *ST* is to understate the truth. *X*'s position in *STm is* not as good as the position we commonly suppose he can be in. The salient point of strength in *P*'s position is this: *after* we (do what *seems* to be only to) 'note' the *HM* fact we *do see* that the perceptual position *X* is in is not as good as the one we thought he was in *before* we 'noted' this fact. Therefore if there is any sleight of mind in *P*'s presentation it lies in the 'noting'. For if what we do amounts simply to noting the *HM* fact then we do genuinely learn, as *P* maintains, that *X*'s perceptual position cannot be as good as Common Sense supposes. We genuinely discover that the *HM* fact has this paradoxical implication unless this 'noting' is not genuine but is really an act which *changes X*'s position, *bringing it about* that he is in a worse position than he was in *ST*. If this 'noting' is in this way counterfeit what we have discovered is that the logic of 'see' is such that a certain act which *seems* to amount only to noting a fact can in reality worsen *X*'s perceptual position.

In sum, *P*'s presentation is characterized by these two propositions:

I. We do what *seems* to be just noting a fact (the *HM* fact) about the sort of situation in which we commonly suppose another person can see a physical object.

II. *After* 'noting' this *HM* fact, we see that the perceptual position *X* is in is inferior to the position we took him to be in before we 'noted' this fact.

Proposition (II) is deliberately ambiguous. It asserts that in *STm X*'s perceptual position *is* worse than the position we would have supposed *X* was in in *ST*, but it leaves open whether 'noting' the *HM* fact is genuine noting, hence just a part of *coming to see* that *X*'s position in *ST* is worse than we had supposed, or whether this 'noting' is spurious, *bringing it about* that *X*'s position is worse than his former position in *ST*. If the 'noting' is genuine, *STm* reveals the true state of affairs in *ST*. If it is not genuine, *ST* and *STm* are essentially different cases.

(I) and (II) together assert that *P* is led to his position not by reasoning or argumentation but by *doing something*, performing an act, which seems to be merely an innocent part of *inquiring* into the facts about a situation. We should, therefore, be well-advised not to speak of the 'arguments' or even of the 'considerations' which lead *P* to his position but rather, as I shall, of the apparently innocent 'inquiry' which does so. Since this inquiry centres on seeing part of the *surface* of a physical object, I shall refer to it, for the sake of brevity, as the 'surface-inquiry'.

Let us look more carefully now into whether (II) is true of *P*'s surface-inquiry. We must also work out exactly in what way *X*'s perceptual position in *STm* is inferior to the position we commonly suppose he is in in *ST*. Is *P* right? That is, is it true in *STm* that *X* can't see the tomato, that all he can *really* see is part of its surface?

It is curious, and important, that although every philosopher who takes the *HM* fact to have paradoxical implications thinks it signifies that in some way the common-sense belief that we can see physical objects is mistaken, no two agree about exactly how it is in error. It is clear from what Descartes says in his 'hats and cloaks' example[1] that he would take the *HM* fact to mean that we *cannot* see physical objects. Moore takes it to signify that 'whenever we talk roughly of seeing any object, it is true that, in another and stricter sense of the word *see*, we only see *a part of* it'.[2] Broad holds that what we discover is that 'the perceptual situation contains as a constituent' not the physical object itself, as, according to Broad, common speech suggests, but at most only part of the surface of the physical object.[3] The question which produces this controversy, expressed in terms of *P*'s surface-inquiry, is: 'Can *X* be said in *STm* to see the tomato?' That a question produces such interminable controversy suggests that something may be wrong with the question itself, and later I am going to argue that, indeed, this question is not as straightforward as these philosophers suppose.

[1] See above, note 1, p. 98.
[2] G. E. Moore, *Some Main Problems of Philosophy*, London 1953, p. 34.
[3] C. D. Broad, *The Mind and Its Place in Nature*, New York 1937, p. 149.

I want now, however, to argue that these several philosophers are each right in one respect, namely that whatever exactly *X*'s perceptual position is in *STm*, it is not as good as the position we would have supposed him to be in in *ST*. In order to show this I shall try now to make plain that *even if X* can be said to see the tomato in *STm*, nevertheless his seeing of this physical object in *STm* is not 'as good as' we suppose it can be in a situation like *ST*.

Consider any physical object in your immediate vicinity that you can see, say a pen. Now imagine that a thin portion of the pen (a portion including that part of the surface towards you that you can see, but also having some thickness) is peeled off and moved slightly towards you and that this portion completely obscures the rest of the pen. What effect does this have on what you, as a plain man (that is putting aside any philosophical convictions you may have about perception), would say you see? Well, you would say, would you not, that now you can see only the peeled-off portion? Before the portion is peeled off one says 'I see a pen'. After it is peeled off and moved forward one says 'Now I see only a thin portion of a pen'.

Now consider these figures:

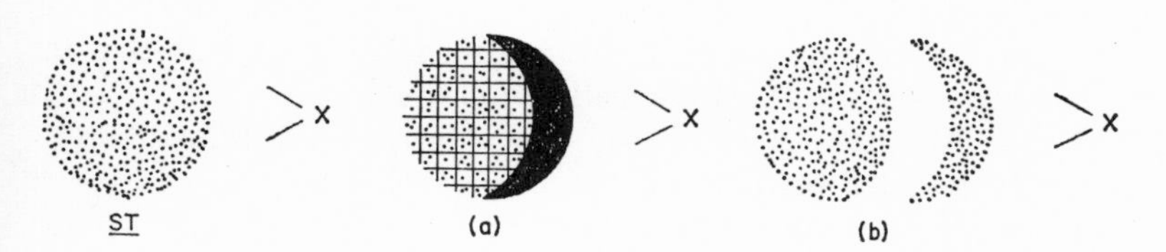

The left-hand figure is *ST* again. Fig. (*a*) is like *STm* except that in (*a*) we have 'marked' in the diagram not the *HM* fact proper but the fact that *X* can't see any more of the tomato than the right quarter (not meaning to imply, of course, that he can see even this much of the tomato). In (*b*) this right quarter is peeled off and moved slightly towards *X*; it hides the rest of the tomato from his sight. If we (as plain men) begin by saying in *ST* 'Here *X* can see the tomato', then when we pass to (*b*) we would in the same vein say '*Here X* can see only the right quarter of the tomato'. Suppose, however, that we begin with (*a*) instead of *ST*, saying of (*a*) 'Here *X* can see the tomato'. What, if we have said this, is it then natural to say *in the same vein* when we pass to (*b*)? Perhaps it is not natural to say anything. Certainly we should not say: 'Here *X* can see only the right quarter'! In respect to being seen *only* the right quarter of the tomato in (*a*) is, as we might put it, 'on a par' with the right quarter in (*b*), whereas in *ST* it is the tomato itself which seems on a par with the right quarter in (*b*). The perceptual position produced by cutting up the tomato is considerably worse than the position *X* seems in *ST* to be in, but it is hardly different (if, indeed, it *is* different) from the position *X* is in *after* the 'marking', that is, in (*a*).

Obviously what is true of 'marking' the fact that *X* can't see any more of the physical object than its right quarter is true also of 'marking' the *HM* fact itself.[1] Even if *X* can be said to see the physical object in *STm*, his seeing of this object is not as good as it seems to be in *ST*. Exactly how it is inferior is not easy to say. One might say that in *STm X* can't see the tomato 'in the way' it seems he can in *ST* (not 'directly', only 'indirectly'), or that in *STm* the tomato does not have quite the 'status' of being seen that it seems to have in *ST*. We need not worry overmuch, however, about the fact that in attempting to characterize the inferiority to which *X*'s seeing in *STm* is subject we seem forced to use distinctions or modes of expression which, at least in this application, seem doubtful, for these difficulties may well be due to the fact that, as I shall suggest later, in conceding it to be true that in *STm X can* see the tomato we allow too much.

I conclude that *P*'s surface-inquiry is properly described by (I) and (II) (restated below).

I. We do what *seems* to be just noting a fact (the *HM* fact) about the sort of situation in which we commonly suppose another person can see a physical object.

II. *After* 'noting' this *HM* fact, we see that the perceptual position *X* is in is inferior to the position we took him to be in before we 'noted' this fact.

Obviously in coming to think that the *HM* fact has paradoxical implications the philosopher (Descartes, Moore, Broad, and others) considers what *he* can see, not, like *P*, what he would say *another* person can see. This difference, however, is in this instance of no consequence, as each of us can verify for himself. Of course,

[1] That *this is* what we find after 'marking the *HM* fact' could have been brought out more directly by comparing *ST*, *STm*, and a case in which the portion of the surface in question is peeled off and moved slightly towards *X*, provided we did not balk at engaging in the fiction that the last case mentioned makes sense.

in order to 'note' the *HM* fact we don't literally mark up a diagram or object, but we can mentally 'mark' the *HM* fact in the object before us by, for example, imagining cross marks on the portions of the object we can't see. Alternatively, this 'noting' can be properly done by imagining a geometrical (two-dimensional) plane inserted in the physical object before us between the near portion of its surface and the rest of the object. Or we may simply, in whatever way seems natural, hold this portion of the surface distinguished ('mentally separated') from the rest of the object. When we do any one of these things, we do *seem* to be just *noting* the fact that all we can see of the physical object before us is the near portion of its surface, and yet this 'noting' has exactly the consequences for our perceptual position that the 'marking' had for *X*'s position. The only reason I have worked here with *P*'s version of the surface-inquiry is that it enabled me to do that requisite act of 'noting' *publicly*, which, in the more fundamental version, each of us must do 'in his head'.

III

We have seen that unless 'noting' the *HM* fact is counterfeit, being in reality an act which, when performed, produces a different, worse, perceptual position, the surface-inquiry is valid, that is to say, we do discover that because we can't see any more of a physical object than part of its surface our perceptual position is worse than we had optimistically supposed. It is a mistake to think that philosophers have deemed Common Sense erroneous in virtue of assuming that it is part of the meaning of 'see' that 'see' is true of *A* only if true of every bit of *A*. This 'assumption', or some approximate version, does in fact hold true *in STm. There* it *is* true that because *X* can't see any more of the physical object than part of its surface he can't be said to see this object 'in the way' it seems he can in *ST* (if, indeed, he can be said to see the object at all). One is blocked from understanding the philosopher if one takes this 'assumption' to be the basis of his view, for to do so is to treat a *conclusion* as if it were a premiss. It is like supposing that Zeno tacitly *assumes* that we can't traverse a finite distance and that his conclusions will come tumbling down once this 'assumption' is brought to light. The only way to show that the philosopher is wrong is to show that 'noting' the *HM* fact involves a sleight of mind, in truth producing a different, poorer, perceptual situation.

In what way might this 'noting' be defective? The truth is, I think, that the '*HM* fact' is the guilty party, for it is not really a fact, and that the 'noting' is comparatively innocent, for to 'note' this 'fact' is to see *what it is like for it to be true* that we can see no more of a physical object than part of its surface.

In order to explain this I must discuss certain peculiar properties of the concept 'see'. It is expedient, however, first to consider a trivial concept 'nibbled at' about which we have no philosophical convictions, preconceptions, or prejudices. I shall go on, I'm afraid, at some length about this unexciting concept; but I hope the nature of perception will be illuminated.

We may begin our examination of 'nibbled at' by considering the examples below. Fig. (1) below represents a piece of cheese which has been nibbled at (as indicated).

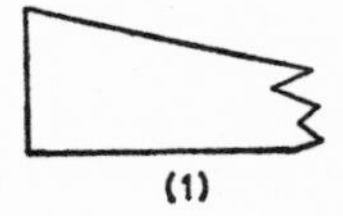
(1)

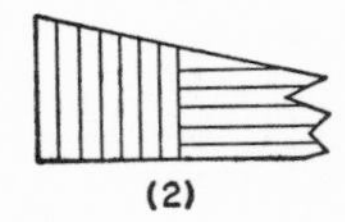
(2)

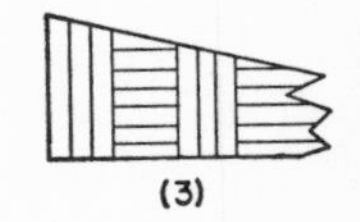
(3)

In reference to (2), which represents the same piece of cheese, this is said: 'Consider the half of the cheese marked with vertical lines and the half[1] marked with horizontal lines. Now, how much of the piece of cheese has been nibbled at?' It is natural to reply 'Only the right half'. In Fig. (3) we are to consider the quarters marked with vertical and horizontal lines. If asked in (3) 'How much of the piece of cheese has been nibbled at?' we should naturally reply 'Only the quarter at the far right'. It is clear from (2) and (3) that physical factors do not by themselves determine how much of the piece of cheese has been nibbled at. What amount is said to have been nibbled at does, of course, depend on physical factors, but not on these factors alone; it depends also on what amounts of the piece of cheese are to be taken as unit portions. It is true *flatly*, as it were, rather than true just *in a manner of speaking*, that in (2) half of the cheese has been nibbled at; there is not in (2) an amount of the piece of cheese which, independently of any specification of

[1] The half is the original (pre-nibbling) half.

relevant unit portions, is *the* amount really nibbled at. In short, that a certain amount of *A* has been nibbled at is not a *physical* fact.

On the other hand, the fact that a certain amount of the cheese has been nibbled *up* is a physical fact. It is also a physical fact that, for example, in (2) most of the right half of the cheese has not been nibbled at, but in spite of this physical fact the right half itself has been nibbled at.

In contexts where there is no indication as to what amounts of *A* are to be taken as relevant units there is no such thing as *an amount* of *A* nibbled at. This does not mean, of course, that in such situations *none* of *A* has been nibbled at but rather that in such contexts the question 'How much of *A* has been nibbled at?' has no answer. Case (1) (p. 106) illustrates this. Imagine that in reference to (1) we are asked: 'How much of this piece of cheese has been nibbled at? The right quarter? The right half? Or . . .?' What are we to reply? The only way to answer this question is to reject it. To say how much had been nibbled at we should first have had to designate some amounts as the relevant units, and there is no basis for choice. It is as if we were presented with a number of rubber balls, all in equally good condition, and without being told anything else except that there was nothing more to tell asked 'Which is the one that should be chosen?' There is no such thing in this context as a ball which should be chosen.

Next let us consider what is to be said about *A* itself having been nibbled at in contexts where there *is* such a thing as an amount of *A* nibbled at.

Suppose we are asked in case (2) (p. 106) 'Has the piece of cheese been nibbled at?' This question may at first sight seem straightforward enough. But instead of answering affirmatively someone might reply: 'No, the piece of cheese has not been nibbled at. All that's *really* been nibbled at is the right half.' What are we to say about this answer? Is it wrong? Is it unintelligible? Neither. Try asserting it. On doing so it strikes one that there is *something* in this reply. Indeed, *while* one is making this reply it seems true! So this negative answer to the question cannot be dismissed as simply wrong or unintelligible. It is not clear exactly what we should say about it.

Furthermore *just* asserting 'In (2) the piece of cheese *has* been nibbled at' leaves something important unsaid. The piece of cheese itself is not in (2) somehow quite as well off in respect to having been nibbled at as it is in (1). Perhaps one might express this difference by saying that in (2) the cheese's 'status' of having been nibbled at isn't as good as the 'status' of having been nibbled at which it enjoys in (1). In (2) only its right *half* is in respect to having been nibbled at 'on a par' with the piece of cheese itself in (1). We acknowledge this difference in our replies to certain questions. Suppose we are asked in reference to (1) 'What is it for the piece of cheese to have been nibbled at?' We should naturally reply in this vein: 'It's for an animal or human being to have been biting off irregular bits of the piece of cheese.' That is, we answer this question by stating, or trying to state, what must be the case if an object is to be correctly said to have been nibbled at. It is natural to answer this question differently if it is asked in (2): 'It's for the right half of the piece to have been nibbled at.' However, we answer in the way we originally did if the same question is asked in (2) about the right half.

To say in (2) that the piece of cheese has been nibbled at is, therefore, not quite as straightforward, not quite the same, as saying this in (1). I have spoken of this unlikeness as a difference in 'status'; whatever exactly it is, it is plainly the same difference that exists, in respect to being seen, between the tomato in *ST* and the tomato in *STm* (cf. pp. 103–4). It is worth noting that if asked in *STm* 'What is it for *X* to see the tomato?' we should naturally reply 'It's for *X* to see the near part of its surface', but if asked the same question in *ST*, or when we were looking at a physical object in front of us (prior to 'noting' the *HM* fact) we should naturally answer the question ostensively, by, for example, holding up a tomato in front of the questioner's nose and saying 'This is what it is to see a tomato'. Only *after* the 'noting' does it seem that seeing the physical object involves seeing a sub-portion of it.

Is it simply *true* that in (2) the piece of cheese itself has been nibbled at? In saying that it has are we merely *reporting* a *fact*? Isn't there something odd about the question 'Has the piece of cheese been nibbled at?' asked in (2) (or in (3))? Consider this series of questions: 'Has the piece of cheese been nibbled at?', asked in (1). 'Yes' (straightforward). 'Has the left half been nibbled at?', asked in (2). 'No' (straightforward). 'Has the right half been nibbled at?', asked in (2). 'Yes' (straightforward). 'Has the piece of cheese been nibbled at?', asked in (2). Doesn't *this* question seem odd? Don't we hesitate? The question doesn't seem appropriate in (2), and in truth it is not. We hesitate because to answer the question affirmatively or negatively means that we must say an object-in-a-certain-context is or is not nibbled at which in fact is neither. We recognize that the piece of cheese in (2) doesn't somehow belong amongst *A*'s that have been nibbled at, but, on the other hand, neither does it belong amongst *A*'s which have not been. But why does it fall in this no-man's land? Take another example. In (2) we don't hesitate to say that the right half has been nibbled at; yet we do hesitate if asked about it in (3). There is no physical difference between (2) and (3). The crucial difference is that in (2) the right half is a *unit* portion, whereas in (3) it is a compound of units. *'Nibbled at' is true only of units*. It is not designed to apply, pro or con, to compounds of units like the right half in (3) and the piece of cheese in (2). Thus, if succumbing to the pressure to say either that the piece of cheese in (2) has, or has not, been nibbled at, we say that it has been, we recognize nevertheless that there is something right about responding instead that it has not *really* been nibbled at. This negative response emphasizes that the piece of cheese in context (2) is not altogether like an *A* of which 'nibbled at' is true. If we deem a compound of units (like the cheese in (2)) nibbled at we then have on our hands a difference to articulate and in attempting to do so find ourselves speaking of such unnerving things as *statuses*, or ways, of having been nibbled at. There aren't two 'ways', nor a better and worse 'status', of having been nibbled at until we *create* the inferior 'status' or second 'way' by forcing 'nibbled at' on to non-units. Finally, an *A*'s having been nibbled at is to be explained in terms of one of its portions having been nibbled at only when this *A* is, again, a compound of units and hence not actually a member of the club anyway.

I conclude, then, that there is an important kind of incompatibility between *A* having been nibbled at and an *amount* of *A* having been so. The concept 'nibbled at' has these special features:

(*a*) The expression 'nibbled at' is true of *A* only when *A* is a unit. But it is an essential part of *A*'s being a unit that no amounts of *A* are fixed as relevant units. Hence when 'nibbled at' is true of *A* there is no such thing as *an amount* of *A* nibbled at.

(*b*) There is *an amount* of *A* nibbled at only when sub-portions of *A* are units. What amount has been nibbled at depends not only on physical conditions but also on which sub-portions are units. Thus in circumstances in which there is such a thing as an amount of *A* nibbled at, *A* is not a unit but a compound of units, and hence 'nibbled at' is neither true nor false of *A* itself.

I shall call any concept which has these properties a *unit* concept.[1]

IV

Let us suppose, for the moment, that 'see' also is a unit concept. If it is, then the truth (rather, *some* of the truth) about the philosopher's position is as stated in the following propositions:

1. The '*HM* fact' is not a fact. It would be true that normally all we can see of a physical object is part of its surface only if it were the case that in most contexts (run-of-the-mill, normal contexts) the near portion of the surface was fixed as one of the relevant units. But this is obviously not the case. It is true that normally we can't see either the far side or the inside of a physical object, but if 'see' is a unit concept this does not mean that, therefore, we can't see any more of the object than the near part of its surface. Consider cases (2) and (3) again (p. 106). In (2) the right half has been nibbled at but in (3) only the right quarter, even though in (2), just as in (3), the second quarter from the right has not itself been nibbled at. That a particular portion *s* of *A* hasn't itself been nibbled at doesn't in itself mean that no more than *A*-minus-*s* of *A* has been nibbled at unless the *s* is a relevant unit. A portion *s* not itself nibbled at can be included in the amount of *A* (properly) nibbled at.

All this holds true of 'see' also if it is a unit concept. 'More' than part of the surface of the physical object may be seen for the same kind of reason that 'more' is nibbled at in (2) than in (3). How much is seen will depend partly on the size of the units.

2. In thinking that the '*HM* fact' has paradoxical implications the philosopher is, *in a sense*, right. *When* it *is* true that all we can see of a physical object is part of its surface 'see' is neither true nor

[1] There are possible exceptions to (*a*) and (*b*) which, however, need not concern us here.

(1) I have not argued directly that 'nibbled at' is not true of a non-unit *A* like the right quarter in case (2), p. 106.

(2) It may be that a compound of units should be said to have been nibbled at when *each* of its units has been.

(3) When there has been no nibbling going on at all in connection with *A*, then it is true *both* that *A* hasn't been nibbled at and that *none* of *A* has been nibbled at.

false of the physical object itself. (For in such contexts the near portion of the surface is a unit, the physical object itself is not.)

Although in discussions of perception one quite frequently hears it said that it is just *trivially* true that seeing a physical object involves seeing part of its surface, some philosophers think, on the contrary, that this represents a surprising discovery, and that it signifies that our seeing of physical objects is not up to Common Sense's expectations. If 'see' is a unit concept, then these philosophers are, again *in a sense*, right. The ordinary seeing of a physical object does not involve seeing part of its surface (or any subportion of it), for when *A* is seen there is no such thing as an amount of *A* seen. That seeing of a physical object which *does* involve seeing part of its surface is the philosopher's own creation, the result of applying 'see' to the physical object in *STm*, that is, to the physical object when it is a compound of units. (The nature of *STm* is discussed further under (3) below.) *This* seeing of a physical object, which is the only seeing of such an object that is possible *when* it is true that all we can see of the physical object is part of its surface, is inferior to ordinary seeing.

3. Finally, what, if 'see' is a unit concept, really happens when we 'note' the '*HM* fact'? In *ST* no amounts of the tomato are fixed as relevant units; the tomato itself is the unit. But in *STm*, that is, when the '*HM* fact' has been 'marked', the tomato itself is no longer a unit, for a portion of its surface is singled out and, as it were, held up to us to be considered. Obviously the other ways of 'noting' the *HM* fact (see p. 105) effect the same change of units. The 'noting' has, however, an intimate connection with the '*HM* fact'. In *ST* (or when, say, in one's study one is looking at a physical object on the desk) there is no such thing as an *amount* of the physical object seen. 'Noting' the '*HM* fact' alters this situation exactly to the extent required in order for it to be true that all we can see of the physical object is part of its surface. Thus, if 'see' is a unit concept, when we 'note' the '*HM* fact' we do see what our perceptual situation is *when* it is true that all we can see of a physical object is part of its surface.

It is interesting that this 'noting' is, except when used in connection with unit concepts, just what it passes itself off as being, and, when used in connection with unit concepts, just what it passes itself off as being when the fact 'noted' or 'marked' in a situation is really a fact of that situation.

This, then, is how the surface-inquiry works if 'see' is a unit concept. The question is, of course, whether 'see' *is* a unit concept.

The sorts of considerations adduced to show that 'nibbled at' is a unit concept, even if adequate for this purpose, will not serve to show that 'see' is such a concept unless, independently of these considerations, we can see that the '*HM* fact' is not a fact. For our conclusions about 'nibbled at' were based essentially on 'what we would say' in certain cases, and I don't see how one can justifiably conclude on the basis of such data alone that it is wrong to subscribe to the *HM* fact. Let me explain. Suppose, for instance, that we begin our examination of 'see' by considering the analogues for 'see' of cases (1), (2), and (3) (p. 106). *ST* would be an analogue of (1), and then the analogues of (2) and (3) would be constructed out of *ST* as (2) and (3) are from (1). Now if asked in the analogue of (2) 'How much of the tomato can *X* see?' we should naturally reply 'Only the right half', and if asked the same question in reference to the analogue of (3) 'Only the right quarter'. However, what we say in these cases would make clear that what amount of an object is seen is dependent on what sub-portions are fixed as the relevant unit amounts (and hence would make clear that the '*HM* fact' is not a fact) only if it is absolutely clear that our answers are, as it were, *flatly* correct rather than just correct *in a manner of speaking*, or *for all practical purposes*. We did not have to worry about showing *this* when we were considering 'nibbled at' for we had no reason in that case for thinking that our answers might be correct only in a manner of speaking, whereas the strong appeal of the belief in the *HM* fact constitutes a powerful reason in the case of 'see'. I doubt that a consideration of further examples of 'what we would say' in particular contexts would suffice to overcome the appeal of this belief and thereby make clear that what we say in such cases is flatly correct.

A direct assault on the *HM* fact is needed. In order to mount this attack let us now examine the surface-inquiry directly.

What is really happening in the surface-inquiry? There are three possibilities. (1) The '*HM* fact' is a fact. 'Noting' this fact is just noting a fact previously overlooked. (2) The '*HM* fact' is not a fact. 'Noting' this 'fact' alters the original situation (*ST*, or its first-person analogue), producing one in which it *is* true that all that can be seen of the physical object is a portion of its surface. That there is yet a third possibility is due to the fact that in 'noting' the '*HM* fact' we do *two* things. (i) We focus on a portion of the physical object's surface, singling it out. (ii) We *hold* this portion singled out when we consider what the real truth is about whether the physical object itself can be seen. (3) The '*HM* fact' is a fact. However, we can see physical objects only because ordinarily the *HM* fact is not to be taken into consideration when we determine what can be seen. Although (i) may be legitimate, being perhaps only a part of attending to the *HM* fact, (ii) is not. For in doing (ii) we alter the original situation (*ST*, or its first-person analogue), producing a situation in which the *HM* fact must be taken into consideration when we determine what can be seen. The force of this third possibility is brought home by noting that when the (undeniable) fact that the tomato has a thin outer skin is marked in *ST*, then *X*'s perceptual position is worsened, and in almost exactly the same way as when the *HM* fact is marked in *ST*.

I shall now argue that (1) and (3) must be rejected. Consider (3) first. When, in the first-person analogue of *ST*, we assert 'All I can see of the physical object is the near portion of its surface', we succeed in meaning our words and seeing what it is for what we are asserting to be true only when we single out this portion of the surface. (Compare uttering these words without singling out this portion and then while singling it out.) But when we *are* meaning what we are saying, we find that for what we are asserting to be true, it is necessary for our seeing to embrace, as it were, this portion of the surface and only this portion. When we cease singling out this portion, the physical object coalesces back into a unit, and we are seemingly in a *different* perceptual position, for now our seeing seems to embrace the physical object itself; the near portion of the surface is now not embraced *per se* but is included in an object which *is* embraced *per se*.[1] This perceptual position is the one we were in, or took ourselves to be in, when we asserted, at the beginning of the surface-inquiry, that we could see the physical object. It is immediately obvious that for it to be true that we see the physical object is for it to be the case that we are in *this* perceptual position. Thus we find, contrary to (3), that not just the *relevance* but the *truth* of 'All we can see of the physical object is the near portion of its surface' is incompatible

[1] It would be desirable, of course, to express these facts less metaphorically, but I shall not attempt to do so here.

with the truth of 'We can see the physical object'. Only if we single out the relevant portion of the surface *and* hold it singled out ((i) *and* (ii)) are we keeping before us the state of affairs in which it is *true* that all we can see of the physical object is the near portion of its surface.

It follows that if the '*HM* fact' is a fact, our perceptual position is worse than 'Common Sense' supposes. This in itself is a good reason for regarding the '*HM* fact' with (at least) suspicion. However, there is, I think, a decisive reason for rejecting the '*HM* fact' (and hence the first possibility). *The* reason for accepting the *HM* fact is that when we single out the near portion of the physical object's surface it is plainly true that all we can see of the physical object is this portion. Thus whether we have a good reason for accepting the *HM* fact depends on whether we have a good reason for believing that this 'singling out' is straightforward, that is, just a part of noting a fact. But an examination of 'see', exactly paralleling the study of 'nibbled at', reveals that 'see' is a unit concept. Specifically, it reveals that this 'singling out', if applied in *ST* (or in its first-person analogue) to any subportion *s* (or rather, to any *s* that completely hides the rest of the physical object from sight), *brings it about* that it is true that *s* is all we can see of the physical object, and, as a consequence, that it is neither true nor false that the physical object itself is seen. Thus to have a good reason for accepting the *HM* fact we should have to have a reason for maintaining, against this study, that this 'singling out' is, *in one application*, that is when applied to the near portion of the surface, straightforward. *But what reason is there for supposing that?*

One final word: There are contexts in which *A* is seen *and* an amount of *A* is seen. This fact, however, does not signify that *A* being seen and an amount of *A* being seen are not mutually incompatible, for it can be shown (although not in the space allowed this paper) that in such contexts *A* is sometimes being treated as a unit, sometimes as a compound of units, and it is true that *A* is seen *only when A* is being treated as a unit and true that an amount of *A* is seen *only when A* is being treated as a compound of units.[1]

[1] I wish to thank the American Council of Learned Societies for a fellowship which provided a period of freedom from teaching partly occupied by the writing of this paper.

VI

AESTHETIC ESSENCE

by MARSHALL COHEN

Associate Professor of Philosophy, The University of Chicago

One of the typical assumptions of traditional aesthetic theory has been that certain features must characterize all objects properly regarded as works of fine art. And the further assumption that some of these features characterize only works (or only successful works) of fine art has occasioned both the search for a definition of art and the attempt to elicit an ultimate ground of critical judgement. It has long been apparent that the traditional theories have made inadequate suggestions as to what these features might in fact be. For most of the suggested properties do not seem even to constitute necessary conditions for the application of the notions of art or of successful art. This is true of beauty and of the expression of emotion; it is true of illusion and of *mimesis*. As Nietzsche has taught us that tragic art is characterized by terror rather than beauty, Eliot has revealed that poetry 'in the tradition' constitutes an escape from, not an expression of, emotion. Since Maurice Denis it has been understood that the canvas may be treated, not as a three-dimensional illusion, but as a two-dimensional reality. And if Le Corbusier has encouraged the doctrine of *mimesis* in designing the chapel at Ronchamp, he has rejected it firmly at the Villa Savoie. Furthermore, if some feature such as significant form, or organic unity, should ever be described with enough clarity to allow us to determine its presence or absence, it seems obvious that it would not be difficult to show that it is, even if a necessary, not a sufficient condition of art. These difficulties have long been apparent, and in recent years they have often been interpreted in the light of Wittgenstein's cautionary observation that the use of a general term need not be supported by the presence of a property common to the 'objects' to which it properly applies. (Like Wittgenstein I do not mean by 'properties' elaborate disjunctive ones.) As a consequence, many writers have begun to suggest that the difficulty in the philosophy of art is not that we have so far failed to discover the required property or properties, but that we have continued to assume without justification that there are such properties to seek.

In this essay I wish to indicate that analogous assumptions and difficulties pervade other areas of aesthetic investigation. For the notion lingers on (even among philosophers of a Wittgensteinian persuasion) that if there is no property common to all works of art there may yet be some property or properties common to our proper experience of these works of art, or to the preconditions of that experience, or to the criteria of our aesthetic judgements. Indeed, it is arguable that such assumptions are more typical of, and more central to, modern aesthetic thinking than the theory more regularly attacked. (Kant's doctrine of disinterestedness, Schiller's doctrine of play, and Coleridge's doctrine of the suspension of disbelief, are not, after all, primarily doctrines about the nature of works of art.) Certain forms of this doctrine of aesthetic essence, as we may call it, are logically independent of the doctrine of artistic essence and have been maintained by writers who explicitly rejected that doctrine. Edward Bullough was in fact driven to his doctrine that there is a feature common to 'all aesthetic impressions' precisely because he believed 'that the discovery in the objective world of Art of a common feature of sufficient concreteness to make it applicable both to all works and to each one separately cannot reasonably be hoped for'. It is because 'theoretical unification of the empirical facts on purely objective lines is either so vague or so artificial as to be practically valueless' that he thought one must turn to psychology and attempt to find some feature 'common to all aesthetic impressions' even if it must be derived from works that are highly 'divergent'. It is in 'aesthetic consciousness', not in artistic objects, that one is to discover the desired 'common meeting ground', the subject of 'the modern conception of aesthetics'.[1] A search for an aesthetic essence may well succeed the search for an artistic essence. And it may take the form either of a psychological search for features common to aesthetic experience, or its preconditions, or of a logical inquiry into the features common to the criteria of specifically aesthetic judgement. In the discussion that follows, I shall wish to show that there is no reason to believe that either the psychological or the logical form of this doctrine of aesthetic essence is true. There is

[1] Edward Bullough, *Aesthetics*, Stanford 1957, p. 57.

no reason to believe any property essential to aesthetic experience or certainly, to believe that such a property distinguishes aesthetic from, say, 'practical', or intellectual experience. And it is doubtful whether there is any feature essential to the criteria employed in aesthetic appraisal, not to speak of one that distinguishes them from the criteria employed in scientific or moral, economic or technical, appraisal. In addition to indicating the dubiousness of these doctrines I shall hope to show some of their unfortunate consequences. For their acceptance encourages unfortunate attitudes in artistic education and scholarship, and it may interfere with the enjoyment of art and with the full exercise of critical judgement. In some of its forms the doctrine is incompatible, too, with what I take to be central features of the modern conception of art.

I

It is habitually assumed that there is an element common to our experiences of works of art (or to experiences called 'aesthetic'). Or if not, it is at least supposed that there are certain mental states necessary for the having of these experiences. I call the first assumption the doctrine of aesthetic experience and the second (in view of its most frequent form) the doctrine of an aesthetic attitude. A straightforward commitment to the doctrine of aesthetic experience may be illustrated by a passage from Roger Fry. He writes:

> If we compare in our minds responses experienced in turn in face of different works of art of the most diverse kinds—as, for instance, architectural, pictorial, musical or literary—we recognize that our state of mind in each case has been of a similar kind . . . and that (there is something) common to all these experiences (and) peculiar to them (which) . . . we might conveniently label . . . the specifically aesthetic state of mind.[1]

Fry tells us that there is some element common, and peculiar, to our experience of all works of art. But he does not mention any marks by which we can identify it. Other writers have been more specific. Thus, Bullough remarks in his classic discussion of the

[1] Roger Fry, *Transformations*, Garden City 1956, pp. 1–2.

various ways, aesthetic and non-aesthetic, of regarding a fog at sea that so long as we regard it practically (or non-aesthetically) we shall experience anxiety, strain, and tension. But he holds that once we adopt the aesthetic attitude toward it we shall experience delight and pleasure.[1] This mode of distinguishing aesthetic from practical experience has a long history in hedonistic aesthetics (and Bullough's specific formulation is an obvious attempt to restate in empirical psychological terms Schopenhauer's conception of art as a release from the pressures of the Will), but it is unworkable. Santayana, the acutest of the hedonistic aestheticians, realized that pleasure characterizes not only aesthetic but also practical activity. He knew the doctrines of the *Nicomachean Ethics* and defined the experience of beauty as the experience of pleasure objectified, because he knew that it must be some very special kind of pleasure that could be peculiar to the aesthetic experience of beauty. But, as we may question whether beauty is, indeed, the essential property of art, we may question whether pleasure, which aestheticians have normally supposed to be characteristic of its apprehension is, truly, an essential feature of aesthetic experience. That beauty is the essence of art has been questioned by Nietzsche and Tolstoy, by Veron and Marinetti, by Eliot and Wittgenstein. And most of them would, I expect, deny that delight or pleasure constitutes the essence of aesthetic experience. Surely, anxiety, tension, and stress, which Bullough takes to be incompatible with aesthetic experience, are in fact essential to the effects not only of detective fiction (from Oedipus to the present) but (to suggest only obvious sources) much metaphysical poetry, *Sturm und Drang* music, and expressionist painting. The muzzles of the battleship *Potemkin*, pointed at the audience, are positively menacing. The element of truth in theories of psychical distance may be that there are limits to the degrees of intensity that such states as anxiety, tension, and stress may attain and yet remain compatible with aesthetic experience. But if this is true, it is probably equally true of such states as those of pleasure and delight.

It does not seem possible to determine *a priori* the variety of sensations, feelings, and attitudes that works of art may engender, and empirical investigation does not seem to have revealed any essential property of those already acknowledged. I do not wish to deny, on the other hand, that certain sensations, feelings, and

[1] Bullough, *op. cit.*, pp. 93–94.

attitudes may be incompatible with the experience of anything we should conceivably regard as art. But it is worth noting that whenever some actual limit has been proposed, in theory or in practice, it has been characteristic of modern artists to attempt to demonstrate its arbitrariness. If there are no specific sensations, feelings, or the like that are peculiarly aesthetic sensations or feelings, it might, nevertheless, be maintained, as by Dewey, that there are certain formal characteristics of experiences that are peculiarly aesthetic. But this thesis, too, is difficult to maintain. It is virtually impossible decisively to refute the various positive suggestions that have been made. For the terms employed, or the uses made of them, are so vague as to defy a confident presentation of counter-examples. Nevertheless, one may wonder whether unity (even unity understood to require that the experience be pervaded by a single individualizing quality)[1] will serve to distinguish aesthetic from non-aesthetic experiences. Surely, the experience of riding a crowded subway, or of being badly beaten, has at least as great a degree of unity as (and is more surely pervaded by a single individualizing quality than) the experience of hearing many a sonata or symphonic suite, or of reading many a picaresque novel or chronicle play. And such supplementary characteristics—I choose the least vague—as consummatory quality,[2] or continuity,[3] do not seem any more persuasive. Consummatory quality is more frequently associated with sexual than with aesthetic experience, and various artistic techniques (of which cinematic *montage* is perhaps the most obvious) are often exploited to create just that gappy, 'breathless', or discontinuous quality that Dewey assigns to practical experience. It is true that a writer such as Dewey would be perfectly content to allow that works of art are not the exclusive sources of aesthetic experience. Yet even those who regard this as a desirable theoretical development may hesitate to subscribe to a formal characterization of aesthetic experience that excludes the experience of central works of art and is satisfied by the experience of brushing one's teeth, or still better, of having them pulled. We do not, and I expect that we cannot, possess a theory about the essential nature of aesthetic experience, if this theory is intended (as perhaps it is not) to encompass the experience of all examples and kinds of art. In what follows I shall, nevertheless, use the

[1] John Dewey, *Art as Experience*, New York 1934, pp. 35 ff.
[2] *Ibid.* [3] *Ibid.*

phrase 'aesthetic experience' to comprehend the experiences that do characteristically arise from the apprehension of works of art.

II

There are plainly certain capacities with which one must be endowed, certain accomplishments one must possess, certain attitudes one must be able to sustain, and certain activities one must be able to perform, if one is to respond adequately to a work of art. Some conditions are logically necessary for particular aesthetic experiences. Thus the man who is tone-deaf cannot enjoy music, and the man who is ignorant of the history of literature cannot apprehend Joyce's *Ulysses*. It is arguable that other conditions are causally necessary. Perhaps one must be capable of patience to enjoy Proust's novel or an Antonioni film, or of concentration to apprehend a complicated fugue. That some such conditions are required for particular aesthetic experiences no one will deny. But whether, as many aestheticians have suggested, there are certain activities or psychological states that are always and everywhere required for (and, even, that insure) the having of aesthetic experience may be questioned. It is important, not only for theoretical reasons, to question such theses. For, in so far as conditions that are not necessary are taken to be so, inappropriate training is proposed, and false instructions are offered, to those who wish to quicken their aesthetic responses. Quickening one's aesthetic responses is not a general problem, but a series of specific problems. In addition, in so far as insufficient conditions are taken to be sufficient, inadequate training and preparation are suggested. I am inclined to believe that there are, in particular, no special activities (such as contemplating) and no psychological states (such as maintaining 'psychical distance') that are required for having aesthetic experience. And as these are, perhaps, the most prestigious candidates I shall discuss them below. But if it is important to question whether any particular states are required, it is even more important to question whether we can know, in advance of the fact, what activities or states of mind will insure the proper apprehension of a work of art. And beyond activities and states of mind, what sensory capacities, what knowledge, courage, or imagination.

The choice of contemplation as the essential precondition (or, indeed, the essential element) of aesthetic experience is, doubtless, influenced by the traditional opposition of the *vita activa* to the *vita contemplativa*. In the modern version that concerns us, however, it is neither philosophical nor religious contemplation that is contrasted with the life of action, but aesthetic contemplation that is contrasted with physical activity, intellectual labour, and practical interest. (In a transitional figure, such as Schopenhauer, the distinction between philosophical or religious and aesthetic contemplation tends to fail.) This elaborate history has left us with a profoundly confused and (as Maritain suggests) perverted term. And this makes a discussion of aesthetic theories in which the concept of contemplation figures crucially exceptionally difficult. The term 'contemplation' is used in aesthetic contexts by many writers simply to comprehend whatever conditions they suppose necessary for obtaining aesthetic experience. But when the term is employed in this manner the question is effectively begged whether there is any feature common to the bewildering variety of psychological states, and even physical activities, that may be required for obtaining the varieties of aesthetic experience. So, too, is the question begged whether the term 'contemplation' can serve both this broad purpose and yet be understood to preclude (as it is normally understood by these same writers to preclude) various physical actions, intellectual operations, or moral interests. There is no point from which one can contemplate Wright's Guggenheim Museum or Le Corbusier's Carpenter Center (the aesthetic experience requires physical movement), no way of appropriating a novel of Broch's or Mann's without engaging in the meditation and cogitation that Richard of St Victor contrasts with contemplation, no way of feeling the excitement of Goya's *The Disasters of War* or Dostoyevsky's *The Possessed* without exercising those moral and political interests that are typically contrasted with aesthetic, ironic, or disinterested contemplation.

It would not do, however, to represent all theorists as presenting us with so unsatisfactory a situation. No contemporary aesthetician has, so far as I know, investigated the subject of contemplation with the kind of detail that can be found in Richard of St Victor, who in addition to distinguishing contemplation from meditation and cogitation noticed its six varieties. But the term 'contemplation' is at least employed with some sense of its non-technical use by an occasional writer on the visual arts. Thus, Pudovkin, who is interested in establishing that 'the camera compels the spectator to see as the director wishes' knows that the camera 'is charged with a conditional relation to the object shot. Now, urged by heightened interest, it delves into details; now it contemplates the general whole of the picture'.[1] Pudovkin observes the difference between delving into and contemplating a scene. And if the camera can force us to see in these different ways so, I think, can the painter. If one ought to contemplate a Redon or a Rothko, one ought to scrutinize the Westminster Psalter, survey a Tiepolo ceiling, regard a Watteau, and peer at a scene of Breughel.[2] If we attend to these distinctions we shall be in a position to deny that we must contemplate these works to have a proper aesthetic experience of them. Nor is it the case, as might be suspected, that writers who observe these distinctions do so because they are innocent of philosophical plans for the concept of contemplation. Here we come upon an instance where a form of the doctrine of aesthetic essence is not independent of a theory about the nature of art.

From the Greeks onward it has been supposed that contemplation requires special kinds of objects, and sometimes that only contemplation is capable of discerning these objects. Modern aesthetics reflects this tradition. For the artistically embodied Ideas of Schopenhauer and the Significant Forms of Bell and Fry require contemplation. And it is assumed that in so far as other modes of vision are present they must be directed to non-aesthetic or aesthetically irrelevant aspects of the work of art. A hint of this may be found in Roger Fry's discussion of Breughel's 'Carrying of the Cross'. 'We are invited,' he writes, 'by the whole method of treatment, to come close and peer at each figure in turn and read from it those details which express its particular state of mind so that we may gradually, almost as we might in a novel, bring them together to build up a highly complex psychological structure.'[3] Fry dislikes Breughel's kind of painting, and what he dislikes about it is what makes it proper to 'peer at it' and 'read it closely' (rather than 'contemplate' it as one would a Cezanne). For peering displays a psychological, rather than an aesthetic, interest, and Breughel is

[1] V. I. Pudovkin, *Film Technique and Film Acting*, London 1958, pp. 154–155.

[2] Cf. Paul Ziff, 'Reasons in Art Criticism', reprinted in Joseph Margolis, ed., *Philosophy Looks at the Arts*, New York 1962, pp. 164 ff. I am grateful to Professor Ziff, as well as to Professors Rogers Albritton and Stanley Cavell, for reading and criticizing an earlier version of this manuscript.

[3] Fry, *op. cit.*, p. 19.

literary, even novelistic, rather than painterly and significantly formalistic. In a word, his painting is non-aesthetic in its appeal, and this is reflected in the fact that it is apprehended by the allegedly non-aesthetic activity of peering. We must, however, stand with Pudovkin and Breughel for the right to delve and peer. The notion that contemplation is the essential condition of aesthetic experience is often no more than a reflection of the theorist's negligent assumption that the rapt Oriental contemplating a Chinese vase is the paradigm of aesthetic experience. When it is not, it is likely to enshrine partisan tastes such as Fry's.

III

In addition to implying misleading accounts of the conditions of aesthetic experience, psychological versions of the theory of aesthetic essence have provided one of the main motivations for false conceptions of the nature and elements of art itself. The notion that some psychological state, such as Bullough's psychical distance, is the necessary (and, indeed, the sufficient) condition of aesthetic experience has led both Bullough and Mrs Langer to attempt to explain its presence or absence by some doctrine about the nature or elements of art. Mrs Langer, for instance, constructs her doctrine that the work of art is an appearance or illusion in order to explain how art imposes an aesthetic 'attitude' and how, by its very nature, it cannot sustain a practical interest.[1] (She falsely assimilates works of art to shadows and rainbows, and forgets the practical uses of signs and wonders.) Bullough's doctrine is less extreme, and despite some remarks in the tradition of Schiller, he does not clearly commit himself to the view of art as appearance or illusion. Nevertheless, it is his view that various features of works of art either encourage, or discourage, the occurrence of a state of mind that he calls 'psychical distance'. I wish to argue that there is no need to assume the presence of such a state as a precondition or element of aesthetic experience. In addition, I shall argue that the interpretation of works of art on

[1] Susanne Langer, *Feeling and Form*, New York 1953. See the discussion of Mrs Langer's views in Marshall Cohen, 'Appearance and the Aesthetic Attitude', *The Journal of Philosophy*, vol. 56 (November 5, 1959), pp. 921–24. The article is reprinted in Marvin Levich, ed., *Aesthetics and the Philosophy of Criticism*, New York 1963.

the assumption that the function of certain of their stylistic traits is to induce this state leads to a misinterpretation of them.

The psychological state supposed to be the necessary condition of aesthetic experience has been described by Prall as involving a loss of the sense of one's body, by Schopenhauer as involving a loss of the sense of one's self, and by Ethel Puffer as being akin to hypnosis. (Schopenhauer discourages an appeal to spirituous drinks or opium to achieve this state, and suggests, rather, a cold bath and a night's sleep.) Bullough's suggestion, if less patently false, is yet communicated in a metaphor susceptible of many interpretations. The most typical interpretation is one under which we may say that James or Brecht, or their readers, maintain their distance from Verena Tarrant or from Galy Gay. However, in this sense, we also say that distance is not maintained from Isabel Archer or Mother Courage. But this cannot be the proper interpretation of Bullough's term, for a lack of distance in this sense is fully compatible with aesthetic experience. (And we may contradict those critics who suppose that the maintenance of distance makes *The Bostonians* a greater novel than *The Portrait of a Lady*. I do not know whether anyone has made so bold a move in the case of Brecht.) How, then, are we to interpret Bullough? While he thinks of distance as a psychic state, we know that on occasion he relates it in an exceptionally straightforward way to certain behavioural manifestations. When we suffer tension, stress, or anxiety we tend to react practically to the situation. It is his view that certain elements of works of art arouse such feelings; in particular, those representing humanly compelling situations. For this reason works of art also include other elements to attenuate or 'distance' those feelings and to inhibit action. In the case of the theatre, for instance, these elements would include the raised stage and the use of costumes and verse. Now Bullough mentions as a clear case of the loss of distance the yokel who leaps upon the stage to save the hapless heroine.[1] Bullough would have us believe that the pressure of his feelings induces the yokel to gain the stage and that the operation of the distancing factors has kept the rest of the audience in their seats. But can we not imagine that the yokel has acted coolly out of an ignorant sense of honour while the carriage-trade has remained in

[1] Bullough, *op. cit.* p. 98. See the discussion of Bullough's views in George Dickie, 'Is Psychology Relevant to Aesthetics?' *The Philosophical Review*, vol. 71 (July 1962), pp. 297–300.

its place seething with emotion? (I assume for the purposes of this discussion that their seething is compatible with the maintenance of sufficient psychical distance.) The operative factors here may not be feelings at all, but rather the presence and absence of knowledge of what a play is and of how one behaves in the theatre. If so, the satisfaction of at least this behavioural criterion of 'psychical' distance, namely, staying put, may be compatible with a wide range of feelings or with none at all. And, indeed, this assumption comports best with the introspective situation.

If knowledge of what a play is should be sufficient to keep the yokel seated, and if no particular feelings or emotions are required to keep the audience in its seats, it will be inappropriate to account for certain elements of a work of art by their tendency to enforce, and others by their tendency to undermine, such psychical states. If the yokel learns what it is to go to a play we shall be able to do the play in a field, without costumes, and in prose, and still expect him to react properly. Thus, the function of the raised stage, costumes, and verse need not be to keep him seated. Indeed, the very stylistic qualities that Bullough supposes to be distancing because of their anti-realistic nature may operate in precisely the opposite fashion. Let us take the theatrical case. The raised stage, appropriate for the performance of Ibsen's plays, tends to make the playgoer less conscious of the rest of the audience. And allowing him to peep into a realistic set peopled with literally costumed characters actually adds to the 'realism' of the play. (Hence the habitual failure of arena-stage productions of Ibsen.) Nor can it plausibly be maintained that the general function of verse is to attenuate responses to the represented events. This does not seem to have been the effect of Aeschylus' verse on the women who gave birth at his plays, or of Shakespeare's on Dr Johnson's reaction to the final scene of King Lear. Alternatively, O'Neill's prosy climaxes (Lavinia's 'O fiddlesticks!') hardly seem to increase the reality of these scenes.

If Bullough's suggestions are often misleading, they are even more often irrelevant. He supposes—it is only an extension of his treatment of the yokel—that anti-realistic (highly-distanced) styles are required mainly to inhibit and to render aesthetic the practical impulses of relatively primitive and unsophisticated peoples. But his hypothesis is quite irrelevant to the problem of the modern anti-realistic style that has occasioned the brilliant speculations of

Ortega and Malraux. For this 'dehumanized' style is the expression, as Ortega indicates, not of the aesthetically unsophisticated masses, but, on the contrary, of an aesthetic elite.[1] And Malraux's argument is of a logical type that Bullough's mode of analysis does not even allow him. For where Bullough's method would lead him to find in the modern renewal of the anti-humanistic or 'transcendental' style a (psychological) purpose similar to that served by this style in the past, it is open to Malraux to suggest that this style has a (non-psychological) purpose exactly opposite to that which it previously served. (It is, he thinks, a 'photographic negative' of previous transcendental styles and serves to express a new humanism rather than to cancel a discredited one.)[2] The possibility of offering quite different accounts of the functions of similar stylistic elements on different occasions and of finding these explanations not in psychological factors but, perhaps, in considerations of history or of *Weltanschauung* seems all to the good. Bullough's attempt to relate such explanations to the fortunes of some otiose and unidentifiable psychological state cannot be regarded as useful procedure. Like Mrs Langer's theory that all works of art are appearances or illusions, Bullough's notion that stylistic elements should be understood as increasing or decreasing distance may be dismissed with its questionable motivation. There is no way of determining the precondition of all aesthetic experience just as there is no way of knowing what qualities such experience must bear.

IV

We have analysed the psychological version of the doctrine of aesthetic essence as it bears on aesthetic experience and its preconditions and on the nature and the analysis of art. It will be useful to conclude by examining the logical version of the doctrine in its relation to the problem of aesthetic judgement and the criticism of art. We are characteristically invited to make aesthetic judgements when making them would not be the obvious thing to do or when it is felt that, although this is the obvious thing to do, it has not been done. Thus, we may be asked to pass an aesthetic judge-

[1] José Ortega y Gasset, *The Dehumanization of Art*, Garden City 1956.

[2] André Malraux, *The Voices of Silence*, Garden City 1953; Joseph Frank, 'Malraux's Metaphysics', *The Sewanee Review*, vol. 70 (Autumn 1962), p. 646.

ment on a car in a conversation in which we have all along been assessing its technical efficacy, or the economics of running it. Alternatively, and this is typical of critical contexts, we may insist that we have, in fact, made an aesthetic (or an artistic, or a literary) judgement. Our point will be to forestall the objection, or to reject the accusation, that we have in fact made a moral, or a technical, or an economic one. It has been suggested that these various kinds of judgement can be distinguished from one another by reference to the criteria that are relevant to making them. Thus, there is a special set of aesthetic criteria, as distinguished from moral, and intellectual, and economic criteria, and it is on the basis of these aesthetic criteria that we make our aesthetic judgements. J. O. Urmson, for instance, regards it as the central task of the philosopher of aesthetics 'to clarify the principles on which we select the special set of criteria of value that are properly counted as relevant to aesthetic judgement'.[1] And, although he does not commit himself to the view that a single principle specifies this special set of 'criteria', the very assumption that there is such a special set supplies a major source of encouragement for the view that some single property does characterize the criteria of aesthetic judgement. In fact, Urmson himself proposes that at least in the simplest cases (and it is not obvious how he would allow more complicated ones to alter his view) aesthetic judgements are judgements of how things look or smell or otherwise present themselves to the senses. It will not be our purpose in this section to propose any alternative analysis of the nature of aesthetic judgements or to suggest any peculiarity of the logic of aesthetic arguments. Our purpose will be to call into question the suggestion that the criteria of aesthetic judgement can be characterized by a feature such as the one Urmson suggests, or that these criteria form a set that characteristically excludes moral, scientific, or ideological criteria. Urmson writes that 'it would be a very odd person who denied that the sound of the words of a poem was one of the criteria of aesthetic judgement of a poem, or who maintained that being scientifically accurate and up to date was another'.[2] Urmson's notion that 'the sound of the words of a poem' is one of the criteria of the aesthetic judgement of poems is simply a manifestation of his more general

[1] J. O. Urmson, 'What Makes a Situation Aesthetic?' reprinted in Margolis, *op. cit.*, p. 20.

[2] *Ibid.*, p. 22.

principle that aesthetic criteria appear to be those concerned with 'the way the object in question looks or presents itself to the other senses'.[1] There is, of course, some plain confusion here. Urmson does not really propose a criterion. 'The sound of the words of a poem' does not constitute a criterion of evaluation. What is it about these sounds that is aesthetically meritorious? Even if we waive this objection, however, it is worth noting that critics as various as Bradley and Croce and I. A. Richards have denied that any feature of the sounds of the words of a poem constitutes an important source of poetic merit. As Eliot puts it 'the music of poetry is not something that exists apart from its meaning'.[2] It does not, of course, follow from what Eliot actually says that our judgements of poems might not be confined to some quality of their sounds. This might be the case even if this quality 'could not exist' outside meaningful contexts. But, as a matter of fact, we rarely, if ever, judge poems (even the poems of Verlaine, Swinburne, or Wallace Stevens) simply by their sounds (a doctrine with which Urmson appears to be flirting) and often enough we do not judge them by their sounds at all. We may by-pass the question whether, in general, music may be said to have sounds or paintings looks. (To be sure, performed music occasionally has a muffled sound, and paintings often have a faded look. But even when they do have such properties, aesthetic judgements may be required positively to ignore them.) The fact is that even the narrowest conception of aesthetic judgement invokes criteria for assessing the formal structure of the work of art or, say, its success in exploiting the medium. It does not seem possible to extend Urmson's principle even to such indisputably aesthetic criteria, and no further principle suggests itself. But even if some feature could be discovered that might cover such aesthetic criteria it would be necessary to question whether those criteria typically classified as moral, scientific, and ideological are, in fact, as Urmson suggests, irrelevant to the making of aesthetic judgements. If they should, in fact, turn out to be relevant, this would not only be of the greatest interest in itself but it would incalculably increase the improbability of discovering some feature common to all the criteria,

[1] J. O. Urmson, 'What Makes a Situation Aesthetic?' reprinted in Margolis, *op. cit.*, p. 25.

[2] T. S. Eliot, 'The Music of Poetry', *On Poetry and Poets*, New York 1961, p. 21.

moral and scientific as well as aesthetic, relevant to aesthetic judgement. And it would indicate that any such property would have to characterize not only aesthetic criteria but certain moral and scientific criteria as well.

A more promising line of objection to the notion that only 'aesthetic' criteria are relevant to aesthetic judgement may seem to be provided by such characteristic critical remarks as that Mary McCarthy's novels are unsuccessful because she is incapable of loving her characters. This may look like a straightforward moral (or psychological) judgement of the novel. And, indeed, it is not impossible to take it that way. But neither is it necessary to take it that way. We may understand the critic to be saying (in an elliptical way that some find misleading) that the characters do not have all the dimensions of life. They lack all those characteristics that only the eye of love can discern. Interpreted in this way the objection may be regarded as an aesthetic judgement criticizing the novels for failing to achieve 'the illusion of life'. If so, it might be argued that Urmson is wrong and that here we have a case where a moral ground (the incapacity to love) is, indeed, 'relevant to' an aesthetic judgement (the novel's lack of verisimilitude). The difficulty with this kind of example is, however, that the 'moral' or psychological fact is relevant to an explanation of why Mary McCarthy cannot write successful 'realistic' novels. What is required is, however, that the fact be relevant to establishing the judgement that the novels do not in fact create 'the illusion of life'. And this it does not do. (Indeed, the psychological fact only becomes relevant to the explanation once the aesthetic fact to be explained has been established.) If the psychological or moral fact is not relevant to making the judgement, certainly it is not its ground. It is true that we say the novels fail to dramatize certain dimensions of reality because Mary McCarthy cannot love her characters. But to take this as establishing that the lack of love is a ground for our judgement is to confuse a causal with a criterial use of 'because'. What we are doing is offering an explanation of the aesthetic failure and not saying that it is in virtue of the fact that Mary McCarthy cannot love her characters that we judge the novels to be unconvincing. Mary McCarthy's alleged moral or psychological failing is not operating as a criterion of aesthetic judgement at all, so it cannot be an example of a moral criterion of such a judgement. A more pertinent example is required.

It will be remembered that Urmson chooses as his example of extreme oddity the person who maintained that being scientifically accurate and up to date was in fact a criterion of aesthetic judgement. (In fact, in one form or another, it is a far more usual criterion of aesthetic excellence than is the possession of some quality of sound.) It is, perhaps, unfair to remind Urmson that Pound was exhibiting one of the central motives of the modern aesthetic creed when he demanded that poets 'make it new'. (Unfair, because the newness he had in mind was a kind of newness impossible for science.) But it is surely fair to cite a judgement like the one Lionel Trilling passes on the recent American novel. 'It is questionable,' he writes, 'whether any American novel since *Babbitt* has told us a new thing about our social life. In psychology the novel relies either on a mechanical or classical use of psychiatry or on the insights that were established by the novelists of fifty years ago.'[1] Unless psychology and social science are ruled out as not really scientific we would appear to have a clear and typical counter-example to Urmson's observation (he rightly sets great store by field work among the critics) and a case of a scientific criterion employed in making an aesthetic judgement. For Trilling means to condemn the recent American novel as an artistic achievement.

It is open to writers of Urmson's persuasion either to deny that such judgements are indeed aesthetic judgements (a position I do not propose to consider here) or to argue that the ostensibly non-aesthetic criteria are in fact really aesthetic ones. Wellek and Warren[2], for instance, feel that they would have to reject Eliot's dictum that the critic must consider whether a poem is 'coherent, mature, and founded on the facts of experience' unless they could show the criteria in question to be aesthetic ones. They observe, then, that coherence is not merely a logical but also an aesthetic criterion. It is not obvious whether they are saying that 'coherence' has two different senses, or whether they are saying that a criterion may fall into a number of different categories. The first, however, seems the more likely. For they go on to suggest that the other criteria, apparently psychological and epistemological, are to be understood as aesthetic. Thus, the psychological criterion of maturity is to be understood as a demand for complexity, and they

[1] Lionel Trilling, *The Liberal Imagination*, New York 1950, p. 263.

[2] René Wellek and Austin Warren, *Theory of Literature*, New York 1949, p. 257.

find that the epistemological criterion of truth to experience 'registers itself in aesthetic terms of vividness, intensity, patterned contrast, width or depth, static or kinetic'. This will not do. Obviously, many works regarded as mature (either for their own qualities or because of their position in an *oeuvre*) are not remarkable for their complexity. The maturity of *Oedipus at Colonus*, *The Tempest*, and *When We Dead Awaken*, is evidenced by the authority of their relative simplicity, and they are less complex than *Oedipus Rex*, *Troilus and Cressida*, and *Peer Gynt*. And, surely, the truth to experience Eliot has in mind displays itself in the calm of Dante (as narrator, not pilgrim) rather than in the intensity of Shelley, in the muted measure of *Four Quartets* rather than in the vividness of 'The Hippopotamus' or 'Mr. Apollinax'. It simply does not seem possible to reduce the criterion of maturity to that of complexity. And more importantly, it does not seem possible to reduce the criterion of truth, either as it is invoked by Trilling or by Eliot, to an aesthetic criterion. If that is so, it would appear to be the case that scientific—and, as it would be still simpler to show, moral—criteria are relevant to the making of aesthetic judgements. Urmson's assumption that the sub-set of such criteria will exclude moral, intellectual, and other criteria, is false. And the hope of discovering some property common to the criteria relevant to aesthetic judgement, in so far as it is based on the assumption that such criteria are, indeed, excluded, will lose its plausibility.

If the aesthetic purists cannot show that ostensibly non-aesthetic criteria are really aesthetic ones, they might try to avoid the conclusion we have reached by denying that they are criteria at all. Or, at least, that they are the real or ultimate criteria of aesthetic judgements. The purists might hold that whenever aesthetic judgements appear to rely on non-aesthetic criteria they can be shown actually or implicitly to invoke some further aesthetic criterion. And it will always be the case that the facts relevant to determining whether the non-aesthetic criteria have been satisfied will be relevant to deciding whether the further aesthetic criteria have been satisfied. If these relations did not obtain, it might be held, the judgement would not be accepted as an aesthetic one. Thus, Trilling may praise James' *The Princess Casamassima* for satisfying just those historical and epistemological criteria he regards the modern American novel as having failed to satisfy. But the aesthetic purists might argue that we accept the judgement as aesthetic only because we take an implicit criterion to be a genuinely aesthetic one. In this case, perhaps, that the demands of the genre are satisfied (and in the case of realistic fiction one of these demands is for genuine historical comprehension). Similarly, they might seek to show that often, at least, when we appear to be appealing to scientific, moral, intellectual, and even economic criteria, we are actually appealing to aesthetic ones. If we merely look at what he writes, we may suppose the critic to be praising Mann's *Dr Faustus* simply for the brilliance of his historical diagnosis, D. H. Lawrence's *Women in Love* for its moral profundity, Schoenberg's Opus 23 piano pieces for their intellectual audacity, and Fabergé jewellery or the Taj Mahal for their expensiveness. But it may be possible to argue that in each case the fundamental criterion of judgement is in fact aesthetic. We are really judging that Mann achieves his artistic intentions, that Lawrence has fully realized the potentialities of the novel, that Schoenberg has renewed an exhausted musical art, and that Fabergé has exploited his materials in the manner best calculated to reveal their peculiar virtue. Whether a position such as the one sketched here can be precisely stated (so that one knows, for instance, how the existence and identity of the implicit criterion is to be determined) and whether it can be defended in detail (some such theory is assumed by many to be *a priori* true) cannot be decided here. I am much inclined to doubt it. But I am still more inclined to doubt whether some property will be found that is essential even to the considerable variety of aesthetic criteria that are likely to be acknowledged if the thesis in question is to be defended at all. For aesthetic criteria are numerous and make reference not only to the sensory and formal features of objects and to expressive and technical qualities of media but also to the intentions of artists, the dialectical demands of particular arts, the expectations of aesthetic elites, and the impersonal progress of the institutions of art.

It is perhaps worth insisting that I do not suppose all judgements of works of art to be aesthetic judgements. And it is important to distinguish those judgements that we regard as aesthetic (even when they are based on moral criteria) from those we do not. For this is to distinguish D. H. Lawrence's judgement of Galsworthy's novels and Santayana's of Whitman's poetry from the Congressional hack's judgement of Martha Graham's dances or the Party hack's judgement of *Dr Zhivago*. But neither do I wish to suggest that we ought never to pass moral or political judgements on works of art. In the Republic it may be necessary to pass Plato's flattering judgement on poets. And in France, at least, it may already be necessary to demand that every writer of fiction ask what would happen if everyone read what he wrote. For the consequences of words are not merely aesthetic consequences. Sartre was, therefore, right to remind us of Mosca's observation beside the coach that carried Fabrice and Sanseverina away.[1] 'If the word Love comes up between them, I'm lost.'

[1] Jean-Paul Sartre, *What Is Literature?* New York 1949. Reprinted as *Existentialism and Literature*, New York 1962, pp. 23–24.

VII

ACTION AND RESPONSIBILITY

by JOEL FEINBERG

Associate Professor of Philosophy, Princeton University

What is the difference between a full-fledged human action and a mere bodily movement? Discussion of this ancient question, long at an impasse, was revitalized a decade and a half ago by H. L. A. Hart's classic article on the subject,[1] in which he argued that the primary function of action sentences is to ascribe responsibility, and that even in non-legal discourse such sentences are 'defeasible' in the manner of certain legal claims and judgements. It is now widely agreed, I think, that Professor Hart's analysis, while containing insights of permanent importance, still falls considerably short of the claims its author originally made for it. Yet, characteristically, there appears to be very little agreement over which features of the analysis are 'insights' and which 'mistakes'. I shall, accordingly, attempt to isolate and give some nourishment to what I take to be the kernel of truth in Hart's analysis, while avoiding, as best I can, his errors. I shall begin with that class of action sentences for which Hart's analysis has the greatest *prima facie* plausibility—those attributing to their subjects various kinds of substandard performance.

I. FAULTY-ACTION SENTENCES AND DEFEASIBILITY[2]

If I throw down my cards at the end of a hand of poker and, with anger in my voice, say to another player, 'You kept an ace up your sleeve!', or more simply, 'You cheated!', then surely I am doing more than 'describing his bodily movements'; I am *charging* him with an offence, *accusing* him of a wrong. It is at least plausible to interpret utterances of that sort as claims that a person is deserving

[1] H. L. A. Hart, 'The Ascription of Responsibility and Rights', *Proceedings of the Aristotelian Society*, Vol. 49 (1948–49), pp. 171–94.

[2] I am grateful to my colleague George Pitcher for pointing out some serious errors in an earlier version of this section. I fear there may still be much in it that he disagrees with.

of censure or punishment for what he did. But though charges of deceit, cruelty, and the like are no doubt the most dramatic examples of pronouncements ascribing sub-par performance, it would probably be a mistake to consider them to the exclusion of other no less 'typical' ascriptions of defective behaviour. While 'condemnatory verbs'[1] such as 'cheat' and 'murder' are of course used to impute faulty actions, they are not the only verbs to do so. Such words as 'miscalculate' and 'stammer' also have faultiness built into their meaning. Miscalculating is a faulty way of calculating, and stammering is a defective way of speaking; and yet miscalculators and stammerers are not (necessarily) deserving of censure or punishment. Similarly, we speak of failing tests and muffing lines, of bumbling, botching, breaking, and spoiling—all defective ways of acting, but none necessarily morally defective.

Let us turn now to that feature of legal language which Hart called 'defeasibility', with the aim of discovering how (and to what extent) it applies to 'faulty-action sentences' interpreted in this broad way. Hart borrowed the term 'defeasible' from the law of property, where it is used to refer to an estate or legal interest in land which is 'subject to termination or "defeat" in a number of different contingencies but remains intact if no such contingencies mature'.[2] He then extended its meaning to cover all legal claims that are regarded as provisionally established at a certain stage of the litigation process but still vulnerable to defeat, annulment, or revocation at some later stage of the proceedings. Defeasibility then, if I understand Hart's intentions, is closely associated with the legal notion of a *prima facie* case: 'A litigating party is said to have a *prima facie* case when the evidence in his favour is sufficiently strong for his opponent to be called upon to answer it. A *prima facie* case, then, is one which is established by sufficient evidence, and can be overthrown only by rebutting evidence adduced on the other side.'[3] If a plaintiff in a civil action fails to state a claim that, if established, would amount to a *prima facie* case, then there is nothing against which the defendant need defend himself and he wins a directed verdict. If the plaintiff does state a claim that, if established, would amount to a *prima facie* case, then there are a

[1] The term is Pitcher's. See his penetrating article 'Hart on Action and Responsibility', *Philosophical Review*, Vol. 69 (1960), pp. 226–35.
[2] Hart, *op. cit.*, p. 175.
[3] *Black's Law Dictionary*, Fourth Edition, p. 1353.

variety of defensive postures open to a defendant. He might deny some of the plaintiff's factual allegations, he might argue that the court lacks jurisdiction, or he might make an 'affirmative defence', that is, in effect, provisionally grant the plaintiff's *prima facie* case, but put forward some one or more of a variety of justifications, excuses, or claimed immunities. The burden of proof switches at this point from plaintiff to defendant, and this is just one of several procedural consequences of the distinction between *prima facie* case and affirmative defence. In a criminal grand jury trial, the *only* question before the court is whether or not there is evidence tending to establish a *prima facie* case against the accused, hence the jury need not even hear the evidence for the defence.

The notion of defeasibility then is inextricably tied up with an adversary system of litigation and its complex and diverse rules governing the sufficiency and insufficiency of legal claims, presumptive and conclusive evidence, the roles of contending parties, and the burden of proof. Of course there are no rules of comparable complexity and precision governing our everyday nontechnical use of 'faulty-action sentences'. At most, then, the assertion that these everyday ascriptions are defeasible suggests only that there are revealing analogies between them and legal claims in respect to their presumptiveness and vulnerability. In particular, I think, Hart would emphasize the vulnerability of both to defeat by excuses (for example, accident, mistake) and justifications (for example, forced choice of the lesser evil, special privilege, consent) but not by such other affirmative defences as diplomatic immunity, expiration of the statute of limitations, and so on. The point is that given certain rules of courtroom procedure, various types of excuse and justification are among those defences which can defeat legal claims and charges even when all the other conditions necessary and normally sufficient for their success (the '*prima facie* case') are satisfied. But in everyday life outside of courtrooms there is rarely a conception of '*prima facie* case' at all comparable in definiteness to the legal model (after all, in the law what is to be included in a *prima facie* case is largely determined by administrative convenience and other considerations having no counterpart in private life); hence outside of the law the notion of 'necessary and normally sufficient conditions' will be necessarily vague, though not necessarily obscure.

Of the several different kinds of nonlegal fault imputations, the most persuasive examples of defeasibility are those ascribing intentional wrongdoing. When we catch a poker player with an ace up his sleeve, we have established a powerful presumption ('*prima facie* case') that he has *cheated*. Now it is up to him to give a satisfactory explanation (he has the 'burden of proof'), and unless he rebuts the presumption (offers an acceptable excuse), the charge will stick. The word 'cheat' is, in fact, an especially clear case, for its character as defeasible by excuses seems part of its very meaning. This is shown by the obvious absurdity of such phrases as 'unintentional cheating' and 'accidental cheating'. (Compare 'accidental murder', 'unintentional lie'.) If the 'defeating' excuse is accepted, the fault-imputation *must* be withdrawn; this is what it means for a fault-imputation to be defeasible, and it allows us to show that 'cheat', 'murder', and 'lie' are defeasible faults. I have widened the notion of 'fault imputation' to include faults of all kinds. Are all fault-imputations then equally defeasible?

It is of considerable philosophical importance, I think, especially for consideration of the free-will problem, to realize that some faults are defeasible while some are not. Consider first of all the faults or defects we might impute to objects other than persons. Flatness is surely a 'fault' in an automobile tyre and rottenness in an egg. When we attribute such defects to tyres and eggs, we leave no space for the reply, 'But that tyre has travelled 50,000 miles and that egg was put in an inefficient refrigerator; therefore you are being too severe to call them flat and rotten respectively'. Ready analogues are found in human beings. Faulty posture (deformity), faulty health (sickness), faulty appearance (ugliness), faulty intelligence (stupidity), and faulty knowledge (ignorance) seem equally clear examples of non-defeasible faults. When we come to faulty character the situation is more difficult. Tactlessness, humourlessness, social obtuseness, are, I think, character faults that are nondefeasible. Of course, we can often explain why a man is tactless, for example, but no explanation in this case will explain away the fact once its normal sufficient conditions have been ascertained to hold; and this is precisely the mark of a nondefeasible fault: it can be explained, but not 'explained away'. Something like defective vision is at the root of these character flaws, and social or moral blindness, like its physical counterpart, can be rued or forgiven or deplored when it clearly shows itself, but not denied.

Other character faults, however, do seem clearly to be defeasible. Perhaps the clearest cases are the highly determinable or generic faults—'wickedness', for example. Any number of defences—mistaken beliefs, defective glands, neurotic compulsion, etc.—will defeat this imputation utterly. Less certain but still probable examples are such flaws as laziness and cruelty. If an apparently normal man is observed spending day after day sleeping until noon, lolling about his rooms, and engaging in only trivial and undemanding activities, there is a presumption that he is lazy. The presumption is not conclusive, however, but only defeasible, as we would soon admit if we learned that he was behaving in an apparently indolent way only because his physician had ordered him to do so, and that he was restless, bored, and impatient to resume an active life. That laziness is defeasible is indicated by the absurdity of such a phrase as 'unintentional' or 'unwilling laziness'. The absurdity is only partly accounted for (if at all) by the fact that laziness is by and large a dispositional word, for it would be equally absurd to say of a man that he spent an hour or a day being unwillingly or unwittingly lazy. The words simply do not go together even when 'lazy' bears an occurrent sense. Similarly, the man who is disposed to act regularly in a way which causes a certain class of people pain may only seem cruel, and the appearance will be a deception if in fact he acts that way because he believes he thereby causes those persons pleasure. Mistaken beliefs usually defeat the charge of cruelty (both cruel habits and cruel acts) as is evidenced by the oddness of the phrase 'unknowing cruelty'. 'Cruelty', however, is typical of a class of fault-words that have evolved or are evolving senses in which they stand for the sort of behaviour normally associated with the fault in the primary (defeasible) sense, even when in fact disassociated from that fault. So, for example, it *can* make sense, in some contexts, to speak of a kind man's (unknowingly) cruel behaviour, although even in these sense-giving contexts, the faintest odour of paradox lingers in the air.

Our main interest here, however, is not with faulty character but with faulty performance, not with fault-imputing nouns and adjectives but with faulty-action verbs. Here again it is possible to find clear examples of both defeasible and nondefeasible imputations. 'He broke the window' and 'He broke down and cried' seem to be nondefeasible, while their distant relative 'He broke faith with his friend' seems defeasible. A man who accidentally breaks a window nevertheless breaks the window. We may forgive him because his faulty performance was accidental, but for all that we do not withdraw the fault-imputing verb or 'defeat' its imputation. He broke down and cried *understandably* perhaps, but the explanation does not cancel the fact of the breakdown. Breaking faith, however, is a fish from another kettle. One cannot break faith unintentionally; for if what one did was done by mistake or accident it cannot properly be called 'breaking faith'. We should have to withdraw the charge of faithbreaking altogether once we acknowledge the excuse. Faithbreaking, in short, is defeasible. Other examples of *non-defeasible* charges of faulty performance are: 'He drove dangerously', 'He dropped the ball' (in a baseball game), 'He spoke falsely'. But 'He drove recklessly', 'He fumbled the ball' (in baseball), 'He lied', are all *defeasible*. All alike are ascriptions of performances that are in some way faulty or defective; but some we would withdraw if the subject had a proper excuse, while the others we cannot withdraw so long as we admit that conditions 'normally sufficient' for their truth are satisfied.

What is the basis of the distinction between defeasible and nondefeasible ascriptions of faulty performance? Both kinds of ascriptions express blame, at least in the very general sense that they attribute to an agent a performance somehow defective or untoward. The distinctive feature of the defeasible ascriptions is that they express a blame *above and beyond* the mere untowardness or defectiveness of the ascribed action. Still, as we have seen, it would be much *too* strong to say that all the verbs in the defeasible ascriptions, unlike their more 'neutral' counterparts, always express moral condemnation (although it is sometimes plausible to say this of some of them). In what way then is their blame 'stronger' and 'beyond' mere ascription of fault?

There is something quasi-judicial or quasi-official about the defeasible ascriptions, I would like to suggest, even when uttered outside of institutional contexts, which helps distinguish them from the nondefeasible ones. To lie or cheat, to fail to show due care, to fumble the ball or flub one's lines, is not merely to do something untoward or defective; it is also to be 'to blame' for doing it. This in turn means that the doing of the untoward act can be *charged* to one, or *registered* for further notice, or 'placed as an entry on one's *record*'. Outside institutional contexts, of course, there are no formal records but only reputations. Perhaps that is what the notion of a 'moral record' comes to. The concept of a record, however, is primarily and originally an institutional concept. Our formal records are found in offices of employment, schools, banks, and police dossiers, and they are full of grades and averages, marks and points, merits, demerits, debits, charges, credits, and registered instances of 'fault'. These records in turn have a hundred different uses, from determining the value of a baseball player to his team to dictating decisions about whether to trust, hire, fire, reward, or punish someone. Without all these records and their informal analogue (reputation) there would be no point to talk of being 'to blame' and no need for the defeasible ascriptions of fault.

To defeat the charge of being to blame by presenting a relevant strong excuse is to demonstrate that an action's faultiness is not properly 'registrable' on one of the agent's records, not chargeable to 'his account'. The reason why a faulty action is sometimes not chargeable to an agent's record even though the action was, under another description, his, is that it was performed under such circumstances that to enter it on the relevant record would make it misleading, and thus defeat its point or purpose. In a baseball game, for example, a fielder is normally said to have fumbled a ball when he is able to get his glove on it without having to run very far and yet is unable to hold on to it once he touches it. If the ball, however, strikes a pebble and takes a bad hop before striking the fielder's glove, the fielder is not then properly chargeable either with an 'error' on his official record or with having 'fumbled the ball' on his 'unofficial record' or reputation. And the reason for the acceptability of this 'strong defence' is found in the very purpose of keeping fielders' records, namely, to allow interested parties to make as accurate as possible an appraisal of the contribution of each player to the success or failure of the team.[1] If we charge fielders for the consequences of fortuitous events the records will lose their accuracy and fail accordingly to achieve their purpose. A similar account, I think, could be given of the rationale of entries on other professional, legal, and even 'moral' records.

[1] This is very close to the function of 'records' in history. Cf. H. L. A. Hart and A. M. Honoré: 'History is written not only to satisfy the need for explanation, but also the desire to identify and assess contributions made by historical figures to changes of importance; to triumphs and disasters, and to human happiness or suffering.' *Causation in the Law*, Oxford 1959, p. 59.

It might be argued against this sketchy account that *any* kind of fault can be put on some sort of record or other, hence 'registrability' cannot very well be the characteristic which distinguishes defeasible from nondefeasible faults. But the point I am endeavouring to make is not one about logical conceivability; it is one about practical plausibility. On what sort of record might we register that Jones drove dangerously, if it should turn out that the risk he created by driving ten miles an hour over the speed limit was amply justified by his purpose in getting a critically ill passenger to the hospital? Should we put this down as a fault on his *driving record*? Surely not, if the point of keeping a driving record is to reveal what kind of driver a man is—safe and capable or careless and dangerous. Jones drove dangerously on this occasion, to be sure, but the circumstances were so special that his behaviour did nothing to reveal his *predominant tendencies*, hence to register it as a fault would not promote the purpose of the record itself. Smith speaks falsely on a given occasion. On what imaginable record might this have a point as an entry? On his *moral record*? Surely not, unless he spoke with intent to deceive, in which case he *lied*—and that *is* registrable. In general, I should think, a person's faulty act is registrable only if it reveals what sort of person he is in some respect about which others have a practical interest in being informed.

There are at least three different types of 'registrable' (defeasible) faults, each exhibiting its own peculiarities. Depending on their purposes, record keepers might register (1) instances of defective skill or ability (for example, 'fumbles'), (2) instances of defective or improper care or effort (negligence, laziness) and (3) instances of improper intention (cheating, breaking faith). There are similarities in the uses to which these three distinct types of entries might be put—and also differences. In all three types of cases, to be forewarned is to be forearmed. If there are numerous instances of cheating on a man's record then we had better not play cards with him, or if we play we should watch him closely. Similarly, if a man's record shows him to be careless and absentminded, then we should hire another and not him to be a night watchman; and if Butterfinger's fielding average is substantially lower than Orthodigit's, we had better install the latter at third base in the ninth inning with our team ahead in a close game.

On the other hand, corresponding to the three types of faults, there are important differences in the modes of treatment we might inflict on their possessors. We should not punish or censure the fumbler, for example, even if we were in a position to do so, except of course to make him try harder; but then the censure is for defective effort, not defective skill. However else we are to analyse punishment and censure, we must include an element of expressed disapproval, perhaps even hostility and resentment; and these attitudes and judgements, while they might intensify desire and even change intention, could have little effect (except perhaps inhibiting) on skill. Censure apparently works best in fortifying the motivation of otherwise careless, distractable, and lazy people, that is, those with faulty records of the second type. There is now apparently some reason to think that manifest hostility, warnings, and threats work less well in correcting faults of improper intention, and in respect at least to the most severe defects of this sort, are useless or self-defeating. To *express* disapproval, for example, to the man with a powerful grudge against society may simply intensify his hatred, and promote rather than hinder further hateful and destructive behaviour.

If we mean by 'blame' any sort of outwardly manifested disapproval of a person for his defective performance, then the relations between blaming and 'being to blame' are diverse and complex indeed. The defeasible fault-imputations charge only that a man is *to blame* for his defective performance (and not merely that the performance *was* defective) but not that he is properly subject to any kind of overt blame for it. Whether to blame him or not depends on what use we wish to make of his 'record', and this in turn depends upon our prior purposes, the nature of the fault, and the prospects of 'utility'.

In summary: I have distinguished three different stages in our responses to faulty performance. We can simply note that a given act is Jones's and that it was in some way faulty or defective. At this stage we need not use the language of defeasible fault-ascriptions at all. We might simply say, for instance, that he dropped the ball, departed from the blueprints, spoke falsely, etc. At a second stage, we might resort to the language of defeasible ascriptions and charge him, for example, with fumbling the ball, botching the job, or lying. At this stage we not only ascribe to him an action which is somehow defective, we also hold him *to blame* for it. This involves registering the defective performance on the agent's relevant record, or in the absence of a formal record and an institutional context, making it part of his reputation. At the third stage, we may put the record or reputation, with the fault duly registered therein, to any one of a great variety of *uses*, including, among other things, overt blame. If we think, on the basis of the record, that overt blame is what the agent deserves, we might say that he is properly subject to—or liable to—blame, and then that judgement could be characterized as an *ascription of liability*. But being 'to blame' and being subject to further blaming performances are two quite distinct things: the former is often a necessary but only rarely a sufficient condition for the latter.

We shall stop at the first stage (nondefeasible fault-ascription) if an appropriate defence defeats the charge that the defect is registrable; or we may stop at the second stage (register that the agent is 'to blame' for the fault) if there is no reason to expect any kind of overt responsive action toward the agent to achieve anything useful. Finally, we may think it necessary to blame or fire or punish him, in which case we hold him (now at the third stage) so liable. In respect to the normal nonfaulty action, however, we do not even get to the first stage.

II. NORMAL-ACTION SENTENCES

Can we conclude by accepting this complicated version of Hart's analysis as holding good for faulty-action sentences only? Was Hart simply misled, as some critics[1] have charged, by his own unrepresentative selection of examples, oddly failing to notice the difference between such accusations as 'He murdered her' (and 'He fumbled the ball') on the one hand, and such normal, non-accusing sentences as 'He closed the door' on the other? This is a tidy way of disposing of Hart's view, but I suspect that it does less than full justice to his insight. Hart must surely have intended, and perhaps with good reason, that the notions of ascriptiveness and defeasibility throw some light on the normal cases of action as well as on defective performance. This is the critical possibility that will be explored in the remainder of this paper.

Is there any sense in which normal-action sentences ascribe responsibility? If we consider the matter closely, we shall discover

[1] *E.g.* Pitcher, *op. cit.*, and P. T. Geach, 'Ascriptiveness,' *Philosophical Review*, Vol. 69 (1960), p. 221.

at least five closely related but distinguishable things that might be meant by the phrase 'ascription of responsibility'.

(1) *Straightforward Ascriptions of Causality*

A meteorologist might ascribe today's weather in New England to yesterday's pressure system over the Great Lakes, meaning simply that the latter is the cause of the former. In similar ways we frequently ascribe causality not only to the presence or absence of impersonal events, states, and properties, but also to the actions, omissions, properties, and dispositions of human beings. Ascriptions of causality, whether to impersonal or to personal sources, often use the language of responsibility. A low pressure system over the Great Lakes, we might naturally say, was *responsible* for the storms in New England; and in precisely the same (causal) sense we might say that a man's action was responsible for some subsequent event or state of affairs, imputing no more blame or credit or guilt or liability to the man than we do to the pressure system when we ascribe causality to it. When we say then that Smith is responsible for *X* we can mean simply that *X* is the result of what Smith did or, in equivalent terms, that Smith did something (e.g. turned the knob) and thereby caused *X* (e.g. the door's opening) to happen.

Gilbert Ryle has argued that we do not speak of persons as responsible for states of affairs unless we are charging them with some sort of offence.[1] There is a point overstated in this claim, but not one which militates against a purely causal sense of 'responsible'. The point is this: we do not ordinarily raise the question of responsibility for something unless that something has somehow excited our interest, and as a matter of fact the states of affairs that excite our interest are very often unhappy ones. But sometimes unexpectedly happy circumstances need accounting for too, and sometimes the interest aroused is the desire to understand, not the desire to give credit or blame. The language of responsibility aside, we do not usually raise the question of the *causation* of something, either, unless that something has somehow excited our interest. The things that cry out for explanation are usually those that first appear somehow 'fishy'; but as Stanley Cavell points out, they need not be 'morally fishy'.[2]

[1] Gilbert Ryle, *The Concept of Mind*, New York 1949, p. 69.

[2] Stanley Cavell, 'Must We Mean What We Say?', *Inquiry*, Vol. I (1958), p. 177.

(2) *Ascriptions of Causal-Agency*

To characterize these properly, we must introduce a rough distinction between complex and simple acts. There are a great number of ways in which actions are complex, but only one of these concerns us here, that which might be called 'causal complexity'. To accomplish such tasks as moving one's furniture to a warehouse or rescuing a drowning swimmer, one must first take a number of other steps, such as lifting chairs, diving into the water, etc. The complex task is performed by means of the performance of a series of teleologically connected 'sub-acts': one closes a door *by* pushing and latching it.

A causally simple case of doing, on the other hand, requires no earlier doing as a means. Smiling and frowning are simple actions, and so are raising one's arm and shutting one's eyes. To do any of these things it is not first necessary to do something else; nor is it necessary to do something in one's mind as a kind of triggering: to set off a volition or 'flex an occult non-muscle'.[1] In very special circumstances, of course, these normally simple acts can be complex. I might have to make myself smile, for social purposes, by a kind of interior girding of my tired facial muscles;[2] but normally one smiles spontaneously without having to 'cause' himself to do so.

Any distinction in terms of simplicity and complexity is, of course, a matter of degree. Winking and smiling are usually perfectly simple actions; grasping, clutching, throwing only slightly more complex; baking a cake, or building a house more complex still. Some relatively complex actions, such as walking, rising, and sitting down, do not involve in their bare descriptions any explicit reference to an external object transformed or manipulated. These can be distinguished from those complex actions typically referred to by transitive verbs, such as 'open', 'close', 'rescue', 'kill', with their objects. Only the latter are referred to here by the phrase 'causally complex actions'.

[1] Ryle, *op. cit.*, p. 74: 'To frown intentionally is not to bring about a frown-causing exertion of some occult non-muscle.'

[2] Cf. Ralph Waldo Emerson: 'There is a mortifying experience . . . I mean "the foolish face of praise", the forced smile we put on in company where we do not feel at ease, in answer to conversation which does not interest us. The muscles, not spontaneously moved but moved by a low usurping wilfulness, grow tight about the outline of the face, with the most disagreeable sensation', *Essays, First Series*, Boston 1895, pp. 56–57.

Now in respect of causally connected sequences of acts and consequences, our language provides us with numerous alternative ways of talking. J. L. Austin describes one of these options: '. . . a single term descriptive of what he did may be made to cover either a smaller or a larger stretch of events, those excluded by the narrower description being then called "consequences" or "results" or "effects" or the like of his act'.[1] Thus we can say that Jones opened the door and thereby caused Smith (who was inside) to be startled, in this way treating Jones's act as the cause of a subsequent effect; or we can say (simply) 'Jones startled Smith' (by opening the door), and thus incorporate the consequence into the complex action. If Smith suffered a heart attack and died, we can say that Jones's opening the door caused his death, or that Jones's startling him caused his death, or simply that Jones killed him (by doing those things).

This well-known feature of our language, whereby a man's action can be described as narrowly or broadly as we please, I propose to call the 'accordion effect', because an act, like the folding musical instrument, can be squeezed down to a minimum or else stretched out. He turned the key, he opened the door, he startled Smith, he killed Smith—all of these are things we might say that Jones *did* with one identical set of bodily movements. Because of the accordion effect we can usually replace any ascription to a person of causal responsibility by an ascription of agency or authorship. We can, if we wish, puff out an action to include an effect, and more often than not our language obliges us by providing a relatively complex action word for the purpose. Instead of saying Smith did *A* (a relatively simple act) and thereby caused *X* in *Y*, we might say something of the form 'Smith *X*-ed *Y*'; instead of 'Smith opened the door causing Jones to be startled', 'Smith startled Jones'.

Ascriptions of causal responsibility, then, are often precisely equivalent to ascriptions of the second type, which we have called ascriptions of causal agency. Whatever difference exists between the two forms of expression is merely a matter of rhetorical emphasis or grammatical convenience.[2] Both say something about

[1] J. L. Austin, 'A Plea for Excuses', *Philosophical Papers*, Oxford 1961, p. 149.

[2] Cf. John Salmond: 'The distinction between an act and its consequences, between doing a thing and causing a thing, is a merely verbal one.' *Jurisprudence*, Eleventh edition, London 1957, p. 402.

causation, the one quite explicitly, the other in the language of agency or authorship.

(3) *Ascriptions of Simple Agency*

These cannot possibly be assimilated to the first two. The purely causal ascriptions can usually be translated into ascriptions of causal-agency, and the latter of course can only be of causally complex actions. Simple actions (as is now widely acknowledged) have no causal component. In order to open a door, we must first do something else which will *cause* the door to open; but to move one's finger one simply moves it—no prior causal activity is required. Hence ascriptions of simple agency are ascriptions of agency through and through. One cannot play the accordion with them.

(4) *Imputations of Fault*

This motley group, discussed in Part I, have, amidst their many dissimilarities, several important features in common. All of them ascribe agency, simple or (more commonly) causal, for a somehow defective or faulty action. Many of them, but not all, are defeasible. Rather than be qualified in certain ways, these will be withdrawn altogether and replaced with nondefeasible faulty-act ascriptions. If they cannot be so 'defeated', however, they are properly entered on a relevant record of the agent's; that is, they are *registrable*. As registered faults, they are *nontransferable*. In the relevant sense of 'being to blame', no one is to blame but the agent; hence no one else can 'take the blame' (or 'shoulder the responsibility') for him.

(5) *Ascriptions of Liability*

These are different in kind from the fault-imputations, even though they are often intertwined or confused with them. The one kind imputes a faulty act, simple or complex, to an agent as its author; the other ascribes, either to the agent or to someone else, liability under a set of rules or customs to some further response for it. Unlike imputations of fault, ascriptions of liability can be transferable, vicarious, or 'strict', that is, independent of actual fault. In some situations under some rules, a faultless spectator may effectively say 'I'll take the responsibility for that', or 'Charge that to my account', and the liability really does transfer as a result.

There are several morals to be drawn immediately from this fivefold classification. First of all, all five types of ascription can be made in the language of responsibility. Sometimes 'responsibility' *means* causal assignability, sometimes authorship, causal or simple, sometimes fault-imputability or creditability, sometimes liability. Often ascriptions of responsibility blend authorship and liability, these being intimately related in virtue of the fact that the most usual (though not the only) reason for holding a person liable for an action (or event) is that he performed (or caused) it. Another thing to notice about the classification is that the first three uses of 'responsible', in ascriptions of straightforward causality, causal agency, and simple agency, apply to the 'normal case' of action, where questions of fault, desert of punishment, and the like, do not arise. Quite clearly, action sentences *do* ascribe responsibility in these senses.

The classification also suggests what it means to say that a sentence *ascribes* responsibility, in any of the senses of 'responsibility'. It was very important to Hart in his original article to argue that action sentences are typically 'ascriptive' rather than 'descriptive'. But this is a confusion. Any kind of action sentence can be *used* either descriptively or ascriptively. We describe a person's actions when we have been considering that person and wondering what he did—when the question before our minds is not 'Who did it?' but rather 'What did *he* do?' When we have occasion to ascribe an action to a person, we have the action, so to speak, in our hands, and we want to know what to do with it, whom to pin it on.

If we wish to know who killed Cock Robin, this must be because we know that *someone* killed Cock Robin, but we don't know *who*. In the case of complex actions this sort of curiosity is common, for we can often examine the effects of an action in separation from the action itself and then wonder to whom to ascribe the consequence. A perfectly simple action, however, has no detachable part to examine in leisurely abstraction from the rest. Except for the simple act itself there is no further 'ascriptum' to ascribe. The statement 'Jones smiled', when it appears routinely in a novelist's narrative or a newspaper article, simply describes or reports what Jones did at a certain moment. In these cases the novelist or journalist has not *assigned* a smile to Jones, as if he had the smile first and then selected Jones to put it on.

Still, rare as they might be, there are occasions for ascribing simple acts. A simple-action sentence is used ascriptively only when a question of personal identity has, for one reason or another, arisen. 'Who was that man who smiled?' one might ask, and another might chime in 'Oh, did someone smile? Who was it?' Now the stage is set for an ascription. An ascription of simple action is but an identification of the doer of an already known doing.

Some philosophers have argued that it is an 'improper way of talking' to speak, after the fact, of a person's being responsible *for his own actions*, that strictly speaking what a person can be held responsible for are the 'consequences, results, or upshots of the things he does'.[1] This is quite true if we mean by 'responsible', *causally* responsible; for with rare exceptions we don't cause our actions, we simply do them. It would be extraordinary however if such a widespread idiom as 'responsibility for one's actions' always embodied such a crude mistake, and our classification reveals several 'proper' uses to which it might be put. First of all, to be responsible for one's own complex actions (e.g. closing a door) is properly to have one's simpler actions identified as the cause of an upshot. The knife cuts both ways: If 'being responsible for the door's being shut (by having caused it to close)' is a permissible way of speaking, then so is talk of being responsible *for closing* the door, which in virtue of the accordion effect is strictly equivalent to it. Secondly, to be responsible for one's simple actions is only to be properly identifiable as their doer. 'It was Mary who smiled' ascribes the responsibility *for smiling* to Mary, and says nothing whatever about causal upshots. This is especially clear when the simple action is faulty, as for example, a socially inappropriate smirk or leer. The report that someone had smiled in church, if it were to have received currency in colonial Massachusetts where such simple activity was a crime, would have set the stage for a noncausal responsibility ascription. To say then that it was Mary who did it would be to ascribe responsibility to Mary *for smiling*, not in the sense of doing something to cause the smile to appear, but rather in the sense of being properly identifiable as the doer of the deed.

III. THE STRONGER SENSE OF 'ASCRIPTIVE'

The fivefold classification of responsibility ascriptions, then, does tend to support Hart's view that action sentences are ascriptive. It

[1] Pitcher, *op. cit.*, p. 227.

suggests at least that, for all kinds of action-sentences, there is some context in which they can be used ascriptively, that is to identify the 'author'. On the other hand it does nothing to support his view that all action-sentences ascribe *liability* to formal responses from others or that they are all defeasible in the manner of legal charges and accusations. In this section the classification will be used to restore still more of Hart's view, though perhaps not in the way he intended it to be understood.

We have already noticed one way in which the puzzling term 'ascription' can be understood. Ascriptions in this sense have a necessary subjective condition or contextual presupposition. What is not an ascription in one context may well be so in another, depending on the concerns of the speaker. If the question is 'What did Jones do?' then the sentence 'Jones did *A*' *describes* what Jones did; but if the question is 'Who did *A*?', then 'Jones did *A*' *ascribes A* to Jones. This simple distinction may seem to have very little importance, since ascriptions and descriptions, so understood, may say the same thing about a man with only different emphases provided by our interests. The distinction between ascriptions and descriptions, however, sometimes reverberates with deeper overtones. Instead of a mere matter of emphasis, the distinction is taken to be one of type. P. T. Geach,[1] for example, in criticizing Hart, compares the distinction between descriptive and ascriptive with the better known contrast between descriptive and *pre*scriptive as if they were distinctions of the same order; and K. W. Rankin contrasts 'matters of ascription' with 'matters of fact'.[2] Now whether the sentence 'Jones did *A*' is used to ascribe *A* to Jones or to describe what Jones did, as we have understood those terms, it surely registers, in either case, a matter of fact. The indicative mood is well suited to express what the sentence does in either use; and ascriptions as well as descriptions can be true or false, and are 'about' what happened. If ascriptions are to be contrasted, then, with 'matters of fact', some new conception of 'ascriptiveness' is involved. The question to be considered now is whether, in this new sense of ascription, there is any reason for treating action sentences as ascriptive.

The stronger notion of ascriptiveness can be explained, I think, in the following way. There is a familiar commonsense distinction

[1] Geach, *op. cit.*, p. 221.
[2] K. W. Rankin, *Choice and Chance*, Oxford 1960, p. 29 *et passim*.

between questions calling for *decisions* and those requiring *discoveries*. I must decide at which restaurant to dine tomorrow, but I must discover the solution of an equation, or the population of a town. In the first case, even when all the facts are in, I have a certain amount of discretion; in the latter case, I am bound or committed totally by the facts—I cannot escape the conclusions they dictate. This distinction has been expressed in a great variety of ways: questions of policy versus questions of fact, practical versus theoretical, regulative versus constitutive, and so on. Some philosophers have denied either the existence or the importance of the distinction: 'Platonists' tend to reduce questions of decision to questions of discovery, and 'Pragmatists' assimilate the theoretical to the practical. Common sense, however, holds firm to the distinction, even when puzzled about how to explain it or where to draw the line. Philosophers who contrast 'ascriptive' with 'factual', I suggest, have this distinction in mind. By 'ascriptive sentences' they mean (among other things) sentences not *wholly* theoretical or factual, having an irreducibly discretionary aspect.

A second characteristic of ascriptions, closely connected with the first, is what may be called their 'contextual relativity'. We may have an option of ascribing *X* to either *A*, *B*, or *C*. To which of these *X* is properly ascribable may depend on numerous factors other than the relevant characteristics of *A*, *B*, *C*. Our decision may turn on our own degree of knowledge or ignorance, on our practical purposes, on the type of ascription or the nature of the 'context', on our long range policies, on institutional rules and practices, on 'values', and so on. Some of these considerations may conflict and thus call for careful weighing up—which is to say that they require not merely decision, but *judgement*. Finally, our well considered ascriptive judgements may exhibit something like what Hart calls 'defeasibility', although outside of legal and quasi-legal contexts, talk of 'cases', and 'claims', and 'defences' may not seem quite at home.

Let us now return to the fivefold classification to see what it can tell us now about 'ascriptiveness' construed as irreducibly discretionary, contextually relative, and 'something-like-defeasible'. The first thing it reveals is that ascriptions of causality, even when they do not involve persons and their actions, commonly exhibit 'ascriptiveness' construed in this fuller way. This is not to suggest that many 'causal laws' are decided upon rather than discovered, or that scientists have any 'discretion' at all in discovering and formulating laws of nature. Where scientists and others have some discretion is in a rather different sort of inquiry—when some unexplained happening has occurred, or some interesting or important state of affairs has been discovered, and we must decide to what cause to attribute it. Here, often, even after all of the facts are in, we have some choice, if what we wish to do is to *select* from the welter of causal factors that made some contribution to the event in question, one to be denominated *the* cause.[1]

Often the selection from among many causal candidates of 'the cause' seems so obvious that we may lose sight altogether of the fact that we are selecting, singling out, deciding. But that causal ascriptions are selective becomes clear to anyone who tries to give a *complete* causal explanation of some event in terms of all the conditions severally necessary and jointly sufficient for its occurrence. *All* of these conditions are equally important to the event, a naive person might argue, in that all were equally necessary to its occurrence. Equally important to the event perhaps, but not equally important to the investigator. The investigator talks of 'the cause' in the first place, only because he suspects that there is some single event or condition among the many causal contributors to the outcome, which it will be of special interest or importance to him or others to identify.

Which 'contributor'[2] to an event is to be labelled the cause of that event then is always a matter of selection, often an occasion for decision, even for difficult judgement, and is generally 'relative' to a variety of contextual considerations. Cataloguing the many forms of causal relativity is a large task but three might be mentioned here. First, selecting the cause of an event is relative to what is usual or normal in a given context. I. M. Copi bids us ponder the

[1] A great deal has been written in recent years about causal ascriptions. I am probably most indebted to W. Dray, *Laws and Explanation in History*, Oxford 1957; D. Gasking, 'Causation and Recipes', *Mind*, Vol. 64 (1955); N. R. Hanson, 'Causal Chains', *Mind*, Vol. 64 (1955); Hart and Honoré, *op. cit.*; and J. L. Mackie, 'Responsibility and Language', *Australasian Journal of Philosophy*, Vol. 33 (1955).

[2] There are circumstances in which 'the cause' need not even be a necessary condition. See Hart and Honoré, *op. cit.*, pp. 116–121. Moreover, we do not have *complete* discretion in selecting, according to our purposes and policies, the cause from the causal conditions, as Hart and Honoré have effectively and thoroughly demonstrated.

fate of the insurance investigator who reports back to his company that the cause of a mysterious fire in the house of a policy holder was 'the presence of oxygen in the air'. What the company clearly wanted him to discover was not just any necessary condition but rather 'the incident or action which in the presence of those conditions normally present, made the difference this time'.[1] Leaving the insurance investigator to be dealt with by his employers, we can without difficulty think of contexts where his ascription would not have raised an eyebrow. '. . . it is easy to imagine cases', write Hart and Honoré, 'where the exclusion of oxygen would be normal, e.g. when some laboratory experiment or delicate manufacturing process depended on its exclusion for safety from fire and hence for success, and in such cases it would be correct to identify the abnormal presence of oxygen as the cause of the fire'.[2] What is 'the cause' then depends on what is 'normal', and what is normal varies with the context.

Another form of causal relativity is relativity to ignorance. Consider how we might explain to a group of workers in a welding shop how an explosion occurred in a nearby warehouse. We might say that the explosion was the result of a spark which, let us suppose, was the last conspicuous event preceding the eruption. But in a welding shop sparks are flying all the time. They are perfectly routine, and hence they can't explain anything as extraordinary as an explosion. Given the context naturally assumed by the welding shop workers, one must cite as the cause much earlier events such as the storing of TNT or leaky gasoline drums. The analogy with history, and its own brand of causal relativity, is plain. Historiographers ascribe the causes of wars, revolutions, and other such explosions, and as a rule they write for their own contemporaries. Historiographers of later ages then write of the same events but for a later group of contemporaries with a later set of conceptions of what is routine. As a result, the earlier writer ascribes 'the cause' to some political or economic equivalent of the spark, and the later opts for some leaky oil can. One of the functions of an explanation of particular occurrences is to render them intelligible, to induce understanding of them. Intelligibility, however, is always intelligibility *to* someone, and understanding is always *someone's*

[1] I. M. Copi, *Introduction to Logic*, First Edition, New York 1952, p. 327.

[2] H. L. A. Hart and A. M. Honoré, 'Causation in the Law', *Law Quarterly Review*, Vol. 72 (1956), Part One, p. 75.

understanding, and these are in part functions of what is already known or assumed to be normal or routine.

A third sort of causal relativity is relativity of practical interest. 'It is a well known fact', wrote R. B. Perry, 'that we describe as the cause of an event that particular condition by which we hope to control it.'[1] Accordingly, we tend to select as 'the cause' of an event, that causal condition which—in Collingwood's felicitous metaphor—has a handle on it which we can grasp and manipulate; and thus even causal generalizations tend to function directively, or as Douglas Gasking puts it, as 'recipes' for cooking up desired effects.

The very meaning we assign the word 'cause' is likely to vary with our purposes. Those who are concerned to produce something beneficial seek 'the cause' of what they wish to produce in some new 'condition', which when conjoined with those usually present, will be *sufficient* for the desired thing to come into existence. On the other hand, those whose primary aim is to eliminate something harmful are for the most part looking for causes in the sense of *necessary condition*. That is because in order to succeed in such a task, one must find some condition in whose absence the undesirable phenomenon would not occur, and then somehow, eliminate *that* condition. Not just any necessary condition, however, will do as 'the cause'; it must be a necessary condition which technicians can get at, manipulate, modify, or destroy. Our purposes here determine what we will accept as 'the cause', and when it is the cause of an illness or a crime wave we are after, accessibility and manipulability are as important to our purposes as the 'necessity' of the condition. Indeed, we will accept as the cause of some unhappy state even some necessary condition which from the point of view of theory is obvious or trivial, provided only it *is* necessary and it is something we can get at.

It would be an oversimplification, however, to identify 'the cause' of an infelicitous condition with *any* manipulable necessary condition, no matter how trivial; and the reason this is so is that it oversimplifies not the processes of nature, but human purposes themselves. No matter how much we wish to get rid of defects and infelicities in our bodies, machines, and societies, we never wish to eliminate them at *any price*. What we want when we look for

[1] Ralph Barton Perry, *General Theory of Value*, Cambridge, Mass. 1926, p. 394.

'the cause' of unfortunate happenings is an *economical* means of eliminating them, the right 'price' being determined by our many implicit 'background purposes'.

A boozy pedestrian on a dark and rainy night steps into the path of a speeding careless motorist and is killed. What caused this regrettable accident? Since liabilities are at stake, we can expect the rival attorneys to give conflicting answers. But more than civil liability is involved. A reformer argues that the liquor laws are the cause, claiming that as long as liquor is sold in that region we can expect to have so many deaths a year. From traffic engineers, city planners, and educators we can expect still different answers; and in a sense they might all be right, if they named genuine 'causal factors'. But that is not what their discussion is all about. Should we prevent such accidents by spending a million dollars as the traffic engineer recommends? Or fifty million as the city planner urges? Each would uproot a necessary condition, but at what expense! Perhaps the moralist is on the right track, but do we really wish to penalize thousands of innocent responsible whisky drinkers in order to prevent the deaths of a careless few? In such ways as these are interests and purposes drawn into the context of ascribing causes. They form an implicit part of every causal field determining in part the direction in which we point when we pick 'the cause' of an event.

In virtue of their discretionary character and their contextual relativity, causal ascriptions characteristically exhibit a kind of vulnerability logically analogous to the defeasibility of some legal claims and accusations. When a humanly interesting event occurs it is always possible to mention dozens of factors that have made important causal contributions to its occurrence. Even events that occurred years earlier may so qualify. (Sometimes the straw that breaks the camel's back is in the middle, or even at the bottom, of the pile.) To cite any one of these as 'the cause' is always to invite a 'rebuttal' from a partisan of one of the other 'causal candidates', just as to make an accusation is always to invite a defence; and to show in a proper way that a certain condition did make a contribution or was an indispensable condition is only to make out a presumption of causal importance which holds unless rebutted in one of the many diverse allowable ways.

In general, properly rebuttable causal ascriptions commit the error, not of misdescribing, but of representing the less important as the more important. When it is said that the presence of oxygen in the air caused the fire, or that the cause of the stomach ache was the drink of whisky (rather than an unsuspected ulcer), or that the riot was caused by the unprecedented presence of a Negro student in the dormitory, it is less to the point to call these statements false than to call them unwise, misleading, or unfair, in the manner of otherwise accurate accounts that put their emphases in the wrong places. To be sure, but for the oxygen, the drink, the presence of the Negro,[1] there would have been no fire, ache, or riot. However, for the purposes of our more comprehensive understanding and control of such events, other equally necessary causal factors are far more important and deserve to be mentioned first.

Given that causal ascriptions, both those that assign 'the cause' to impersonal factors and those that select out human actions, are 'ascriptive' in the stronger sense, it follows immediately, in virtue of the accordion effect, that ascriptions of causal agency are so too. If 'Jones caused the door to close' is ascriptive, then 'Jones closed the door' must be so equally. If 'causing a war by an act of assassination' is ascriptive, then the still more complex 'act' of 'starting a war' must be so too. We have found a sense, then, in which one large class of action-sentences—those attributing causal agency—are ascriptive and 'something-like-defeasible' *even when the activity in question is in no way faulty*.

Ascriptions of simple agency, however, cannot be analysed in this way, for a simple doing is not the upshot of a prior doing to which it may be ascribed, and *a fortiori* we have no discretion to *decide* whether *to select* a prior doing as 'the cause' of the simple doing in question. Whether or not a man smiled is entirely a question of fact whose answer is to be discovered, not 'decided' or 'selected' presumptively.

In so far as the word 'smile' is *vague*, of course, there is room for discretion in its application to a borderline case; but the discretion here, which is hardly peculiar to simple-action words, is of a

[1] For an account of the difficult integration of the University of Georgia, see Calvin Trillin, 'An Education in Georgia', *New Yorker*, July 13, 1963—'On the . . . night of the riot, their [the white girls'] behaviour changed drastically. After the first brick and the first coke bottle had crashed into her room, Charlayne [Hunter] went to a partly partitioned office . . . and stayed there during most of what followed. A group of [white] coeds soon formed a circle in front of the office and marched around, each screaming an insult as she got to the door. "They kept yelling 'Does she realize she's causing all this trouble?' " '

different sort. Whether we call a borderline coloured object blue or green, we are likely to say, is a matter of indifference, or 'a mere question of words'. But when we deny that a question of causation is wholly factual, we are not contrasting 'question of fact' with 'question of language'; nor are we implying that its resolution by a decision is indifferent or arbitrary. We are implying instead that a decision cannot be made without a reference to our own practical purposes and values, which is quite another thing.

Simple-action sentences, then, such as 'Jones moved his finger', can be used ascriptively to identify an agent, but they are not ascriptive in the further strong sense that we are left with discretion to accept or reject them even after all the facts are in. Thus, in summary, Hart's critics are right in charging him with over-burdening the notion of ascriptiveness, for we have seen one class, at least, of action sentences, the action-simples, which are not ascriptive in the sense that is opposed to 'wholly factual'. But we have restored a good part of Hart's original theory (considerably reinterpreted) that is often rejected, for we have shown that one substantial class of action sentences that do not necessarily impute faults are nevertheless very often ascriptive in a strong sense, and that these sentences, as is shown by the characteristic ways in which they might be rebutted, are 'something-like-defeasible' as well.

IV. TWO VERSIONS OF 'THE PROBLEM OF ACTION'

How important is this restoration of a part of Hart's original thesis? That depends in large measure on one's philosophical interests and strategies. For problems of jurisprudence and moral psychology, I should think, the ascriptive and defeasible character of the action-sentences of most interest to those disciplines is a matter of great importance indeed. But for 'the problem of action' (or of 'voluntary action'), construed as a problem of metaphysics, where the concern is to distinguish activity from passivity as very general conceptual categories, the notions of ascriptiveness and defeasibility appear to be of no help whatever. It is no accident that writers in ethics and jurisprudence, when troubled by 'the problem of action', typically select as their examples more or less complex, teleologically connected sequences of behaviour that cause harm or happiness, success or failure, to self or others. They are likely to ask, for example, what distinguishes a voluntary killing from a mere accidental homicide, or a voluntary from an involuntary signing of a contract, or in general an act freely and deliberately performed from one done in circumstances that gave the agent 'no choice'. The best answer to *this* question about voluntary action, it seems to me, is that of Hart and Honoré in *Causation in the Law*: 'In common speech, and in much legal usage, a human action is said not to be voluntary or not fully voluntary if some one or more of a quite varied range of circumstances are present . . .'[1] These circumstances make a lengthy enumeration. They include, Hart and Honoré inform us,[2] physical compulsion, concussion, shock, dizziness, hypnosis; the motives of self-preservation, preservation of property, safeguarding of other rights, privileges, or interests of self or others; legal or moral obligation; unreflective, instinctive, or automatic movement; mistake, accident, or even negligence. Voluntariness ('actness'?) in this sense is a matter of degree. An action done under a threat of physical violence, for example, comes closer to being fully voluntary than an act done under the threat of death. Further, voluntariness in this sense has no direct and invariant connection with liability. An agent may be held strictly accountable for an action which is considerably 'less than fully voluntary' if the act is sufficiently harmful; and where the harm is enormously great (e.g., giving military secrets to the enemy) no degree short of complete involuntariness may relieve the agent of liability.[3]

Writers concerned with the metaphysical problem of action typically select as *their* examples such simple movements as raising one's arm or moving one's finger. When they ask what distinguishes a voluntary from an involuntary act they are inquiring about the difference between an *action* (said with emphasis) and a mere bodily movement, for example between a wink and a mere eye-twitch. Involuntariness in this sense (lack of muscular control) is only one of the circumstances that can render an act less than fully voluntary in the other sense. That is, some actions which *are* actions through and through and not automatic twitches or 'mere bodily movements' are nevertheless not fully voluntary in the sense

[1] Hart and Honoré, *Causation in the Law*, p. 38.
[2] *Ibid.*, pp. 134 ff.
[3] Cf. Aristotle, *Nichomachean Ethics*, 1110ª 20–1110ᵇ, and Hart and Honoré, *op. cit.*, p. 147.

discussed earlier because they may be done from threats or under moral obligation, etc. Now, whether an action in the sense opposed to mere bodily motion is properly to be ascribed to a person whose arm has moved is not a question that has anything to do with excuses, presumptions, and practical purposes. It has every appearance of being strictly about 'the facts', although just what kind of facts it is about is part of the metaphysical perplexity that the question naturally engenders.

On the other hand, whether or not a causally complex act is to be ascribed to a person whose relatively simple act was a causal factor in the production of some upshot depends, as we have seen, on how important a causal contribution it made, as determined by our prior assumptions and practical purposes. It is misleading to attribute '*X*-ing *Y*' to a man as his doing when other factors made more important contributions. When the action in question is 'faulty', then sometimes the 'other conditions' are mitigating *excuses* (the agent's sickness or fatigue); sometimes not—as when between the agent's act and the upshot a dozen unanticipated causal factors intervened. 'Burning down a forest' cannot be ascribed to a camper whose campfire is suddenly scattered by unprecedented hurricane winds, even though but for his relatively simple act of making a fire, the forest would never have burned; and to cite the abnormal winds as causally more important factors is not to cite an excuse. Nor does one offer an excuse when he points out that Jones did not 'burn down the forest' because twelve other campfires also burned out of control and any one of them would have been sufficient to consume the whole forest. This consideration does not necessarily relieve Jones of *fault*. What it does is override the presumption that Jones's action is the crucial causal factor in the production of the outcome. But 'overriding presumptions of causal importance' and 'defeating imputations of personal fault', while of course not one and the same thing, are still sufficiently similar for their comparison to be mutually illuminating; and the discretionary character, contextual relativity, and presumptiveness of the causal ascription, while perhaps not identical with Hart's 'ascriptiveness' and 'defeasibility', are strongly analogous to them.

Simple noncausal doings, however, resist these comparisons; and to Wittgenstein's puzzling question 'What is left over if I subtract the fact that my arms goes up from the fact that I raise my arm?'[1] the notions of ascriptiveness and defeasibility can provide no answer. Here as elsewhere in philosophy, analytic techniques help to answer the penultimate questions, while the ultimate ones, being incapable of *answer*, must be come to terms with in some other way.

[1] *Philosophical Investigations* I, 621.

VIII

EXPLANATIONS IN PSYCHOLOGY[1]

by JERRY A. FODOR

Assistant Professor, Department of Humanities, Massachusetts Institute of Technology

In this paper I will try to say what a psychological explanation is. This project should be distinguished from others to which it is indirectly related. Thus, I shall not be trying to settle the mind-body problem, nor shall I examine the alleged incompatibility between freedom of choice and the existence of psychological laws. What I shall have to say will be relevant to those problems only in this respect: Philosophers who have argued that psychology could (or could not) account for consciousness or for choice have sometimes supported their arguments by reference to features psychological explanations are alleged to have: that they employ causal laws, that they are concerned only with motions, that they are concerned only with aberrant behaviour, that they consist solely in the delineation of stimulus-response connections, and so on. In so far as philosophical claims have been based upon such analyses of psychological explanation, what I have to say should be relevant to assessing those claims. Moreover, there is at least one philosophical issue to which this paper is directly relevant. It is sometimes said that the programme implicit in the doctrine of the unity of science cannot be carried through unless it is possible to reduce the concepts employed in psychology to neurological concepts. We shall see that, though such reduction is not possible in principle, this fact is nevertheless compatible with the unity of science.

In so far as psychology affords explanations of behaviour, saying what a psychological explanation is involves saying what it is to explain behaviour.[2] However, not all explanations of behaviour are

[1] This paper has been influenced by several discussions of psychological explanation, and not least by those with which it explicitly takes issue. I wish to acknowledge a particular indebtedness to J. A. Deutsch, *The Structural Basis of Behaviour*, Chicago, 1960, and Hilary Putnam, "Minds and Machines," in Sidney Hook, (ed.) *Dimensions of Mind*, New York 1960.

[2] Throughout this paper I shall follow the current psychological practice of using 'behaviour' in a much more general way than ordinary language would

psychological explanations. You bought the chocolate one and I want to know why. Well, because you prefer chocolate, because vanilla was more expensive, because chocolate keeps better, because you were asked to buy chocolate, because you felt like it. Any or all of these may do as explanations, for any or all of them may be what I want to know. None of them, however, is a psychological explanation. To say what a psychological explanation is involves distinguishing psychological explanations from such explanations as those.

'But surely what you propose to do would be a waste of effort? Psychological explanations are what psychology texts supply. If you want to know what a psychological explanation is, go and look.' Psychologists do not always agree about what sort of thing a psychological explanation is or about what sort of things are psychological explanations. Such disagreements are important because they affect the course of research and the constraints that psychological theories are required to meet. Lashley showed that the presence of conductive metal strips in the cortex of a chimpanzee did not materially interfere with shape recognition and hence that the 'fields' some gestalt theorists had supposed must function in visual perception could not involve macroscopic variation of the electrical potential of the chimpanzee's brain.[1] What, then, must we say about field theories of perception? That depends in part upon what we say about the status of theoretical constructs in psychological explanations, and, in particular, upon whether we hold such constructs admissible even when their identification with neurological states or processes seems unlikely or impossible. What is involved is a question about the constraints theories in psychology ought to be required to meet, hence a question about what a psychological explanation is.

appear to warrant. It is, perhaps, not an accident that ordinary language often fails to supply words sufficiently general to describe the subject-matter of a special science (Cf. the use of 'matter' and 'energy' in physics); among the insights a science may achieve is the discovery that phenomena that appear dissimilar to uninstructed intuition are susceptible of similar explanations and thus ought to fall within the domain of a single discipline. The fact that we must invent a term like 'matter' to say what physics is about is related to the fact that it is not *obvious* (for example) that the laws determining the trajectory of missiles also account for the orbit of the moon.

[1] Cf. Lashley, K. S., K. L. Chow, and J. Semmes, 'An Examination of the Electrical Field Theory of Cerebral Integration,' *Psychological Review*, Vol. 58, 1951, pp. 123–136.

'Psychological explanations are what psychology texts supply. If you want to know what a psychological explanation is, go and look.' An account of psychological explanation on which *no* psychological theory turned out to be an explanation would be *ipso facto* unacceptable. One must start by assuming some clear cases if one is to start at all. But we need not suppose even the clear cases immaculate. It will be no surprise if it turns out that the best available psychological theories could be improved by simplification, by integration with theories in related disciplines, and so on. One reason for wanting to characterize psychological explanation is that an acceptable account would afford a basis for the criticism and improvement of theories psychologists propose.

We want an account of psychological explanation that shows what makes the clear cases clear. One might say we are trying to discover the criteria psychologists use to assess the adequacy of psychological explanations, except that this formulation is misleading in two ways. First, it fails to do justice to the extent to which an account of psychological explanation may require reconstruction: the criteria psychologists use may, on some occasions or to some extent, be inconsistent, or unreasonable, or too weak, or too strong, and in such cases we would wish to substitute criteria that are consistent, and reasonable and just strong enough. Secondly, we must not confuse the task of saying what a psychological explanation is with that of saying how psychologists use the verb 'explain'. The former investigation is not linguistic in any of the usual senses of that term, nor do I suppose that the account of psychological explanation I will propose is analytically true by virtue of the meaning of 'explain'. That is, I reject the view that the metatheory of a science must consist solely of analytic statements. On the contrary, it may well be characteristic of psychological explanations that they presuppose the truth of some such empirical assumptions as: that all behaviour is directed towards drive reduction, or that it is under the control of the central nervous system, or that it tends towards the achievement of a state of equilibrium, or whatever. If this is the case, then such assumptions will be built into our characterization of psychological explanation: to explain behaviour will involve showing how it affects reduction of drive, how it is controlled by the central nervous system, or how it tends towards the establishment of an equilibrium.

Philosophers have often remarked that consonance with very general propositions about the world sometimes achieves the status of a necessary condition upon explanations in the sciences. But the conclusion they have drawn is only that such propositions serve as implicit definitions of key terms and are thus effectively analytic despite their empirical appearance. If, however, this entails that we could never have grounds for abandoning such propositions, it would appear to be false.

I want to claim that not only psychological theories, but also the metatheory of psychology may, in the relevant sense, be subject to empirical disconfirmation. To show that learning can occur without reward is to show both that some behaviour is *not* directed towards the reduction of drive and that an account of psychological explanation according to which explaining learned behaviour invariably consists in showing how it affects drive reduction is an inadequate account.

This view may seem simply paradoxical. 'If consonance with the proposition *P* is a necessary condition placed upon the acceptability of psychological theories by some metatheory, then surely no disconfirmation of *P* is possible since, *ex hypothesis*, no theory incompatible with *P* is acceptable.' What that argument overlooks is that major revolutions in scientific thought often affect not only our beliefs as to what explanations are true, but also our notions about what constitutes an explanation. Thus, it may be true both that our notion of a satisfactory explanation includes consonance with some very general empirical assumptions and that such assumptions could be abandoned in face of overwhelmingly persuasive counter-explanations of a previously unanticipated type.

I want to say what a psychological explanation of behaviour is, for I hold that behaviour is susceptible of psychological explanation. Some philosophers deny this. They maintain either that psychological explanation is concerned solely with *aberrant* behaviour or that psychological explanation is not concerned with behaviour at all, but only with motions. We shall have to examine these views. An account of psychological theories is required to say what psychological theories are about.

In the *Concept of Mind*, Gilbert Ryle writes:[1]

[1] Ryle, G., *The Concept of Mind*, New York 1949, p. 326.

The classification and diagnosis of exhibitions of our mental impotences require specialized research methods. The explanation of the exhibitions of our mental competences often requires nothing but ordinary good sense, or it may require the specialized methods of economists, scholars, strategists and examiners. But their explanations are not cheques drawn on the accounts of some yet more fundamental diagnoses. So not all, or even most, causal explanations of human actions and reactions are to be ranked as psychological.

It is clear that Ryle has been careful not to burn his bridges. He says only that explaining mental competences *often* requires nothing but good sense. This might equally be said of 'impotences' and lapses, for 'his attention wandered', 'it slipped his mind', 'he was tired', 'he didn't think what he was doing', etc. may all be satisfactory explanations. If, however, Ryle holds that psychological explanations can be given only in cases of failure to perform, or in cases where the performance somehow runs contrary to expectations, then Ryle is simply wrong.

That normal functioning often needs to be accounted for is clear enough in cases other than behaviour. To explain how an internal combustion engine works is to account for its normal performance; the account will not include an explanation of backfires, misfires, and overheating. Backfires and misfires can be explained, but explaining them is not part of explaining how an internal combustion engine works. And backfires and misfires are certainly not *all* that can be explained. Engineering schools offer courses in the theory of the internal combustion engine, not in the theory of backfires and misfires.

If the situation is less obvious in the case of behaviour, that is because, of the variety of types of explanation we can give to account for what someone did, the one we want for practical purposes is rarely couched in terms of underlying psychological mechanisms. Analogously, if the insurance agent wants an explanation of the fire, we do not offer him physics. Yet presumably a physical explanation could be given and would be appropriate on certain occasions. Roughly: the appropriateness of an explanation is determined not by the phenomena it seeks to account for but by the question it seeks to answer.

It is clear from myriad examples that psychological explanations of normal behaviour can be (and often are) given and accepted. Thus, consider:

1. Freud explained that the occurrence of dreams is a mechanism for dealing with stimuli which would otherwise interrupt sleep.[1]

2. An explanation of the perceptual constancies accounts for our ability to see true colour even under adverse lighting conditions.[2]

3. Broadbent explained our ability to follow two conversations at once by reference to a hypothetical system of filters and stores.[3]

4. Skinner explained learned perceptual distinctions by reference to histories of reinforcement.[4]

It is irrelevant whether the explanations instanced in 1–4 are in fact correct accounts of the phenomena with which they are concerned. I am interested only in the point that what each purports to explain is either a 'competence' or a bit of perfectly normal human behaviour. It is a sufficient argument against Ryle's account of psychological explanation that it renders such explanations as 1–4 logically inappropriate. If a certain view of explanation entails that most of psychology will have to be abandoned without hope of replacement, that shows something is wrong with the view, not that something is wrong with psychology.

It appears that neither an appeal to explanations of phenomena other than behaviour nor an appeal to the received practices of psychologists uncovers support for the claim that psychological explanations must be limited to accounting for aberrations. On the contrary, the psychologist's concern with aberrant phenomena is often motivated primarily by the belief that they represent the automatic consequence of the application to atypical situations of the principles governing normal behaviour. What Teuber has said about the motivation for studying illusions applies, *mutatis mutandis*, to areas of psychology other than perception: '. . . to speak of illusions as special cases—curiosa of perception, as it were —is tendentious . . . the explanation for perceptual illusions will

[1] Cf. e.g. Freud, S., *General Introduction to Psychoanalysis*, New York 1920.

[2] Cf. Teuber, H.-L., 'Perception,' *Handbook of Physiology*, Vol. 3, Washington 1960.

[3] Cf. Broadbent, D. E. *Perception and Communication*, New York 1958.

[4] Cf. Skinner, B. F. *The Behaviour of Organisms*, New York 1938.

be sought among the general laws of perception. Once these laws are known, the illusions themselves will be understood'.[1]

In so far as psychology is concerned to explain behaviour at all, it is concerned to explain normal behaviour *inter alia*. But philosophers have sometimes argued that psychological explanations are not (that is, cannot be) explanations of behaviour. In an article entitled 'Behaviour', Hamlyn writes:[2]

> No mechanism of any sort can do more than account for movements, reactions, and the like. It may, of course, be the case that a particular movement or series of movements may exemplify a kind of behaviour; it may be classifiable as such, and capable of such an interpretation. It is this possibility which permits us on any particular occasion to describe both the movements and the behaviour, though to do these things will by no means be to do the same thing. Thus, no mechanism can be given which will account for behaviour *per se* however much we may feel that the behaviour will have been accounted for incidentally in providing a mechanism for the movements which constitute behaviour on a particular occasion. At other times, however, the movements involved may be different, though we may still describe the behaviour in the same way.

Unlike Ryle's, this view of psychological explanation is found among psychologists. Thus, to choose an example at random, Tinbergen[3] characterizes the domain of the behaviour sciences as '. . . the total *movements* made by the intact animal'.

There are two sorts of reasons for holding that psychology is concerned to explain movements in the sense in which movements are contrasted with behaviour. First, one may be impressed, as Hamlyn is, with the fact that why-questions about behaviour are appropriately answered by citing reasons rather than causes. Hence, it is argued, if psychology is a causal science, its explanations cannot be explanations of behaviour. Second, one may be impressed, as psychologists often are, by the need to eliminate from the 'observation base' of the science (i.e. from the vocabulary

[1] Teuber, *op. cit.*, p. 1601.

[2] Hamlyn, D. W. 'Behaviour,' reprinted in Chappell, V. C. (ed.) *The Philosophy of Mind*, Englewood Cliffs, N.J., 1962, p. 65.

[3] Tinbergen, N. *The Study of Instinct*, Oxford 1951, p. 2. Emphasis mine.

in which its predictions are couched) any term whose application requires interpretation of the phenomena. It must be possible to determine by purely observational procedures whether a prediction of the theory has been verified, since to use theoretical constructs in describing the phenomena upon which the confirmation of the theory depends is held to be circular. 'To describe behaviour requires interpretation of movements according to certain standards . . .'[1] Hence, it is only by limiting the theory to accounting for motions that we can assure ourselves that its explanations and predictions will be susceptible of purely objective verification.

It is notable that this position is open to a *reductio ad absurdum* argument similar to that to which Ryle's succumbed. That is, if we were literally to proscribe the psychological explanation of behaviour, it would turn out that not even learning theory is properly part of psychology, since *not even so basic a psychological notion as that of a response can be characterized in terms of movements alone.*[2] In laboratory situations, an organism is said to have mastered a response when it regularly produces any of an indefinite number of types of functionally equivalent motions under the appropriate stimulus conditions. That some reasonable notion of functional equivalence can be specified is essential, since we cannot in general require that two motions manifesting the same response be identical either in their observable properties or in their physiological basis. Thus, a rat has 'got' the bar pressing response if and only if it habitually presses the bar upon food deprivation. Whether it presses with its left or right front paw or with three or six grams of pressure is, or may be, irrelevant. Training is to some previously determined criterion of homogeneity of performance, which is to say that we permit variation among the *motions* belonging to a response so long as each of the variants is functionally equivalent to each of the others: *viz.* so long as each of the motions is correctly related to the bar, to the general stimulus situation, and to the history of the organism.

Not only does the requirement that psychology concern itself with motions alone prohibit the employment of such basic notions as 'response', it also prohibits the construction of a reasonable criterion of identity for motions themselves. An otherwise indis-

[1] Hamlyn, *op. cit.*, pp. 63–64.

[2] Cf. Chomsky, N. 'Review of Skinner's *Verbal Behaviour*', *Language*, Vol. 35 No. 1, 1959.

tinguishable pair of motions may be produced by quite different physiological mechanisms and hence be the outcome of quite different psychological processes. In order to take account of this fact, it may very often be necessary to determine identity and difference of motions by identity and difference of the muscular contractions that produce them[1] and, in case the same muscular contractions are sometimes under the control of different central processes, we may finally have to determine identity and difference of motions by identity and difference of hypothetical underlying causal mechanisms at the neural level.[2]

In short, the requirement that we characterize the events upon which the confirmation of a theory depends *only* in terms of their immediately observable properties may render the systematic explanation of those events impossible. Among the goals of theory construction is that of providing a conceptual framework for the coherent description of the phenomena with which the theory is concerned. That is, it is one of the achievements of a satisfactory theory that it provides a way of determining identity and difference of the confirming events such that, *on that determination*, the occurrence of those events is rendered susceptible of explanation. The view that such determinations can in principle be made on the basis of purely observable features of behaviour is so far from being obviously true as to make its adoption as a methodological rule extremely ill-advised. In the present case, it is by no means clear that a science of the motions of organisms is possible: that is, it is unclear that anything systematic could be said about the motions of an organism unless we permitted ourselves to identify motions not solely on the basis of their immediately observable properties, but also by their relation to such hypothetical states as drives, needs, goals, muscle contractions, neurological firings, and so on. To put it somewhat differently, among the facts which drive us to theory construction in psychology is the existence in non-verbal behaviour of the counterparts of ambiguity and synonymy. Just as, in linguistics, not every utterance of the phonemic sequence 'bank' is an utterance of the same word, so in psychology, not every occurrence of a given movement or muscular contraction is an instance of the same behaviour. Conversely, in linguistics two

[1] This is, in fact, what Tinbergen does in the volume cited above.

[2] For an interesting example, Cf. Luria, A. R., *Speech and the Development of Mental Processes in the Child*, London 1959.

phonemically distinct utterances ('bachelor', 'unmarried man') may be equivalent in significant respects. So, in psychology, two quite different patterns of motions (swimming to the right and running to the right in a T-maze) may be instances of the same behaviour: a fact we notice when we discover that an organism trained to produce one will, under appropriate circumstances, produce the other without further training. The consequences of such facts are identical in both sciences. If we are to capture the relevant generalizations, identity and difference of the events with which the science is concerned must often be determined by reference to properties other than those that are directly observable. In particular, in both sciences we attempt to construct theories containing levels sufficiently abstract to enable us to mark the respects in which events whose observable properties are identical may nevertheless be functionally distinct and the respects in which events whose observable properties are distinct may nevertheless be functionally identical.[1]

But it may still be said that the explanation of behaviour requires reasons while causal explanations provide not reasons but causes. There is, I think, something to this argument: explanations of behaviour are very often given by appealing to motives, utilities, strategies, goals, needs, desires, and so on.[2] It seems clear that such explanations will not be forthcoming from a causal science where this is understood to be a science which affords explanations *only* by appealing to causal chains and causal laws.[3] I shall argue that psychology is not a causal science in *that* sense. At any event, at the present stage there is no need to suppose that, because some explanations of behaviour are not causal, psychology must be limited to saying '. . . that in certain circumstances people behave

[1] Cf. Chomsky, N., *Syntactic Structures*, The Hague 1957; J. J. Katz and J. A. Fodor, 'The Structure of a Semantic Theory', *Language*, Vol. 39, No. 2, June 1963.

[2] Which need not blind us to the fact that causal explanations of behaviour are sometimes precisely what the situation requires. 'It was the liquor he drank that made him behave so badly.'

[3] The notion of a causal explanation is not itself so clear that it is evident precisely what is being asserted or denied when it is claimed that psychology is or is not a causal science. I shall follow Hamlyn in adopting the most restricted interpretation of this notion. In particular, I shall use 'causal explanation' and 'mechanistic explanation' as roughly interchangeable. To deny that psychological explanations are causal in this sense is not, of course, to deny that they may be causal in some broader sense.

in certain ways . . .'[1] or that we should ' . . . content ourselves with the programme of accounting for behaviour in terms of the capacities or dispositions from which it is derivable',[2] an undertaking which, as Hamlyn rightly remarks, 'is not a scientific programme, but one which may be carried out by anyone with sufficient experience of human affairs'.[3] Rather, the argument shows that we need to understand how a science can afford explanations and predictions of events in terms which do not refer solely to the causes of those events.

Psychology is the systematic attempt to explain and predict the behaviour of organisms. It is assumed that at any instant behaviour is the joint product of two sorts of factors:

1. Stimuli currently impinging upon the sensory receptors of the organism.
2. Internal states of the organism.

The relative contribution of each of these factors to the determination of behaviour probably varies greatly for behaviour of different kinds. While knowledge of local stimulus conditions contributes greatly to accurate prediction of certain kinds of instinctive behaviour and certain kinds of conditioned behaviour, in the case of verbal behaviour knowledge of the stimulus situation often affords very little grounds for predicting what the organism will do.

I shall argue that psychological explanation is essentially a two-phase process, the first phase of which is the development of a theory of the internal states of the organism such that (*a*) the terms of the theory which do not refer to behaviour are functionally characterized and (*b*) the theory is capable of adequately predicting the behaviour of the organism given knowledge of the current stimulus situation. Each of these conditions must be discussed at length.

Quite aside from any physiological considerations, it is possible to say a number of things about the kinds of internal states organisms must be supposed to have if characteristic features of their behaviour are to be accounted for. For example: the behaviour of an organism in a specified stimulus situation is very often partly determined by the previous stimulations it has encountered. Much of the most careful work in recent psychology

[1] Hamlyn, *op. cit.* p. 66. [2] *Ibid.* [3] *Ibid.*

has been devoted to exhibiting the differences between naive and sophisticated behaviour and to determining which patterns of stimulation are conducive to the development of sophistication. But though it is obvious that organisms of identical genetic endowment often differ profoundly in their response to novel stimulations depending on features of their individual life histories, it is not obvious how this fact should be accounted for. The problem becomes apparent when we notice that the degree to which, and the conditions under which, prior stimulations determine current behaviour differ markedly from species to species: discriminations difficult for the octopus to learn are easy for the rat, imprinting is known in birds but not in monkeys, operant conditioning is easier with fish than with planaria, verbal learning occurs only in man. The susceptibility of behaviour to alteration by experience would thus appear to vary from species to species.[1]

If we are to account for the alteration of behaviour as a result of prior stimulation, we must assume that some at least of the internal states that determine the way an organism responds to current stimulation are themselves the product of its previous experiences. Since the laws governing the formation of such states may be supposed to differ from species to species, it becomes understandable that the same history of stimulation produces very different behaviour in organisms of sufficiently different biological types. Conversely, if genetically identical organisms have such internal states in common only in case their life histories have been similar in relevant respects, then we expect relevantly dissimilar life histories to produce differences in behaviour. Finally, the assumption that some such experientially induced states are inherently unstable and tend to decay in a lawful fashion provides for the possibility of explaining such characteristic features of long term memory as stereotyping, elimination of detail, tendency towards 'good form', etc.[2]

It goes without saying that the laws which presumably determine the careers of such internal states (and, in particular, the laws which determine under what stimulus conditions they arise and how they contribute to the production of behaviour) are arrived at indirectly. The internal states of the organism are assumed to have

[1] Cf. Thorpe, W. H. *Learning and Instinct in Animals*, London 1956.

[2] Cf. e.g. Bartlett, F. C. *Remembering*, New York 1932, for a discussion of characteristic features of the decay of memories.

those properties required to account for the observed features of its behaviour. This is a sort of reasoning that is perfectly ordinary in sciences other than psychology. Radio telescopy shows the star to be very active, light telescopy shows it to be very dim. Perhaps we are dealing with a bright star very far away. The function of the theory is, *inter alia*, to save the appearances.

The sense in which terms referring to internal states are functionally characterized in theories developed in the first phase of psychological explanation may now be made clear. Phase one psychological theories characterize the internal states of organisms only in respect of the way they function in the production of behaviour. In effect, the organism is thought of as a device for producing certain behaviour given certain sensory stimulations. A phase one psychological explanation attempts to determine the internal states through which such a device must pass if it is to produce the behaviour the organism produces on the occasions when the organism produces it. Since, at this stage, the properties of these states are determined by appeal to the assumption that they have whatever features are required to account for the organism's behavioural repertoire, it follows that what a phase one theory tells us about such states is what role they play in the production of behaviour. It follows too that the evidence to be adduced in favour of the claim that such states exist is just that assuming they do is the simplest way of accounting for the behavioural capacities the organism is known to have.

It should be noticed that explanations afforded by phase one theories are *not* causal explanations, although a fully elaborated phase one theory claims to be able to predict behaviour given sufficient information about current sensory stimulations. Phase one explanations purport to account for behaviour in terms of internal states, but they give no information whatever about the mechanisms underlying these states. That is, theory construction proceeds in terms of such functionally characterized notions as memories, motives, needs, drives, desires, strategies, beliefs, etc. with no reference to the physiological structures which may, in some sense, correspond to these concepts. Now, if I say 'He left abruptly upon remembering a prior engagement' I am giving an explanation in terms of an internal event postulated in order to account for behaviour (including, perhaps, behaviour which consists in his telling me why he left). Moreover, it is an explanation which, *ceteris paribus*, might have been adequate for the prediction of behaviour since I might have known that *if* he had been reminded of his engagement he would certainly have left. Yet, it is not a causal explanation in the sense in which that term is usually used. That is, it is not at all like a reflex-arc explanation of a knee-jerk response or an explanation of the trajectory of a billiard ball; no causal laws are invoked, nor is any notion of a causal chain at issue.

We thus arrive at the following view of phase one psychological explanations. Organisms are observed to produce certain types of behaviour either spontaneously or as the consequence of certain types of stimulation. A phase one psychological theory attempts to account for these observations by reference to hypothetical internal states which, together with the relevant stimulation, are supposed to produce the observed behaviour. The regularity of the observed behaviour is thus explained and rules provided which enable us to predict what the organism will do in any of indefinitely many novel situations. Phase one explanations are arrived at indirectly in that we attribute to the organism whatever internal states are required to account for its behavioural repertoire. The characterization of these states is thus purely functional since we know about them only what role they play in the production of behaviour.

A characteristic feature of phase one explanations is that they are compatible with indefinitely many hypotheses about the physiology of the organism. We have seen that phase one explanations are *not* causal explanations precisely because they make no claims about the mechanisms underlying internal states. In a phase one explanation, we picture the organism as proceeding through a series of internal states that terminate in the production of observable behaviour. But we make no attempt to say what these states are states of: what internal mechanisms correspond to the functionally defined states we have invoked. Now, the set of mechanisms capable of realizing a series of such functionally defined states is indefinitely large. Only our ingenuity limits the number of mechanisms we could devise which, upon exposure to the relevant stimulations, would go through a sequence of internal states each functionally equivalent to a corresponding state of an organism and would then produce behaviour indistinguishable in relevant respects from the behaviour of the organism.

We may say that each mechanism capable of realizing the series of states a phase one theory attributes to an organism is a *model* of the theory. And we may now see why phase one explanations are inadequate accounts of behaviour. For, in the first phase of psychological explanation, we say no more of an organism than that it is one of an indefinitely large number of possible models of a theory. Which such model the organism is is something a phase one explanation does not determine.

Many psychologists would claim that this last question is not properly within the domain of their science. J. A. Deutsch, for example, has argued persuasively that the production of adequate phase one theories exhausts the psychologist's professional responsibilities.

For instance, to attempt to guess at the particular change which occurs in the central nervous system during learning in the framework of a theory purporting to explain behaviour is not only unnecessary but also purely speculative. That some type of change occurs may be inferred from the behaviour of an animal. What this type of change is cannot be arrived at, nor is it very important for the psychologist to know. This can be shown by taking the example of an insightful learning machine. . . . To be told that the semipermanent change in the machine which occurs when it learns is due to a uniselector arm coming to rest does not help us to understand the behavioural properties of the machine. Nor can it be checked by performing experiments on the behaviour of the machine. For the change could equally well be due to a self-holding relay, a dekatron selector, or any type of gadget known to technology capable of being turned from one steady state into another. In the same way, to speculate about terminal end boutons in the way that Hebb does or about changes of synaptic resistance seems to be trying to answer a question irrelevant, strictly speaking, to the psychological theorist. What behaviour would one of these assumptions explain which the others would not?[1]

Border disputes tend to be philosophical in the sense of that term in which it is synonymous with 'uninteresting'. But more is at issue here than whether the determination of the physical representation of a phase one theory in the nervous system of an organism is the duty of the psychologist or the neurologist or both.

It must be remembered that the talk of a first and second phase

[1] Deutsch, *op. cit.* p. 12.

of psychological explanation cannot be understood as expressing a chronological relation between types of psychological theories. It is offered as a reconstruction of psychological explanation, not as a history of the development of psychology. In historical fact, what happens is that research directed towards a functional account of behaviour is simultaneous with research directed towards determining the nature of the mechanisms whose functional characteristics phase one theories specify. This fact has two fairly important consequences. First, information about the mechanisms underlying behaviour may sometimes lead to hypotheses that are most naturally stated in functional terms and tested in terms of behaviour. The history of psychological research on memory is filled with experiments originally inspired by speculations about the neurology of the memory trace, just as the history of perception theory is filled with experiments inspired by speculations about the character of the neural events triggered by a stimulus array. Secondly, and more important, it seems reasonable to maintain that any phase one theory that is incompatible with known facts of neurology must be, *ipso facto*, unacceptable. To put it slightly differently, it is sufficient to disconfirm a functional account of the behaviour of an organism to show that its nervous system is incapable of assuming states manifesting the functional characteristics that account requires. To accept this principle is, of course, to build into our characterization of psychological explanation a blatantly empirical assumption about the causation of behaviour: namely that the nervous system does, in fact, constitute a model of some phase one theory. This may be an incorrect view of the relation between neural and molar events (we had anticipated the possibility that the metatheory of psychology might itself prove susceptible of empirical disconfirmation). But, if it is correct, it provides an extremely important constraint upon phase one theories. Moreover, it provides motive for precisely the sort of neurological speculations about which Deutsch professes suspicion. If consonance with neurological fact is a condition upon the adequacy of phase one theories, it is clearly good strategy for the psychologist to construct such theories in awareness of the best estimates of what the neurological facts are likely to be.

It should be noticed that the view of the relation between psychological and neurological theories espoused here is to be distinguished from all varieties of reductionism. On this view, neurological structures are models of certain functionally characterized relations. A neurological theory thus provides an account of the mechanics of systems whose functional characteristics are given by phase one theories. But to attempt to reduce a functional account to a mechanistic account would be patently absurd; the relation between functional analysis and mechanistic analysis is not at all like the relation between macroanalysis and microanalysis, though the two have sometimes been confused.

In microanalysis one asks: 'What does *X* consist of?' and the answer has the form of a specification of the microstructure of *X*s. Thus: 'What does water consist of?' 'Two molecules of hydrogen linked with one molecule of oxygen.' 'What does lightning consist of?' 'A stream of electrons.' And so on. In functional analysis, one asks about a part of a mechanism what role it plays in the activities characteristic of the mechanism as a whole: 'What does the camshaft do?' 'It opens the valves, permitting the entry into the cylinder of fuel which will be detonated to drive the piston.' Successful microanalysis is thus often contingent upon the development of more powerful instruments of observation or more precise methods of disection. Successful functional analysis, on the other hand, requires an appreciation of the sorts of activities characteristic of a mechanism and of the contribution of the functioning of each part of the economy of the whole.

Explanation in psychology consists of a functional analysis and a mechanistic analysis: a phase one theory and a determination of which model of the theory the nervous system of the organism represents. Neither aspect of the explanation is dispensible. In particular, a neurological account without the corresponding phase one account would amount to no more than a description of a series of biochemical and electrical interactions. It would fail to describe the role of these interactions in the production of behaviour.[1] To put it succinctly, a complete psychological explanation requires more than an account of what the neurological circuitry is; it requires also an account of what such circuitry does. This second sort of account is given in terms of the familiar constructs of psychology: drives, motives, strategies, and so forth.

[1] I want to make it clear that I do *not* deny that accounts of functional relations may play an important role within neurology. There is, of course, nothing wrong with saying that the firing of a certain neuron inhibits the firing of some other. My point is rather that, *vis-à-vis* explanations of behaviour, neurological theories specify mechanisms and psychological theories do not.

Notice that explanations outside psychology often have this same double aspect: functional analysis plus mechanistic analysis. We say 'The camshaft functions to lift the valves at the proper time by displacing the tappets.' That is, we say what the camshaft does and we say how it does it. Neither account is adequate without the other.

Psychologists and philosophers who have complained that it is possible to trace an input from afferent to central to efferent neurological systems without once encountering motives, strategies, drives, needs, hopes, and so forth have thus been right in one sense but wrong in another, just as one would be if one argued that a complete causal account of the operation of an internal combustion engine never encounters such a thing as a valve lifter. In each case, the confusion occurs when a term properly figuring in functional accounts of mechanisms is confounded with terms that properly appear in causal accounts. From a functional point of view, a camshaft is a valve lifter. But a mechanistic account of the operations of internal combustion engines does not seek to replace the concept of a valve lifter with the concept of a camshaft, nor does it seek to reduce the former to the latter. What it does do is explain how the valves get lifted, what mechanical transactions are involved when the camshaft lifts the valves.

There is no sense to the question 'What does a valve opener consist of?' where this is understood as a request for a microanalysis. Functions do not have parts; valve openers are not made of rods, springs and atoms in the sense that camshafts are.[1] There is a sensible question: 'How are the valves opened in this (sort of) engine?' This question invites a mechanistic account, and in such an account the term 'camshaft' may appear. Analogously, there is a sensible question: 'What is the mechanism of drive reduction in this (sort of) organism?' This question invites a neurological account, and in such accounts the term 'circuit' may appear.

Drives, motives, strategies, etc. are internal states postulated in attempts to account for behaviour in phase one theories. In

[1] To add to the confusion, however, it may be observed that some *mechanisms* are designated by their function. This is why in one sense it does and in another sense it does not make sense to ask: 'What is a can opener made of?' Again, it is because 'mousetrap' is ambiguous between function and mechanism that it makes sense to talk of building a better one. Analogously, it is customary to designate *neurological* structures in terms of their supposed *psychological* functions: hence, the 'speech centre', the 'association cortex', etc.

completed psychological explanations they serve to characterize the functional aspects of neurological mechanisms. That is, they function in accounts of the relation between the operation of such mechanisms and the molar behaviour of organisms. But drives, motives and strategies are not themselves neurological mechanisms nor do they have a microanalysis in terms of neurological mechanisms. The remark 'A drive is not a neurological state' has the same logical status as the remark 'A valve lifter is not a camshaft.' That is, it expresses a necessary truth.

If the position just presented is correct, it would appear that much of the discussion of theoretical identification[1] that has arisen in attempting to determine the relation between neurological and psychological concepts must in fact be irrelevant to that problem. It need not be denied that, in general, no *a priori* determination can be made of the cases in which considerations of economy or elegance may require scientists to identify states or events previously held to be distinct. Nor need it be denied that, far from being arbitrary decisions, such identifications often have the status of major scientific discoveries. Above all, there is no reason to suppose an adequate view of language would require us to hold that such identifications invariably involve changes of meaning. But, important though these insights are for a proper understanding of scientific explanation, on the present view they do not apply to the relation between neurological and psychological theories; since psychological terms are understood to be names for functions, psychological states are not available for microanalysis and theoretical revision could identify them only with other functions, not with mechanisms.

[1] Cf. Place, U. T. 'Is Consciousness a Brain Process', reprinted in Chappell, *op. cit.*, Smart, J. J. C. 'Sensations and Brain Processes', reprinted in Chappell, *op. cit.*; and Putnam, *op. cit.*

IX

FREGE'S THEORY OF NUMBER

by CHARLES D. PARSONS

Associate Professor of Philosophy, Columbia University

It is impossible to compare Frege's *Foundations of Arithmetic*[1] with the writings on the philosophy of mathematics of Frege's predecessors—even with such great philosophers as Kant—without concluding that Frege's work represents an enormous advance in clarity and rigour. It is also hard to avoid the conclusion that Frege's analysis increases our understanding of the elementary ideas of arithmetic and that there are fundamental philosophical points that his predecessors grasped very dimly, if at all, which Frege is clear about.

I mention this impression which Frege's book makes because it is often forgotten in critical discussion of his ideas, and still more forgotten in discussion of 'the Frege–Russell view', 'the reduction of mathematics to logic', or 'logicism'. Frege's main thesis, that arithmetic is a part of logic, is not fashionable now. It seems to me that this is justified, and the accumulated force of the criticisms of this thesis is overwhelming. But even though Frege is more studied now than at the time when his thesis was regarded by many as having been conclusively proved, I find that we still lack a clear view of what is true and what is false in his account of arithmetic. What follows is intended as a contribution toward such a view.

It will help with this task not to focus our attention too exclusively on the thesis that arithmetic is a part of logic. An examination of the argument of the *Foundations* shows that this thesis is introduced only *after* some of the confusions of his predecessors have been cleared up by other analyses. It seems to me that we might best divide Frege's view into three theses, which I shall discuss in turn.

[1] *Die Grundlagen der Arithmetik* (Breslau 1884). Reprinted with a translation by J. L. Austin as *The Foundations of Arithmetic* (Oxford 1950; 2d ed. 1953). References are to the second Oxford edition, and quotations are in that translation. The pagination of the German in the Oxford editions is the same as in the original.

(1) Having a certain cardinal number is a property of a *concept* in what we may take to be Frege's technical sense. It appears that the basic type of singular term referring to numbers is of the form 'the number of objects falling under the concept *F*', or, more briefly, 'the number of *F*'s', or in symbolic notation '$N_x\, Fx$'.

(2) Numbers are *objects*—again in Frege's technical sense.

(3) Arithmetic is a part of logic. This may be divided into two:

  (*a*) The concepts of arithmetic can be defined in terms of the concepts of logic.

  (*b*) The theorems of arithmetic can be proved by means of purely logical laws.

The first thesis does not require much discussion. The appeal to Frege's special sense of 'concept' is of course something which would give rise to difficulty and controversy, but it is not essential to the main point. Everyone will agree that we cannot get far in talking about cardinal numbers without introducing singular terms of the form mentioned, or others in which the general term is replaced by a term referring to a class or similar entity.

There is a further question whether, in elementary examples involving perceptual objects, we could attribute the number to something more concrete, or more in accord with the demands of nominalism, than a class or a concept. Frege himself was apparently not interested in this question, and it does not seem to me very important for the foundations of mathematics.

I shall now discuss the thesis that numbers are objects. It will prove to be closely connected with the third thesis, that arithmetic is a part of logic. The first thing to note is that for Frege the notion of an object is a *logical* one. He held that linguistic expressions satisfying certain syntactical conditions at least purport to refer to objects. I do not have a precise general account of what these conditions are. Being a possible subject of a proposition is the primary one, but it must be so in a *logical* sense; otherwise 'every man' in 'Every man is mortal' would refer to an object. The occurrence of the definite article is an important criterion. Such examples as 'The number 7 is a prime number' seem to show that numerical expressions satisfy the syntactical criteria.

Another criterion of great importance in the *Foundations* is that *identity* must have sense for every kind of object.

Frege took this in a very strong sense: if we think of '_ _ _' and '. . .' as object-expressions, then '_ _ _ = . . .' must have sense even if the objects to which they purport to refer are of quite different categories, for example, if ' ___ ' is 'the Moon' and '. . .' is 'the square root of 2'.[1] Moreover, the principle of substitutivity of identity must be satisfied.

> Now for every object there is one type of proposition which must have a sense, namely the recognition-statement, which in the case of numbers is called an identity. . . . When are we entitled to regard a content as that of a recognition-judgement? For this a certain condition has to be satisfied, namely that it must be possible in every judgement to substitute without loss of truth the right-hand side of our putative identity for its left-hand side.[2]

This is a view which Quine expresses succinctly by the maxim, 'No entity without identity'. One of the main efforts of the positive part of the *Foundations* is to explain the sense of identities involving numbers.

That terms satisfying these conditions, and perhaps others besides, occur in places accessible to quantification, and that we make such inferences as existential generalization (e.g. from '2 is an even prime number' to 'There is an even prime number') might be taken to show that numerical terms purport to refer to objects. From Frege's point of view, however, I should think that this shows only that they purport to *refer*, for quantification could also occur over functions, including concepts.

Shall we accept Frege's criteria for expressions to purport to refer to objects? We might, I think, separate those explicitly stated by Frege from the criterion, added from Quine, of accessibility to quantification. The latter has some complications having to do with mathematical constructivity and predicativity. These do not make it an unacceptable criterion, but might lead us to distinguish 'grades of referential involvement'. With this reservation, I do not know any better criteria than the ones I have mentioned. I am still not very clear about their significance, what it is to *be* an object. In particular, the central role of identity is something which I do

[1] This follows from Frege's general doctrine that a function must be defined for every object as argument, since identity is for Frege a function of two arguments. See P. Geach and M. Black (eds.), *Translations from the Philosophical Writings of Gottlob Frege* (Oxford 1952), pp. 32–33, 159–70. Cf. *Foundations*, pp. 78, 116–17.

[2] *Foundations*, pp. 116–17.

not know how to explain. Perhaps it has to do with the fact that the cognitive activities of human beings are spread out over space and time.

I have been very careful to speak of criteria for expressions to *purport* to refer to objects. Indeed, it would seem that if we explain number-words in such a way that they will be shown in at least some of their occurrences to satisfy these criteria, then we shall at most have shown that they purport to refer to objects but not that they actually *do* refer to them, i.e. that in these occurrences they actually *have* reference. I shall now consider how this matter stands in Frege's analysis of number.

The simplest account of it is as follows: Frege finds[1] that a necessary and sufficient condition for the number of F's to be *the same* as the number of G's is that the concept F and the concept G stand in a relation he called *Gleichzahligkeit*, which may be translated as 'numerical equivalence'. The concept F is numerically cquivalent to the concept G if there is a one-to-one correspondenee of the objects satisfying F and the objects satisfying G. If we express this by '$Glz_x(Fx, Gx)$', we may express the result of this stage of Frege's analysis as the principle

$$(A) \qquad N_xFx = N_xGx \,.\equiv Glz_x(Fx, Gx).$$

He then gives an *explicit definition* whose initial justification is that (A) follows from it. The number of F's is defined as the extension of the concept *numerically equivalent to the concept F*, in other words the class of all concepts numerically equivalent to the concept F.

Then it seems that the problem of the existence of numbers is merely reduced to the problem of the existence of extensions. If this is so, Frege is in two difficulties.

The first is that the paradoxes make it not very clear what assumptions as to the existence of extensions of concepts are permissible. Frege sought a general logical law by which one could pass from a concept F to its extension $\hat{x}Fx$, but his axiom (V):

$$\hat{x}Fx = \hat{x}Gx \,.\equiv (x)(Fx \equiv Gx)^2$$

[1] *Foundations*, pp. 72–81.

[2] My symbolism, essentially that of Quine's *Methods of Logic* (New York 1950), follows the *Foundations* rather than the ideas of the *Grundgesetze der Arithmetik* (Jena, vol. I, 1893, vol. II, 1903; reprinted Hildesheim 1962). Throughout I largely neglect the fact that in Frege's later writings concepts are

led directly to Russell's paradox. What stands in its place in later set theory is a variety of possible existence assumptions of varying degrees of strength.

Frege may have seen no alternative to the recourse to extensions in order to secure a reference for numerical terms. It may be for that reason that he saw Russell's paradox as a blow not just to his attempt to prove that arithmetic is a part of logic, but also to his thesis that numbers are objects:

And even now I do not see how arithmetic can be scientifically established; how numbers can be apprehended as logical objects, and brought under review, unless we are permitted—at least conditionally—to pass from a concept to its extension.[1]

He never mentions the possibility of apprehending numbers as objects of a kind other than logical.

It is possible to identify at least finite numbers with quite unproblematic extensions. A natural way of doing this is to identify each number with some particular class having that number of members, as is done in von Neumann's construction of ordinal numbers.[2]

The second difficulty is that if we admit enough extensions, on some grounds or other, then there are too many possible ways of identifying them with numbers. In fact, *any* reasonably well-behaved sequence of classes can be chosen to represent the natural numbers.

Frege must have thought that his own choice was more natural than any alternative. The relation of numerical equivalence is reflexive, symmetric, and transitive; and he thought of a number as an equivalence class of this relation. He motivates it by discussing the notion of the direction of a line as an equivalence class of the relation of parallelism.[3] But this will not do. Ordinary

a special kind of function; the axiom stated is more special than the actual axiom V of the *Grundgesetze*, which relates arbitrary functions and what Frege calls their *Werthverläufe*. This expository convenience is not meant to exclude the *Grundgesetze* from the scope of my discussion.

[1] Geach and Black, *op. cit.*, p. 234. From *Grundgesetze*, II, 253.

[2] See for example W. V. Quine, *Set Theory and its Logic* (Cambridge, Mass. 1963), ch. VII.

[3] Cf. M. Dummett, 'Nominalism', *Philosophical Review*, vol. 65 (1956), pp. 491–505, esp. pp. 501–2. Dummett seems to accept the analogy.

equivalence classes are subclasses of some given class. But the application of numbers must be so wide that, if *all* concepts (or extensions of concepts) numerically equivalent to a concept F are members of N_xFx, then it is by no means certain that N_xFx is not the sort of 'unconditioned totality' that leads to the paradoxes. The difference is reflected in the fact that in the most natural systems of set theory, such as those based on Zermelo's axioms, the existence of ordinary equivalence classes is easily proved, while, if anything at all falls under F, the *non-existence* of Frege's N_xFx follows.

It is odd that we should have to identify numbers with extensions in order to insure that number terms have a reference, but that we should then be able to choose this reference in almost any way we like. We might entertain the fantasy of a tribe of mathematicians who use the ordinary language of number theory and who also all accept the same set theory. In their public life, the question whether the numbers are to be identified with classes never arises. However, each one *for himself* identifies the natural numbers with a certain sequence of classes but does not tell the others which it is. If one says that two terms of number theory refer to the same number, whether another assents or dissents in no way depends on whether *his* natural numbers are the same as the speaker's.

The reader will be reminded of a well-known passage in the *Philosophical Investigations* (I, 293). If it makes no difference in mathematics to which class a term of number theory refers, what is the relevance to the thesis that numbers are objects of the *possibility* of an identification of numbers and classes?

Dummett, in the above-cited paper,[1] suggests another way of looking at this problem. He appeals to Frege's principle that 'only in a proposition have words really a meaning',[2] that 'we must never try to define the meaning of a word in isolation, but only as it is used in the context of a proposition'.[3] Dummett takes this to mean that in order to determine the sense of a word, it is sufficient to determine the sense of the sentences in which the word is used. This is a matter of determining their truth-conditions. If a word functions syntactically as a proper name, then the sense of the sentences in which it occurs will determine its sense; and which sentences, as a matter of extra-linguistic fact, express true propositions will determine its reference.

[1] See note 3, p. 184. [2] *Foundations*, p. 71. [3] *Ibid.*, p. 116.

Although Dummett says that when this position is stated it is a 'banality', it seems to me to have a serious ambiguity which makes it doubtful that it can get around the difficulties we have mentioned. Dummett apparently takes the principle to mean that if the specification of truth-conditions of the contexts of a name can be done at all, then the name *has* a reference. But this comes into apparent conflict with Frege's principles. For a sufficient explanation of the sense of a name by no means guarantees that it has a reference, and therefore that the sentences in which it occurs express propositions that are true or false. So it seems that there will be a further question, once the sense has been specified, whether the reference actually exists, which must be answered before one can begin to answer questions about the truth-values of the propositions. Or perhaps it will prove impossible to specify the sense of all the expressions required without in the process specifying the reference or presupposing that it exists. In either case, the usefulness of Frege's principle for repudiating philosophical questions about existence would be less than Dummett thinks.

However, I do not think that these considerations show that Dummett's interpretation of Frege is wrong. Another possible way of taking the principle is that if we can show that sentences containing a certain name have well-determined truth-values, then we are sure this name has a reference, and we do not have to discover a reference for the name antecedently to this. Frege indicates that the contextual principle is the guiding idea of his analysis of number in the *Foundations*; I shall try taking it this way. I shall also suppose that the same principle underlies Frege's attempted proof in the *Grundgesetze der Arithmetik*[1] that every well-formed name in the formal system there set forth has a reference.

There is a general difficulty in the application of the principle which will turn up in both these cases: it is hard to see how it can be applied unless it provides for the elimination of the names by contextual or explicit definitions. We shall see that, for a quite simple reason, the kind of contextual definition Frege's procedure might suggest is impossible. And in the case of the *Grundgesetze*

[1] I, 45–51. I am indebted to M. D. Resnik for pointing out to me the relevance of this argument to my discussion. A detailed analysis of the argument occurs in his Ph.D. thesis, *Frege's Methodology* (Harvard University 1963).

argument, where the crucial case is that of names of extensions,[1] it seems obvious that explicit definition is impossible.

Frege regarded identity contexts of an object-name as those whose sense it is most important to specify. His procedure in the *Foundations* can be regarded as an effort to do this. These identities are of three forms:

(1) the number of F's = the number of G's,

(2) the number of F's = 7,

where '7' could be replaced by any other such expression which we take to refer to a number.

(3) the number of F's = . . .

where '. . .' represents a name of a quite different type, such as 'the moon', 'Socrates', or 'the extension of the concept *prime number*'.

The truth-conditions of identities of form (1) are determined by the above-mentioned principle (A): (1) is to be true if and only if there is a one-to-one correspondence of the F's and the G's. This in turn can be defined without appealing to the concept of number, as we shall see.

Frege analysed identities of form (2) by defining individual numbers as the numbers belonging to certain particular concepts, so that they are in effect assimilated to identities of form (1). Thus 0 is the number of the concept *not identical with itself* and turns out to be the number of any concept under which nothing falls. $n + 1$ is the number of the concept *member of the series of natural numbers ending with n*. I shall not raise now any problems concerning such identities or Frege's way of handling them.

Thus we can regard the explicit definition mentioned above (p. 183) as necessary only to handle identities of form (3), as Frege intimates.[2] By supposing that the notion of the extension of a concept is already understood, Frege provides that the sense of (3) is to be the sense of:

the extension of the concept *numerically equivalent to the concept F* = . . . ,

and the sense of the latter is already determined. Then, as I said, (A) follows from the explicit definition, so that this definition also serves for other contexts.

That Frege did not regard the introduction of extensions as

[1] More generally, *Werthverläufe* of functions. See note 2, p. 183.

[2] *Foundations*, p. 116.

essential to his argument is insisted upon by Peter Geach.[1] He seems to think that the analysis of identities of form (1) is by itself sufficient to establish the thesis that numbers are objects:

> Having analysed 'there are just as many *A*s as *B*s' in a way that involved no mention of numbers or of the concept number, Frege can now offer this analysis as a criterion for numerical identity—for its being the case that the number of *A*s is the same number as the number of *B*s. Given this sharp criterion for identifying numbers, Frege thought that only prejudices stood in the way of our regarding numbers as objects. I am strongly inclined to think he is right.[2]

It would seem that we could deal with identities of type (3) very simply, by specifying that they are all either nonsense or false. The first alternative is plausible enough in such examples as 'the number of planets = the moon' or '(the number of roots of the equation $x^2 + 3x + 2 = 0$) = the class of prime numbers'. It would, however, be an abandonment of Frege's position that objects constitute a single domain, so that functions and concepts must be defined for all objects.[3] The second is plausible enough when '. . .' is a closed term; it means rejecting the demand that we identify numbers with objects given in any other way.

However, both these solutions have a fatal defect: apparently we must explain the sense of (3) when '. . .' is a *free variable*. We cannot declare that '$N_xFx = y$' is to be true of *nothing*, for that will contradict our stipulation concerning (1) and lead to the consequence that our universe contains no numbers. It seems that the only ways to take care of this fact are either to give an explicit definition of 'N_xFx' or to assume we understand what the number of *F*'s is and say that '$N_xFx = y$' is to be true of just that object. But this in effect begs the question of reference. This is a quite general difficulty which does not depend on the fact that numbers are to be in the same universe of discourse with other objects. For it is essential to the use of *quantification* over a universe of discourse which is to include numbers that 'N_xFx' should occur in places

[1] 'Class and Concept', *Philosophical Review*, vol. 64 (1955), p. 569; *Three Philosophers* (Oxford 1961), p. 158.

[2] *Three Philosophers*, p. 161. It is not clear what Geach intends to be the final relation between numbers and extensions.

[3] See the references given in note 1, p. 182.

where it can be replaced by a variable. And not to quantify over numbers is surely to renounce the thesis that numbers are objects.

However, it seems that explanation of '$N_x Fx = \ldots$' where '...' is a *closed* term (in Frege's language, a proper name) might be regarded as sufficient if it is presupposed that the quantifiers range only over such objects as have names in one's formalism. Indeed, if this is so then it seems that we *have* explained for what objects '$N_x Fx = y$' is to be true, so that the above objection has no force. The condition, however, cannot be met if the formalism is to express (in the standard way) enough classical mathematics to include a certain amount of set theory or the theory of real numbers, since in that case the universe will contain indenumerably many objects, while the formalism contains only denumerably many names.

In the *Grundgesetze* (I, 45–51), Frege tries to show on the basis of what seems to be a generalization of the contextual principle that each well-formed name of his formal system has a reference. This is, in particular, the only attempt he makes at a direct justification of his introduction of *Werthverläufe* and his axiom (V) about them. The principle on which he operates is that an object name has reference if every name which results from putting it into the argument place of a referential first-level function name has reference. Similarly, a function name (of whatever level) has reference if every result of putting in a referential name of the appropriate type has reference. Since any sentence (i.e. name purporting to refer to a truth-value) containing a given object name can be viewed as the result of applying a function name to the given object name, the first principle is a generalization of Dummett's principle that a proper name has reference if every sentence in which it occurs has a truth-value.

In applications it is sufficient to show that simple names have reference. The difficult case, and that which is of interest to this discussion, is that of abstracts. The problem of showing that '$\hat{x}(\ldots x \ldots)$' has a reference reduces to that of showing that '$\hat{x}(\ldots x \ldots) = \_\,\_\,\_$' has a well-determined truth-value, whatever object the name '_ _ _' represents.

However, the argument fails for two reasons. First, the principles do not require him to determine the truth-value in the case where '_ _ _' is a free variable, so that the same problem arises in interpreting quantification. The other difficulty arises from impredicative constructions. Frege argues that if '. . . *x* . . .' is referential, then so is '$\hat{x}$(. . . *x* . . .)'. But to show that '. . . *x* . . .' is referential we need to show that '. . . _ _ _ . . .' is referential if '_ _ _' is *any* referential object name. But one of these is '$\hat{x}$(. . . *x* . . .)', if everything turns out right. So that it is not at all clear that the rules exclude circularities and contradiction, as indeed they do not if we let '. . . *x* . . .' be '$x \varepsilon x$' or '—($x \varepsilon x$)'.

Frege could meet both difficulties, at the sacrifice of some of classical mathematics, by restricting himself to predicative set theory. This would, however, also not be in the spirit of his philosophy. It seems incompatible with Frege's realism about abstract objects to admit only such as have names and not to allow quantification over all of them (as would happen if predicativity were realized in the traditional way, by arranging the variables in a ramified hierarchy). Since the same considerations would dictate a predicative interpretation of quantification over concepts and relations, it seems there will no longer be a single relation of numerical equivalence, so that the notion of cardinal number will diverge from the (Cantorian) one which Frege intended. However, the elementary arithmetic of natural numbers would not be affected by this. So the thesis that numbers are objects might be sustained on this basis, if its application were restricted to natural numbers. But the divergence from Frege's intentions which this possibility involves justifies us in not pursuing it further.

From his realistic point of view, Frege cannot complete the specification of the senses of numerical terms and class abstracts. He cannot avoid making some assumptions as to their reference which could in principle be denied. The situation can, however, be viewed as follows: The information given about the *sense* of such terms by the principle (*A*) and the axiom (V) is not useless, since it enables one to eliminate the reference to numbers and classes from some contexts at least, and to decide the truth-values of some propositions referring to them. We can call (*A*) or (V) or similar principles *partial contextual definitions*. They give some justification for the assumption of entities of a certain kind. But they are no guarantee even against contradiction, as is shown by the fact that an instance of (V) gives rise to Russell's paradox.

I shall make some further remarks about explicitly defining 'the number of *F*'s' in terms of classes. The objection mentioned above loses much of its force if one drops the idea that it is the possibility of definition of this kind which guarantees that numbers exist. This does not mean that such an explicit definition cannot be used, even in a theory which is to serve as a philosophically motivated 'rational reconstruction'. The point is that the kind of general explanation and justification of the introduction of classes, to which that of numbers can be reduced by a definition, could be done directly for numbers. The identification of numbers with classes could still serve the philosophical purpose of showing that numbers are not more problematic entities than classes. There is still, however, a general difficulty about abstract entities which is illustrated by the fact that infinitely many different definitions, or perhaps none at all, are possible. This is that the concepts of different categories of abstract entities, even in highly developed mathematical theories, do not determine the truth-value of identities of entities of one category with those of another. There is perhaps some presumption in favour of regarding them as false or nonsense, but this is weakened by the fact that if it is disregarded for the sake of simplicity, no harm ensues to the logical coherence of the theories, and in practical application the worst that occurs is misunderstanding which can be dissipated easily. There is a similar difficulty even within categories, which is illustrated by Frege's observation that if X is a one-one mapping of the universe of discourse onto itself, then if (V) holds and we set

$$\tilde{x}Fx = X(\hat{x}Fx)$$

then

$$\tilde{x}Fx = \tilde{x}Gx \,.\equiv (x)(Fx \equiv Gx)$$

also holds. So that the only condition he assumes about extensions does not suffice to determine which individual objects they are.[1]

Thus we still have a weaker form of our earlier difficulty: numbers and classes are regarded as definite objects while we seem able to choose freely between infinitely many incompatible assumptions about their identity and difference relations. One may regard this as just a failure of analogy between abstract and concrete entities[2] or regard it as resolvable by some kind of appeal to intuition.

[1] *Grundgesetze*, I, 17. Frege lessens this indeterminacy by identifying certain *Werthverläufe* with the True and the False.

[2] Similar difficulties may arise in the concrete case, e.g. between physical and psychical events.

I shall now discuss the thesis that arithmetic is a part of logic. We are led into this by reminding ourselves that Frege's identification of numbers and extensions was part of the argument for this thesis. He regarded *Werthverläufe* as the most general kind of 'logical objects'; the passage from a concept to its extension was the only way of inferring the existence of an object on logical grounds.[1] I shall give reasons for denying that set theory is 'logic' once commitment to the existence of classes is introduced, but it is certainly a significant fact that in formal mathematical theories Frege's programme of replacing postulation of objects by explicit definition in terms of classes can actually be carried out.

I do not know quite how to assess it. Dummett suggests that taking an equivalence relation of entities of one kind as a criterion of identity for entities of a new kind is the most general way of introducing reference to abstract entities, and if this is so then all abstract entities can be construed as classes. This may not be enough to make axioms of class-existence logical principles, but if true it is striking and important.

The first part of Frege's argument for the thesis that arithmetic is a part of logic consists in his analysis of the general notion of cardinal number: he argues that the cardinal numbers belonging to concepts must be objects satisfying the principle (*A*) and then gives the above-mentioned explicit definition of '$N_x Fx$' so that (*A*) becomes provable. In order to give an analysis of the notion of natural (finite) number, he must pick the natural numbers out from the class of cardinals.

We might ask whether the analysis so far is sufficient for the general notion of cardinal number. So far, I have talked as if what is essential to the notion of cardinal numbers is that they should be objects with the identity condition given by (*A*). Beyond that, it does not matter what objects they are, for example, whether a cardinal number is even identical with an object given in some other way. The emphasis of the *Foundations* suggests that Frege thinks this is all that is essential, but I doubt that he really does think so. To be clear about this, I shall consider a possible justification of (*A*) arising from the question, What is it to *know* the number of *F*'s for a given *F*? It could hardly be simply to know

[1] See in addition to the quotation above (p. 184) *Grundgesetze* II, 148–49 and the quotations from letters to Russell in J. M. Bartlett, *Funktion und Gegenstand* (Munich 1961).

the name of an object with the given identity conditions, for 'the number of F's' is already such a name.

The basis of indisputable fact on which Frege's analysis rests can be brought out by the following considerations. In the finite case, we know the number of F's if we can name, in some standard fashion, a *natural number n* such that the number of F's is n. The primary way of obtaining such a number is by *counting*. To determine by counting that there are n F's involves correlating these objects, one-by-one, with the numbers from 1 to n. Thus we can take as a necssary condition for there to be n F's that it should be possible to correlate the F's one-to-one with $1 \ldots n$, i.e. that F and the concept *number from* 1 *to n* are numerically equivalent. The role of one-to-one correspondence in explaining the notion of number can be developed from this condition and the following mathematical considerations:

(1) If the F's can be correlated one-by-one with the numbers from 1 to n, then the objects falling under the concept G can be correlated with the numbers from 1 to n if and only if they can be correlated with the F's.

From (1) and our condition for there to be n F's, it follows:

(2) If there are n F's, then there are the same number of F's as G's if and only if there is a one-to-one correspondence of the F's and the G's; that is, the principle (A) holds in the finite case.

(3) That a relation H establishes a one-to-one correspondence of the F's and the G's can be expressed by a formula of the first-order predicate calculus with identity. The condition is

$$(x)[Fx \supset (\exists ! y)(Gy \,.\, Hxy)] \,.\, (y)[Gy \supset (\exists ! x)(Fx \,.\, Hxy)]$$

where '$(\exists ! z)\, Jz$', which can be read as 'there is one and only one z such that Jz', is an abbreviation for

$$(\exists z)[Jz \,.\, (x)(Jx \supset x = z)] \,.$$

Thus, since F and G are numerically equivalent if and only if there is a relation H establishing a one-to-one correspondence of the F's and the G's, '$Glz_x(Fx, Gx)$' can be explicitly defined in the second-order predicate calculus with identity, in particular without appealing to the concept of number.

(4) For each natural number n, a necessary and sufficient condition for there to be n F's can also be expressed by a formula

of the first-order predicate calculus with identity. If, following Quine,[1] we write 'there are exactly n objects x such that Fx' as '$(\exists x)_n Fx$', then we have

$$(a)\ (\exists x)_0 Fx \equiv -(\exists x)Fx$$
$$(b)\ (\exists x)_{n+1} Fx \equiv (\exists x)[Fx.\ (\exists y)_n (Fy \,.\, y \neq x)],$$

so that for a particular n, the numerical quantifier can be eliminated step by step. Thus '$(\exists x)_2 Fx$' is equivalent to

$$(\exists x)\{Fx \,.\, (\exists y)[Fy \,.\, y \neq x \,.\, -(\exists z)(Fz \,.\, z \neq x \,.\, z \neq y)]\},\ \text{i.e.}$$
$$(\exists x)(\exists y)[Fx \,.\, Fy \,.\, x \neq y \,.\, (z)(Fz \supset .\, z = x \vee z = y)].$$

Frege followed Cantor in taking (*A*) as the basic condition cardinal numbers had to satisfy in the infinite case as well as the finite. He went beyond Cantor in using it as a basis for the ordinary arithmetic of natural numbers, and in observing that numerical equivalence could be expressed in terms merely of second-order logic. Without these two further steps, the procedure has, of course, no claim at all to be a reduction of arithmetic to logic.

As I have said, the remainder of Frege's argument consists in picking out the natural numbers from the cardinals. Although this was not Frege's actual procedure, we can put it in the form of defining Peano's three primitives, '0', 'natural number', and 'successor', and proving Peano's axioms. '0' and the successor relation are defined in terms of '$N_x Fx$':

$$0 = N_x(x \neq x)$$
$$S(x, y) \equiv (\exists F)[N_w F_w = y \,.\, (\exists z)(Fz \,.\, N_w(Fw \,.\, w \neq z) = x)]$$

Then the natural numbers can be defined as those objects to which 0 bears the ancestral of the successor-relation, i.e.

$$NN(x) \equiv (F)\{F0 \,.\, (x)(y)[Fx \,.\, S(x, y) \,.\supset Fy] \,.\supset Fx\}$$

From these, Peano's axioms can be proved; it is not necessary to use any axioms of set existence except in introducing terms of the form '$N_x\, Fx$' and in proving (*A*), so that the argument could be carried out by taking (*A*) as an axiom. Lest this statement mislead, I should point out that I am provisionally counting the second-order predicate calculus as logic rather than as set theory; for from Frege's point of view the range of the higher-type variables will be

[1] *Methods of Logic*, § 39.

concepts, while the extensions with which he identifies the numbers must be *objects* in the same domain with the objects numbered.

The definition of Peano's primitives and the proof of Peano's axioms can be carried out in one way or another not only in Frege's own formal system but also in Russell's theory of types and in the other systems of set theory constructed in order to remedy the situation produced by the paradoxes, which of course showed Frege's system inconsistent. We have seen that it is possible to give these definitions in infinitely many ways. It is sometimes said that what the logicists achieved in trying to prove that arithmetic is a part of logic is the proof that arithmetic can be modelled in set theory. But it should be pointed out that the modelling of the Peano arithmetic in set theory does not need to make use of the facts (1)–(4) above cited or the general analysis of cardinal number in terms of numerical equivalence, if Frege's choice of the sets to represent the numbers is abandoned.

I intend to discuss two main lines of criticism of the thesis that arithmetic is a part of logic. The first points to the fact that the formal definitions and proofs by which the thesis is justified make use of the notion of extension, class, or set, and assume the existence of such entities. It is denied that set theory is logic. It is also denied that a reduction merely to set theory will suffice for a philosophical foundation of arithmetic or for a refutation of the epistemological theses about arithmetic (e.g. Kant's and Mill's views) against which the reduction is directed.

In discussing the thesis that numbers are objects, we found a difficulty for Frege in justifying assumptions of the existence of classes. Indeed, set theory will be logic only if propositions which assert the existence of classes are logical laws. Paul Benacerraf points out[1] that this would not be in accord with the usual definition of logical validity, according to which a formula is logically valid if and only if it is true under all interpretations in any non-empty universe, i.e. regardless of what objects, and how many, there are in the universe.[2] This definition applies to higher-order logic such as the one we have used in formulating Frege's views. But if numbers and classes are to be *objects*, a law which provides

[1] *Logicism, Some Considerations* (Ph.D. thesis Princeton University 1960), p. 196 n.

[2] The qualification 'non-empty' may be regarded merely as excluding a special case for the sake of simplicity.

for the existence of any at all will require the universe over which the quantifiers range to contain *specific* objects, and if it provides for the existence of enough for even elementary number theory, it will require the universe to be infinite.

Thus there is a clear sense in which the predicate calculus is a more general theory than any set theory, and therefore more entitled to be called 'logic'. This observation is confirmed by the fact that there are infinitely many possible assumptions of the existence of classes which can be ordered by logical strength, if the notion of strength is construed as what one may prove from them by the predicate calculus. Moreover, the stronger assumptions are in many ways more complex, obscure, and doubtful. Each well-defined system of such assumptions is incomplete in a strong sense and extendable in a natural way, in contrast to the completeness of the predicate calculus. But it is hard to see that the principles involved in such extensions are self-evident or logically compelling. This is particularly true when they allow impredicatively defined classes. Thus the existential commitments of set theory are connected with a number of important formal differences between it and the predicate calculus, and it seems that the predicate calculus is much closer to what was traditionally conceived as formal logic.

As a concession to Frege, I have accepted the claim of at least some higher-order predicate calculi to be purely logical systems. Our criticisms of Frege hold under this condition. The justification for not assimilating higher-order logic to set theory would have to be an ontological theory like Frege's theory of concepts as fundamentally different from objects, because 'unsaturated'. But even then there are distinctions among higher-order logics which are comparable to the differences in the strength of set theories. Higher-order logics have existential commitments. Consider the full second-order predicate calculus, in which we can define concepts by quantification over *all* concepts. If a formula is interpreted so that the first-order variables range over a class D of objects, then in interpreting the second-order variables we must assume a well-defined domain of concepts applying to objects in D which, if it is not literally the domain of *all* concepts over D, is comprehensive enough to be closed under quantification. Both formally and epistemologically, this presupposition is comparable to the assumption which gives rise to both the power and the difficulty of set theory, that the class of all subclasses of a given class exists. Thus it seems that even if Frege's theory of concepts is accepted, higher-order logic is more comparable to set theory than to first-order logic.

It is also sometimes claimed that the concept of class is intrinsically more problematic than that of numbers, so that the reduction of arithmetic to set theory is not a suitable philosophical foundation for arithmetic. There are several reasons which can be cited to support this contention—the multiplicity of possible existence assumptions, questions about impredicative definitions, the paradoxes, the possible indeterminacy of certain statements in set theory such as the continuum hypothesis. However, it should be pointed out that a quite weak set theory suffices for elementary number theory. Most of the difficulties arise only in the presence of impredicatively defined classes, and for the development of elementary number theory we do not have to suppose that any impredicative classes exist. If the modelling in set theory of a part of mathematics requires the existence of such classes, this can only be because the mathematics itself involves impredicativity, so that this is not a difficulty about the reduction to set theory.

However, it still seems that in order to understand even the weak theory, one must either have a general concept of set or assume it to be restricted in some way which involves the notion of number. The theory may be such that only finite sets can be proved to exist in it, but the reduction is not very helpful if the quantifiers of the theory are interpreted as ranging over finite sets. It seems that for a proposition involving quantification over *all* sets to have a definite truth-value, it must be objectively determined what sets exist. I think one might get around this, but it is certain that the assumption that any such proposition *has* a definite truth-value, which seems to be involved already in applying classical logic to such propositions, is stronger and more doubtful than any principle which needs to be assumed in elementary number theory.

The second criticism which I want to consider denies that arithmetic is reducible to set theory in the most important sense. This objection is as old as those concerning the foundations of set theory, but on the surface at least independent of them. It is to be found in Brouwer and Hilbert, but was probably argued in greatest detail by Poincaré.[1] Recently it has been taken up by Papert.[2] It

[1] *Science et Méthode* (Paris 1908), ch. iv.

[2] 'Sur le réductionnisme logique', *Problèmes de la construction du nombre* (Études d'épistémologie génétique, XI, Paris 1960).

is closely related to the criticisms of Wittgenstein[1] and Wang.[2]

This objection holds that the reduction is circular because it makes use of the notion of natural number. This obviously does not mean that the notion of natural number, or one defined in terms of it, appears as a primitive term of any set theory by which the reduction could be carried out, for this would be obviously false. Rather, the claim is that we must use the notion of natural number either to set up the set theory, to see the truth of the set-theoretical propositions to which number-theoretical propositions are reduced by explicit definitions, or to see the equivalence of the set-theoretical propositions and their number-theoretical correlates. This can in fact be seen by a quite simple argument. Inductive definitions, especially, play an essential role both in setting up a system of set theory and in establishing the correspondence between it and the system of number theory. For example, typically the definition of *theorem* for each system will be an inductive definition of the following form: Certain axioms and rules of inference are specified. Then to be a theorem is either to be an axiom or to be obtainable from theorems by a single application of one of the rules of inference. Then the model of number theory in set theory is established by defining for each formula A of number theory a set-theoretical translation $T(A)$. To prove that if A is a theorem of number theory then $T(A)$ is a theorem of set theory, we first prove this for the case where A is an axiom. Then suppose A follows from, say, B and C by a rule of inference in number theory, where B and C are theorems. We then show that $T(A)$ is deducible from $T(B)$ and $T(C)$ in the set theory. By hypothesis of induction, $T(B)$ and $T(C)$ are theorems of set theory. Therefore so is $T(A)$. By an induction corresponding to the definition of theorem of number theory, $T(A)$ is a theorem of set theory whenever A is a theorem of number theory.

Although the observation on which this objection is based is true, this is not sufficient to refute the reductionist. For the latter may maintain that the notion he defines is capable of *replacing* that of natural number (and equivalent notions involving induction) in all contexts, in particular those uses which are involved in describing the logical systems and in establishing the correspondence. So

[1] *Remarks on the Foundations of Mathematics* (Oxford 1956), part II.

[2] 'Process and Existence in Mathematics', *Essays on the Foundations of Mathematics*, in honour of A. A. Fraenkel (Jerusalem 1961).

that we can imagine that in both the number-theoretical and the set-theoretical formal systems 'A is a theorem' is defined, say, as 'A belongs to every class of formulas which contains all axioms and is closed under the rules of inference', as is done in some writings of Tarski. Whenever natural numbers are used ordinally for indexing purposes, they are to be replaced by their set-theoretical *definientia*.

We might consider in this connection a form of Poincaré's objection due to Papert.[1] Papert says in effect that the Frege-Russell procedure defines *two* classes of natural numbers, such that mathematical induction is needed to show them identical. For we give explicit definitions in the set theory of 'o', 'So', 'SSo' . . . and *also* define the predicate '$NN(x)$'. How are we to be sure that '$NN(x)$' is true of what o, So, SSo, . . . are defined to be and only these? Well, we can prove 'NN(o)' and '$NN(x) \supset NN(Sx)$'.

If '$NN(S^{(n)}\text{o})$'[2] is the last line of a proof, then by substitution and *modus ponens*, we have a proof of '$NN(S^{(n+1)}\text{o})$'. By induction, we have a proof of '$NN(S^{(n)}\text{o})$' for every n.

We can likewise prove by induction that every x for which '$NN(x)$' is true is denoted by a numeral. For o clearly is. If $n = S^{(m)}\text{o}$, then $Sn = S^{(m+1)}\text{o}$. So by induction (the derived rule of the set theory), if $NN(x)$, then $x = S^{(m)}\text{o}$ for some $m > \text{o}$.

What we have proved is a meta-linguistic proposition. The reply to Papert would be to say that we can define the class of symbols $S^{(m)}\text{o}$ by the same device; i.e. if $Num(x)$ is to be true of just these symbols, we define:

$$Num(x) \equiv (F)\{F(\text{'o'}) \,.\, (x)[Fx \supset F(\text{'}S\text{'}{}^\frown x)] \,.\supset Fx\} \,.$$[3]

Then the first of the above two inductive proofs will be an application of this definition, just as the second is an application of the definition of $NN(x)$.

Papert can raise the same question again. We can prove formally that if $NN(x)$ holds, then x is denoted by an object y such that $Num(y)$. Moreover, we can prove formally that if $Num(y)$ then the result of substituting y for the variable 'x' in '$NN(x)$' is provable. But how do we know that the extension of '$Num(x)$' consists just of 'o', 'So', 'SSo', etc.?

[1] *Loc. cit.*

[2] '$S^{(n)}$o' is an abbreviation for 'o' preceded by n occurrences of 'S'.

[3] If x and y are expressions, $x^\frown y$ is their concatenation, that is, the result of writing x followed by y.

This is clearly the beginning of a potentially infinite regress. What is happening is this. If we replace an inductive definition by an explicit one, it takes an inductive *proof* to show that they define coextensive concepts. *This* difficulty can be avoided by denying that we have an independent understanding of inductive definitions. That is, if we ask Papert what he means by ' "o", "*S*o", "*SS*o", etc.', he would have to reply by an explicit definition which would turn out to be equivalent to '*Num*(*x*)'. But this last reply to Papert depends on the claim that the apparatus in terms of which such explicit definitions as that of '*NN*(*x*)' are given can be understood independently of even the most elementary inductive definitions. This is implausible since the explicit definitions involve quantification over all concepts. It is hard to see what a concept is, or what the totality of concepts might be, without something like the inductive generation of linguistic expressions which (on Frege's view) refer to them.

There is another difficulty which Papert's exposition shows he has in mind.[1] It is independent of the question whether inductive definitions are replaced by explicit ones. Consider some numeral, say '*SSSS*o', and a proposition of the form '*F*(*SSSS*o)'. If we have proved '*F*o' and '(*n*) [*Fn* ⊃ *F*(*Sn*)]', we have two independent ways of proving a proposition '*F*(*SSSS*o)'. We might infer '(*n*)*Fn*' by induction and '*F*(*SSSS*o)' by universal instantiation. Or we might prove it without induction, by successive applications of *modus ponens:*

$$\cfrac{\cfrac{\cfrac{\cfrac{Fo \quad Fo \supset F(So)}{F(So) \quad F(So) \supset F(SSo)}}{F(SSo) \quad F(SSo) \supset F(SSSo)}}{F(SSSo) \quad F(SSSo \supset F(SSSSo)}}{F(SSSSo)}$$

We say that the proof by way of induction gives us the assurance that we *can* construct such a proof by successive applications of *modus ponens*. And the complexity of such proofs is unbounded. (But how do we see that we *always* can? By induction!) The application of the procedure involves the iteration of certain steps *n* times for the proof of $F(S^{(n)}o)$. Neither the reduction of induction

[1] Especially in the subsequent essay in the volume cited in note 2, p. 197 above, 'Problemès épistemologiques et génétiques de la récurrence'.

to an explicit definition nor the Wittgensteinian doctrine[1] that '$F0 . (n)[Fn \supset F(Sn)]$' constitutes the *criterion* for the truth of 'for all natural numbers n, Fn' gives us an assurance that there will be no *conflict* between the two methods for proving individual cases. When Poincaré said that a step of induction contained an infinity of syllogisms, he was saying that it guaranteed the possibility of all the proofs of the instances by reiterated *modus ponens.* He was right at least to this extent: if we do have an *a priori* assurance that there will be no conflict between construction in individual cases and inference from general propositions proved by induction, then this assurance is not founded on logic or set theory.

Let us now return to the question which we left in the air in our discussion of the thesis that numbers are objects: What *does* guarantee that the singular terms of arithmetic have reference?

If we consider two different systems of numerals,

$0, S0, SS0, \ldots$
$0, T0, TT0, \ldots$

then the order-preserving correspondence between them fixes when two numerals shall *denote the same number*. Indeed, I do not think there is a more fundamental criterion of this. For this reason I should say that if the critics of logicism intend to deny Frege's assertion that the notion of one-to-one correspondence plays a constitutive role in our notion of number, they are wrong. It also follows that the ordinal and cardinal notions of number are interdependent. One might hold that cardinals are 'applied ordinals'; i.e. if we are given the numbers with their order, then the relation to one-to-one correspondence and therefore to numerical equivalence is something that arises only in the application of numbers and does not belong to their nature as pure mathematical objects. However, I do not see how we could be said to be *given* the numbers except through a sequence of numerals or some other representatives of the same type of order. And if it is not part of the concept of number that the sequence in question should be a paradigm which could be replaced by some other equivalent sequence, the unnatural conclusion follows that features of the representative sequence which one would expect to be quite accidental, such as the particular design of the numerals, *are* relevant. But Frege's

[1] F. Waismann, *Introduction to Mathematical Thinking* (New York 1951), Ch. 9.

definitions *do* bring some avoidable complexity into the notion of natural number, because it defines them in terms of *explicit assertions* of the existence of one-to-one correspondences, and this need *not* be part of the sense of statements about natural numbers.

Suppose we regard it as essential to a system of numerals that it be formed by starting with some initial numeral and iterating some basic operation (representing the successor function). Let us try the following model of how the numerals come to have reference: At first they function like indexical expressions, in that in counting each refers to the object with which it is correlated, as is actually true of the expressions 'the first', 'the second', etc. Then by a kind of abstraction, the reference of the numeral is taken to be the *same* on all occasions. What guarantees the *existence* of the number *n* is the existence of an ordered set in which some object is the *n*th. For any numeral, the numerals up to that one will be such a set. Then no ulterior fact beyond the generation of the numerals is needed to guarantee that they have reference.[1]

In the case of small numbers, the guarantee of their existence is somewhat analogous to that which sense-experience gives of the existence of physical objects. But because any instance of a certain type of order will do, and because such instances can be found in sense-experience, and we cannot imagine what it would be like for us to be *unable* to find such instances, we are inclined to regard the evidence of the existence of small numbers as *a priori*.

We speak of its being *possible* to continue the construction of numerals to infinity. On the basis of this possibility we can say that numbers exist for which we have no numerals. However, this is an extrapolation from the concrete possibilities, and the only reason for favouring *it* as the guarantee for the existence of large numbers over the hypothesis of an actual infinity of sets, from which representatives of the numbers can be chosen, is that it is weaker. It is comparable to Kant's assumption that the 'possibility of experience' extends to regions of space too small or too distant for us to perceive.

With respect to the thesis that arithmetic is a part of logic, our conclusion is that although the criticisms which have been made of it over the years *do* suffice to show that it is false, it ought not to be rejected in the unqualified way in which it appears to have been

[1] Cf. Benacerraf, *op. cit.*, pp. 162–74, and his paper 'What Numbers Could Not Be' to appear in *The Philosphical Review* (1965).

rejected by Poincaré, Brouwer, and Hilbert. It seems to me that Frege *does* show that the logical notion of one-to-one correspondence is an essential constituent of the notion of number, ordinal as well as cardinal. The content of arithmetic that is clearly additional to that of logic, which Frege failed to acknowledge, is in its existence assumptions, which involve an appeal to intuition and extrapolation. (The same kind of intuitive construction as is involved in arithmetic is also involved in *perceiving the truth* of logical truths.) The same appeal is involved in set theory, although if we go beyond general set theory and assume the existence of infinite sets, the extrapolation is of course greater. Concerning the relation of the notion of natural number to the notion of finite set, it seems clear to me that they go together, and that neither can be understood without the other. I should like to argue, although I do not have the space to do so now, that there is a reciprocal relation between such arithmetical identities as '$2 + 2 = 4$' and the logical truths closely associated with them under the Frege–Russell analysis, so that it will not do to regard one as a mere abbreviation of the other.

X

THE FREE WILL DEFENCE

by ALVIN PLANTINGA

Associate Professor of Philosophy, Calvin College

Since the days of Epicurus many philosophers have suggested that the existence of evil constitutes a problem for those who accept theistic belief.[1] Those contemporaries who follow Epicurus here claim, for the most part, to detect logical inconsistency in such belief. So McCloskey:

Evil is a problem for the theist in that a *contradiction* is involved in the fact of evil, on the one hand, and the belief in the omnipotence and perfection of God on the other.[2]

and Mackie:

I think, however, that a more telling criticism can be made by way of the traditional problem of evil. Here it can be shown, not that religious beliefs lack rational support, but that they are positively irrational, that the several parts of the essential theological doctrine are *inconsistent* with one another . . .[3]

and essentially the same charge is made by Professor Aiken in an article entitled 'God and Evil'.[4]

These philosophers, then, and many others besides, hold that traditional theistic belief is self-contradictory and that the problem of evil, for the theist, is that of deciding which of the relevant propositions he is to abandon. But just which propositions are involved? What is the set of theistic beliefs whose conjunction

[1] David Hume and some of the French encyclopedists, for example, as well as F. H. Bradley, J. McTaggart, and J. S. Mill.

[2] H. J. McCloskey, 'God and Evil'. *The Philosophical Quarterly*, Vol. 10 (April 1960), p. 97.

[3] 'Evil and Omnipotence.' J. L. Mackie, *Mind*, Vol. 64, No. 254 (April 1955), p. 200.

[4] *Ethics*, Vol. 48 (1957–58), p. 79.

yields a contradiction? The authors referred to above take the following five propositions to be essential to traditional theism: (*a*) that God exists, (*b*) that God is omnipotent, (*c*) that God is omniscient, (*d*) that God is wholly good, and (*e*) that evil exists. Here they are certainly right: each of these propositions is indeed an essential feature of orthodox theism. And it is just these five propositions whose conjunction is said, by our atheologians,[1] to be self-contradictory.

Apologists for theism, of course, have been quick to repel the charge. A line of resistance they have often employed is called *The Free Will Defence*; in this paper I shall discuss and develop that idea.

First of all, a distinction must be made between *moral evil* and *physical evil*. The former, roughly, is the evil which results from human choice or volition; the latter is that which does not. Suffering due to an earthquake, for example, would be a case of physical evil; suffering resulting from human cruelty would be a case of moral evil. This distinction, of course, is not very clear and many questions could be raised about it; but perhaps it is not necessary to deal with these questions here. Given this distinction, the Free Will Defence is usually stated in something like the following way. A world containing creatures who freely perform both good and evil actions—and do more good than evil—is more valuable than a world containing quasi-automata who always do what is right because they are unable to do otherwise. Now God can create free creatures, but He cannot causally or otherwise determine them to do only what is right; for if he does so then they do not do what is right *freely*. To create creatures capable of moral good, therefore, he must create creatures capable of moral evil; but he cannot create the possibility of moral evil and at the same time prohibit its actuality. And as it turned out, some of the free creatures God created exercised their freedom to do what is wrong: hence moral evil. The fact that free creatures sometimes err, however, in no way tells against God's omnipotence or against his goodness; for he could forestall the occurrence of moral evil only by removing the possibility of moral good.

[1] *Natural theology* is the attempt to infer central religious beliefs from premises that are either obvious to common sense (e.g., *that some things are in motion*) or logically necessary. *Natural atheology* is the attempt to infer the falsity of such religious beliefs from premises of the same sort.

In this way some traditional theists have tried to explain or justify part of the evil that occurs by ascribing it to the will of man rather than to the will of God. At least three kinds of objections to this idea are to be found both in the tradition and in the current literature. I shall try to develop and clarify the Free Will Defence by restating it in the face of these objections.

I

The first objection challenges the assumption, implicit in the above statement of the Free Will Defence, that free will and causal determinism are logically incompatible. So Flew:

> . . . to say that a person could have helped doing something is not to say that what he did was in principle unpredictable nor that there were no causes anywhere which determined that he would as a matter of fact act in this way. It is to say that if he had chosen to do otherwise he would have been able to do so; that there were alternatives, within the capacities of one of his physical strength, of his I.Q., of his knowledge, open to a person in his situation.
>
> . . . There is no contradiction involved in saying that a particular action or choice was: *both* free, and could have been helped, and so on; *and* predictable, or even foreknown, and explicable in terms of caused causes.
>
> . . . if it is really logically possible for an action to be both freely chosen and yet fully determined by caused causes, then the key-stone argument of the Free Will Defence, that there is contradiction in speaking of God so arranging the laws of nature that all men always as a matter of fact freely choose to do the right, cannot hold.[1]

Flew's objection, I think, can be dealt with in a fairly summary fashion. He does not, in the paper in question, explain what he means by 'causal determination' (and of course in that paper this omission is quite proper and justifiable). But presumably he means to use the locution in question in such a way that to say of Jones' action *A* that it is *causally determined* is to say that the action in question has causes and that given these causes, Jones could not

[1] 'Divine Omnipotence and Human Freedom', in *New Essays in Philosophical Theology*, ed. A. Flew and A. MacIntyre, London 1955, pp. 150, 151, 153.

have refrained from doing *A*. That is to say, Flew's use of 'causally determined', presumably, is such that one or both of the following sentences, or some sentences very much like them, express necessarily true propositions:

(*a*) If Jones' action *A* is causally determined, then a set *S* of events has occurred prior to Jones' doing *A* such that, given *S*, it is causally impossible for Jones to refrain from doing *A*.

(*b*) If Jones' action *A* is causally determined, then there is a set *S* of propositions describing events occurring before *A* and a set *L* of propositions expressing natural laws such that

(1) the conjunction of *S*'s members does not entail that Jones does *A*, and
(2) the conjunction of the members of *S* with the members of *L* does entail that Jones does *A*.

And Flew's thesis, then, is that there is no contradiction in saying of a man, both that all of his actions are causally determined (in the sense just explained) and that some of them are free.

Now it seems to me altogether paradoxical to say of anyone all of whose actions are causally determined, that on some occasions he acts freely. When we say that Jones acts freely on a given occasion, what we say entails, I should think, that either his action on that occasion is not causally determined, or else he has previously performed an undetermined action which is a causal ancestor of the one in question. But this is a difficult and debatable issue; fortunately we need not settle it in order to assess the force of Flew's objection to the Free Will Defence. The Free Will Defender claims that the sentence 'Not all free actions are causally determined' expresses a necessary truth; Flew denies this claim. This strongly suggests that Flew and the Free Will Defender are not using the words 'free' and 'freedom' in the same way. The Free Will Defender, apparently, uses the words in question in such a way that sentences 'Some of Jones' actions are free' and 'Jones did action *A* freely' express propositions which are inconsistent with the proposition that all of Jones' actions are causally determined. Flew, on the other hand, claims that with respect to the ordinary use of these words, there is no such inconsistency. It is my opinion that Flew is mistaken here; I think it is he who is using these words in a non-standard, unordinary way. But we need not try to resolve that issue; for the Free Will Defender can simply make

Flew a present of the word 'freedom' and state his case using other locutions. He might now hold, for example, not that God made men free and that a world in which men freely do both good and evil is more valuable than a world in which they unfreely do only what is good; but rather that God made men such that some of their actions are *unfettered* (both free in Flew's sense and also causally undetermined) and that a world in which men perform both good and evil unfettered actions is superior to one in which they perform only good, but fettered, actions. By substituting 'unfettered' for 'free' throughout this account, the Free Will Defender can elude Flew's objection altogether.[1] So whether Flew is right or wrong about the ordinary sense of 'freedom' is of no consequence; his objection is in an important sense merely verbal and thus altogether fails to damage the Free Will Defence.

II

Flew's objection, in essence, is the claim that an omnipotent being could have created men in such a way that although free they would be *causally determined* to perform only right actions. According to a closely allied objection, an omnipotent being could have made men in such a way that although free, and free from any such causal determination, they would nonetheless *freely refrain* from performing any evil actions. Here the contemporary spokesman is Mackie:

> . . . if God has made men such that in their free choices they sometimes prefer what is good and sometimes what is evil, why could he not have made men such that they always freely choose the good? If there is no logical impossibility in a man's freely choosing the good on one, or on several occasions, there cannot be a logical impossibility in his freely choosing the good on every occasion. God was not, then, faced with a choice between making innocent automata and making beings who, in acting freely, would sometimes go wrong; there was open to him the obviously better possibility of making beings who would act freely but always go right. Clearly, his failure to avail himself of this possibility is inconsistent with his being both omnipotent and wholly good.[2]

[1] And since this is so in what follows I shall continue to use the words 'free' and 'freedom' in the way the Free Will Defender uses them.

[2] *Op. cit.*, p. 209.

This objection is more serious than Flew's and must be dealt with more fully. Now the Free Will Defence is an argument for the conclusion that (*a*) is not contradictory or necessarily false:[1]

(*a*) God is omnipotent, omniscient, and all-good and God creates free men who sometimes perform morally evil actions.

What Mackie says, I think, may best be construed as an argument for the conclusion that (*a*) *is* necessarily false; in other words, that *God is omnipotent, omniscient and all good* entails *no free men He creates ever perform morally evil actions.* Mackie's argument seems to have the following structure:

(1) God is omnipotent and omniscient and all-good.
(2) If God is omnipotent, He can create any logically possible state of affairs.
∴(3) God can create any logically possible state of affairs. (1, 2)
(4) That all free men do what is right on every occasion is a logically possible state of affairs.
∴(5) God can create free men such that they always do what is right. (4, 3)
(6) If God can create free men such that they always do what is right and God is all-good, then any free men created by God always do what is right.
∴(7) Any free men created by God always do what is right. (1, 5, 6)
∴(8) No free men created by God ever perform morally evil actions. (7)

Doubtless the Free Will Defender will concede the truth of (4); there is a difficulty with (2), however; for
(*a*) that there are men who are not created by God is a logically possible state of affairs
is clearly true. But (2) and (*a*) entail
(*b*) If God is omnipotent, God can create men who are not created by God.
And (*b*), of course, is false; (2) must be revised. The obvious way to repair it seems to be something like the following:
(2′) If God is omnipotent, then God can create any state of affairs *S* such that *God creates S* is consistent.

[1] And of course if (*a*) is consistent, so is the set (*a*)–(*e*) mentioned on page 205, for (*a*) entails each member of that set.

Similarly, (3) must be revised:

(3′) God can create any state of affairs *S* such that *God creates S* is consistent.

(1′) and (3′) do not seem to suffer from the faults besetting (1) and (3); but now it is not at all evident that (3′) and (4) entail

(5) God can create free men such that they always do what is right

as the original argument claims. To see this, we must note that (5) is true only if

(5*a*) God creates free men such that they always do what is right

is consistent. But (5*a*), one might think, is equivalent to:

(5*b*) God creates free men and brings it about that they always freely do what is right.

And (5*b*), of course, is *not* consistent; for if God *brings it about* that the men He creates always do what is right, then they do not do what is right *freely*. So if (5*a*) is taken to express (5*b*), then (5) is clearly false and clearly not entailed by (3′) and (4).

On the other hand, (5*a*) could conceivably be used to express:

(5*c*) God creates free men and these free men always do what is right.

(5*c*) is surely consistent; it is indeed logically possible that God creates free men and that the free men created by Him always do what is right. And conceivably the objector is using (5) to express this possibility—i.e., it may be that (5) is meant to express:

(5*d*) the proposition *God creates free men and the free men created by God always do what is right* is consistent.

If (5) is equivalent to (5*d*), then (5) is true—in fact necessarily true (and hence trivially entailed by (3′) and (4)). But now the difficulty crops up with respect to (6) which, given the equivalence of (5) and (5*d*) is equivalent to

(6′) If God is all-good and the proposition *God creates free men and the free men He creates always do what is right* is consistent, then any free men created by God always do what is right.

Now Mackie's aim is to show that the proposition *God is omnipotent, omniscient and all-good* entails the proposition *no free men created by God ever perform morally evil actions*. His attempt, as I outlined it, is to show this by constructing a valid argument whose premise is the former and whose conclusion is the latter.

But then any additional premise appealed to in the deduction must be necessarily true if Mackie's argument is to succeed. (6′) is one such additional premise; but there seems to be no reason for supposing that (6′) is true at all, let alone necessarily true. Whether the free men created by God would always do what is right would presumably be up to them; for all we know they might sometimes exercise their freedom to do what is wrong. Put in a nutshell the difficulty with the argument is the following. (5*a*) (God creates free men such that they always freely do what is right) is susceptible of two interpretations ((5*b*) and (5*c*)). Under one of these interpretations (5) turns out to be false and the argument therefore fails. Under the other interpretation (6) turns out to be utterly groundless and question begging, and again the argument fails.

So far, then, the Free Will Defence has emerged unscathed from Mackie's objection. One has the feeling, however, that more can be said here; that there is something to Mackie's argument. What more? Well, perhaps something along the following lines. It is agreed that it is logically possible that all men always do only what is right. Now God is said to be omniscient and hence knows, with respect to any person he proposes to create, whether that person would or would not commit morally evil acts. For every person P who in fact performs morally evil actions, there is, evidently, a possible person P' who is exactly like P in every respect except that P' never performs any evil actions. If God is omnipotent, He could have created these possible persons instead of the persons He in fact did create. And if He is also all-good, He *would*, presumably, have created them, since they differ from the persons He did create only in being morally better than they are.

Can we make coherent sense out of this revised version of Mackie's objection? What, in particular, could the objector mean by 'possible person'? and what are we to make of the suggestion that God could have created possible persons? I think these questions can be answered. Let us consider first the set of all those properties it is logically possible for human beings to have. Examples of properties *not* in this set are the properties of *being over a mile long; being a hippopotamus; being a prime number; being divisible by four;* and the like. Included in the set are such properties as *having red hair*; *being present at the Battle of Waterloo; being the President of the United States; being born in 1889;* and *being a pipe-smoker*. Also included are such moral properties as *being kind to one's maiden aunt, being a scoundrel, performing at least one morally wrong action*, and so on. Let us call the properties in this set H properties. The complement $\bar{P}$ of an H property P is the property a thing has just in case it does not have P. And a *consistent set of H* properties is a set of H properties such that it is logically possible that there be a human being having every property in the set. Now we can define 'possible person' in the following way:

> x is a possible person $=$ x is a consistent set of H properties such that for every H property P, either P or $\bar{P}$ is a member of x.

To *instantiate* a possible person P is to create a human being having every property in P. And a set S of possible persons is a *co-possible set of possible persons* just in case it is logically possible that every member of S is instantiated.[1]

Given this technical terminology, Mackie's objection can be summarily restated. It is granted by everyone that there is no absurdity in the claim that some man who is free to do what is wrong never, in fact, performs any wrong action. It follows that there are many possible persons containing the property *is free to do wrong but always does right*. And since it is logically possible that all men always freely do what is right, there are presumably several co-possible sets of possible persons such that each member of each set contains the property in question. Now God, if he is omnipotent, can instantiate any possible person and any co-possible set of possible persons he chooses. Hence, if He were all-good, He would have instantiated one of the sets of co-possible persons all of whose members freely do only what is right.

In spite of its imposing paraphernalia the argument, thus restated, suffers from substantially the same defect that afflicts Mackie's original version. There are *some* possible persons God obviously cannot instantiate—those, for example, containing the property *is not created by God*. Accordingly it is *false* that God can instantiate just any possible person He chooses. But of course the interesting question is whether

(1) God can instantiate possible persons containing the property of always freely doing what is right

is true; for perhaps Mackie could substitute (1) for the premise just shown to be false.

[1] The definiens must not be confused with: For every member M of S, it is logically possible that M is instantiated.

Is (1) true? Perhaps we can approach this question in the following way. Let P be any possible person containing the property *always freely does what is right*. Then there must be some action A such that P contains the property of being free with respect to A (i.e., the property of being free to perform A and free to refrain from performing A). The *instantiation* of a possible person S, I shall say, is a person having every property in S; and let us suppose that if P were instantiated, its instantiation would be doing something morally wrong in performing A. And finally, let us suppose that God wishes to instantiate P. Now P contains many properties in addition to the ones already mentioned. Among them, for example, we might find the following: *is born in 1910, has red hair, is born in Stuttgart, has feeble-minded ancestors, is six feet tall at the age of fourteen*, and the like. And there is no difficulty in God's creating a person with these properties. Further, there is no difficulty in God's bringing it about that this person (let's call him Smith) is free with respect to A. But if God *also* brings it about that Smith refrains from performing A (as he must to be the instantiation of P) then Smith is no longer free with respect to A and is hence not the instantiation of P after all. God cannot cause Smith to refrain from performing A, while allowing him to be free with respect to A; and therefore whether or not Smith does A will be entirely up to Smith; it will be a matter of free choice for him. Accordingly, whether God can instantiate P depends upon what Smith would freely decide to do.

This point may be put more accurately as follows: First, we shall say that an H property Q is *indeterminate* if *God creates a person and causes him to have Q* is necessarily false; an H property is *determinate* if it is not indeterminate. Of the properties we ascribed to P, all are determinate except *freely refrains from doing A* and *always freely does what is right*. Now consider P_1, the subset of P containing just the determinate members of P. In order to instantiate P God must instantiate P_1. It is evident that there is at most one instantiation of P_1, for among the members of P_1 will be some such individuating properties as for example, *is the third son of Richard and Lena Dykstra*. P_1 also contains the property of being free with respect to A; and if P_1 is instantiated, its instantiation will either perform A or refrain from performing A. It is, of course, possible that P_1 is such that if it is instantiated its instantiation I will perform A. If so, then if God allows I to remain free with respect to *A*, *I* will do *A*; and if God prevents *I* from doing *A*, then *I* is not free with respect to *A* and hence not the instantiation of *P* after all. Hence in neither case does God succeed in instantiating *P*. And accordingly God can instantiate *P* only if P_1 is *not* such that if it is instantiated, its instantiation will perform *A*. Hence it is possible that God cannot instantiate *P*. And evidently it is also possible, further, that *every* possible person containing the property *always freely does what is right* is such that neither God nor anyone else can instantiate it.

Now we merely supposed that P_1 is such that if it is instantiated, its instantiation will perform *A*. And this supposition, if true at all, is merely contingently true. It might be suggested, therefore, that God could instantiate *P* by instantiating P_1 and bringing it about that P_1 is *not* such that if it is instantiated, its instantiation will perform *A*. But to do this God must instantiate P_1 and bring it about that P_1 is such that if it is instantiated, its instantiation *I* will *refrain* from performing *A*. And if God does this then God brings it about that *I* will not perform *A*. But then *I* is not free to perform *A* and hence once more is not the instantiation of *P*.

It is possible, then, that God cannot instantiate any possible person containing the property *always freely does what is right*. It is also possible, of course, that He *can* instantiate some such possible persons. But *that* He can, if indeed He can, is a contingent truth. And since Mackie's project is to prove an entailment, he cannot employ any contingent propositions as added premises. Hence the reconstructed argument fails.

Now the difficulty with the reconstructed argument is the fact that God cannot instantiate just any possible person he chooses, and the possibility that God cannot instantiate any possible persons containing the property of always freely doing what is right. But perhaps the objector can circumvent this difficulty.

The *H* properties that make trouble for the objector are the indeterminate properties—those which God cannot cause anyone to have. It is because possible persons contain indeterminate properties that God cannot instantiate just any possible person He wishes. And so perhaps the objector can reformulate his definition of 'possible person' in such a way that a possible person is a consistent set *S* of *determinate* properties such that for any determinate *H* property *P*, either *P* or $\bar{P}$ is a member of *S*. Unfortunately the following difficulty arises. Where *I* is any indeterminate H property and D a determinate H property, D or I (the property a person has if he has either D or I) is determinate. And so, of course, is $\bar{D}$. The same difficulty, accordingly, arises all over again—there will be some possible persons God can't instantiate (those containing the properties *is not created by God or has red hair* and *does not have red hair*, for example). We must add, therefore, that no possible person *entails* an indeterminate property.[1]

Even so our difficulties are not at an end. For the definition as now stated entails that there are no *possible free persons*, i.e., possible persons containing the property *on some occasions free to do what is right and free to do what is wrong*.[2] We may see this as follows: Let P be any possible free person. P then contains the property of being free with respect to some action A. Furthermore, P would contain either the property of performing A (since that is a determinate property) or the property of refraining from performing A. But if P contains the property of performing A and the property of being free with respect to A, then P entails the property of freely performing A—which is an indeterminate property. And the same holds in case P contains the property of refraining from performing A. Hence in either case P entails an indeterminate property and accordingly is not a possible person.

Clearly the objector must revise the definition of 'possible person' in such a way that for any action with respect to which a given possible person P is free, P contains neither the property of performing that action nor the property of refraining from performing it. This may be accomplished in the following way. Let us say that a person S is *free with respect to a property* P just in case there is some action A with respect to which S is free and which is such that S has P if and only if he performs A. So, for example, if a person is free to leave town and free to stay, then he is free with respect to the property *leaves town*. And let us say that a set of properties is free with respect to a given property P just in case it contains the property is *free with respect to* P. Now we can restate the definition of 'possible person' as follows:

> x is a possible person = x is a consistent set of determinate H properties such that (1) for every determinate H property

[1] Where a set S of properties entails a property P if and only if it is necessarily true that anything having every property in S also has P.

[2] This was pointed out to me by Mr. Lewis Creary.

P with respect to which x is not free, either P or $\overline{P}$ is a member of x, and (2) x does not entail any indeterminate property.

Now let us add the following new definition:

Possibly person P has indeterminate property I = if P were instantiated, P's instantiation would have I.

Under the revised definition of 'possible person' it seems apparent that God, if he is omnipotent, can instantiate any possible person, and any co-possible set of possible persons, he chooses. But, the objector continues, if God is also all-good, He will, presumably, instantiate only those possible persons who have some such indeterminate H property as that of *always freely doing what is right*. And here the Free Will Defender can no longer make the objection which held against the previous versions of Mackie's argument. For if God can instantiate any possible person he chooses, he can instantiate any possible free person he chooses.

The Free Will Defender can, however, raise what is essentially the same difficulty in a new guise: what reason is there for supposing that there are *any* possible persons, in the present sense of 'possible person', having the indeterminate property in question? For it is clear that, given any indeterminate H property I, the proposition *no possible person has I* is a contingent proposition. Further, the proposition *every possible free person freely performs at least one morally wrong action* is possibly true. But if every *possible* free person performs at least one wrong action, then every *actual* free person also freely performs at least one wrong action; hence if every possible free person performs at least one wrong action, God could create a universe without moral evil only by refusing to create any free persons at all. And, the Free Will Defender adds, a world containing free persons and moral evil (provided that it contained more moral good than moral evil) would be superior to one lacking both free persons and moral good and evil. Once again, then, the objection seems to fail.

The definitions offered during the discussion of Mackie's objection afford the opportunity of stating the Free Will Defence more formally. I said above (p. 209) that the Free Will Defence is in essence an argument for the conclusion that (*a*) is consistent:

(*a*) God is omnipotent, omniscient, and all-good and God creates persons who sometimes perform morally evil actions.

One way of showing (*a*) to be consistent is to show that its first conjunct does not entail the negation of its second conjunct, i.e., that

(*b*) God is omnipotent, omniscient and all-good

does not entail

(*c*) God does not create persons who perform morally evil actions.

Now one can show that a given proposition *p* does not entail another proposition *q* by producing a third proposition *r* which is such that (1) the conjunction of *p* and *r* is consistent and (2) the conjunction of *p* and *r* entails the negation of *q*. What we need here, then, is a proposition whose conjunction with (*b*) is both logically consistent and a logically sufficient condition of the denial of (*c*).

Consider the following argument:

(*b*) God is omnipotent, omniscient and all-good.
(*r*1) God creates some free persons.
(*r*2) Every possible free person performs at least one wrong action.
∴(*d*) Every actual free person performs at least one wrong action. (*r*2)
∴(*e*) God creates persons who perform morally evil actions. ((*r*1), (*d*))

This argument is valid (and can easily be expanded so that it is *formally* valid). Furthermore, the conjunction of (*b*), (*r*1) and (*r*2) is evidently consistent. And as the argument shows, (*b*), (*r*1) and (*r*2) jointly entail (*e*). But (*e*) is the denial of (*c*); hence (*b*) and (*r*) jointly entail the denial of (*c*). Accordingly (*b*) does not entail (*c*), and (*a*) (God is omnipotent, omniscient and all-good and God creates persons who perform morally evil acts) is shown to be consistent. So stated, therefore, the Free Will Defence appears to be successful.

At this juncture it might be objected that even if the Free Will Defence, as explained above, shows that there is no contradiction in the supposition that God, who is all-good, omnipotent and omniscient, creates persons who engage in moral evil, it does nothing to show that an all-good, omnipotent and omniscient Being could create a universe containing as *much* moral evil as this one seems to contain. The objection has a point, although the fact that there seems to be no way of measuring or specifying amounts of moral evil makes it exceedingly hard to state the objection in any way which does not leave it vague and merely suggestive. But let us suppose, for purposes of argument, that there is a way of measuring moral evil (and moral good) and that the moral evil present in the universe amounts to ϕ. The problem then is to show that

(*b*) God is omnipotent, omniscient and all-good

is consistent with

(*f*) God creates a set of free persons who produce ϕ moral evil.

Here the Free Will Defender can produce an argument to show that (*b*) is consistent with (*f*) which exactly parallels the argument for the consistency of (*b*) with (*c*):

(*b*) God is omnipotent, omniscient and all-good.

(*r*3) God creates a set *S* of free persons such that there is a balance of moral good over moral evil with respect to the members of *S*.

(*r*4) There is exactly one co-possible set *S′* of free possible persons such that there is a balance of moral good over moral evil with respect to its members; and the members of *S′* produce ϕ moral evil.

Set *S* is evidently the instantiation of *S′* (i.e. every member of *S* is an instantiation of some member of *S′* and every member of *S′* is instantiated by some member of *S*); hence the members of *S* produce ϕ moral evil. Accordingly, (*b*), (*r*3) and (*r*4) jointly entail (*f*); but the conjunction of (*b*), (*r*3) and (*r*4) is consistent; hence (*b*) is consistent with (*f*).

III

The preceding discussion enables us to conclude, I believe, that the Free Will Defence succeeds in showing that there is no inconsistency in the assertion that God creates a universe containing as much moral evil as the universe in fact contains. There remains but one objection to be considered. McCloskey, Flew and others charge that the Free Will Defence, even if it is successful, accounts for only *part* of the evil we find; it accounts only for moral evil, leaving physical evil as intractable as before. The atheologian can therefore restate his position, maintaining that the existence of *physical evil*, evil which cannot be ascribed to the free actions of human beings, is inconsistent with the existence of an omniscient, omnipotent and all-good Deity.

To make this claim, however, is to overlook an important part of traditional theistic belief; it is part of much traditional belief to attribute a good deal of the evil we find to Satan, or to Satan and his cohorts. Satan, so the traditional doctrine goes, is a mighty non-human spirit, who, along with many other angels, was created long before God created men. Unlike most of his colleagues, Satan rebelled against God and has since been creating whatever havoc he could; the result, of course, is physical evil. But now we see that the moves available to the Free Will Defender in the case of moral evil are equally available to him in the case of physical evil. First he provides definitions of 'possible non-human spirit', 'free non-human spirit', etc., which exactly parallel their counterparts where it was moral evil that was at stake. Then he points out that it is logically possible that

(*r*5) God creates a set *S* of free non-human spirits such that the members of *S* do more good than evil,

and

(*r*6) there is exactly one co-possible set *S′* of possible free non-human spirits such that the members of *S′* do more good than evil,

and

(*r*7) all of the physical evil in the world is due to the actions of the members of *S*.

He points out further that (*r*5), (*r*6), and (*r*7) are jointly consistent and that their conjunction is consistent with the proposition that God is omnipotent, omniscient and all-good. But (*r*5) through (*r*7) jointly entail that God creates a universe containing as much physical evil as the universe in fact contains; it follows then, that the existence of physical evil is not inconsistent with the existence of an omniscient, omnipotent, all-good Deity.

Now it must be conceded that views involving devils and other non-human spirits do not at present enjoy either the extensive popularity or the high esteem of (say) the Theory of Relativity. Flew, for example, has this to say about the view in question:

To make this more than just another desperate *ad hoc* expedient of apologetic it is necessary to produce independent evidence for launching such an hypothesis (if 'hypothesis' is not too flattering a term for it).[1]

But in the present context this claim is surely incorrect; to rebut the charge of contradiction the theist need not hold that the hypothesis in question is probable or even true. He need hold only that it is not inconsistent with the proposition that God exists. Flew suspects that 'hypothesis' may be too flattering a term for the sort of view in question. Perhaps this suspicion reflects his doubts as to the meaningfulness of the proposed view. But it is hard to see how one could plausibly argue that the views in question are nonsensical (in the requisite sense) without invoking some version of the Verifiability Criterion, a doctrine whose harrowing vicissitudes are well known. Furthermore, it is likely that any premises worth considering which yield the conclusion that hypotheses about devils are nonsensical will yield the same conclusion about the hypothesis that God exists. And if *God exists* is nonsensical, then presumably theism is not self-contradictory after all.

We may therefore conclude that the Free Will Defence successfully rebuts the charge of contradiction brought against the theist. The Problem of Evil (if indeed evil constitutes a problem for the theist) does not lie in any inconsistency in the belief that God, who is omniscient, omnipotent and all-good, has created a world containing moral and physical evil.

[1] *Op. cit.*, p. 17.

XI

WHAT IS A SPEECH ACT?

by JOHN SEARLE

Associate Professor of Philosophy, University of California at Berkeley

I. INTRODUCTION

In a typical speech situation involving a speaker, a hearer, and an utterance by the speaker, there are many kinds of acts associated with the speaker's utterance. The speaker will characteristically have moved his jaw and tongue and made noises. In addition, he will characteristically have performed some acts within the class which includes informing or irritating or boring his hearers; he will further characteristically have performed acts within the class which includes referring to Kennedy or Khrushchev or the North Pole; and he will also have performed acts within the class which includes making statements, asking questions, issuing commands, giving reports, greeting, and warning. The members of this last class are what Austin[1] called illocutionary acts and it is with this class that I shall be concerned in this paper, so the paper might have been called 'What is an Illocutionary Act?' I do not attempt to define the expression 'illocutionary act', although if my analysis of a particular illocutionary act succeeds it may provide the basis for a definition. Some of the English verbs and verb phrases associated with illocutionary acts are: state, assert, describe, warn, remark, comment, command, order, request, criticize, apologize, censure, approve, welcome, promise, express approval, and express regret. Austin claimed that there were over a thousand such expressions in English.

By way of introduction, perhaps I can say why I think it is of interest and importance in the philosophy of language to study speech acts, or, as they are sometimes called, language acts or linguistic acts. I think it is essential to any specimen of linguistic communication that it involve a linguistic act. It is not, as has generally been supposed, the symbol or word or sentence, or even

[1] J. L. Austin, *How To Do Things With Words*, Oxford 1962.

the token of the symbol or word or sentence, which is the unit of linguistic communication, but rather it is the *production* of the token in the performance of the speech act that constitutes the basic unit of linguistic communication. To put this point more precisely, the production of the sentence token under certain conditions is the illocutionary act, and the illocutionary act is the minimal unit of linguistic communication.

I do not know how to *prove* that linguistic communication essentially involves acts but I can think of arguments with which one might attempt to convince someone who was sceptical. One argument would be to call the sceptic's attention to the fact that when he takes a noise or a mark on paper to be an instance of linguistic communication, as a message, one of the things that is involved in his so taking that noise or mark is that he should regard it as having been produced by a being with certain intentions. He cannot just regard it as a natural phenomenon, like a stone, a waterfall, or a tree. In order to regard it as an instance of linguistic communication one must suppose that its production is what I am calling a speech act. It is a logical presupposition, for example, of current attempts to decipher the Mayan hieroglyphs that we at least hypothesize that the marks we see on the stones were produced by beings more or less like ourselves and produced with certain kinds of intentions. If we were certain the marks were a consequence of, say, water erosion, then the question of deciphering them or even calling them hieroglyphs could not arise. To construe them under the category of linguistic communication necessarily involves construing their production as speech acts.

To perform illocutionary acts is to engage in a rule-governed form of behaviour. I shall argue that such things as asking questions or making statements are rule-governed in ways quite similar to those in which getting a base hit in baseball or moving a knight in chess are rule-governed forms of acts. I intend therefore to explicate the notion of an illocutionary act by stating a set of necessary and sufficient conditions for the performance of a particular kind of illocutionary act, and extracting from it a set of semantical rules for the use of the expression (or syntactic device) which marks the utterance as an illocutionary act of that kind. If I am successful in stating the conditions and the corresponding rules for even one kind of illocutionary act, that will provide us with a pattern for analysing other kinds of acts and consequently for explicating the notion in general. But in order to set the stage for actually stating conditions and extracting rules for performing an illocutionary act I have to discuss three other preliminary notions: *rules*, *propositions*, and *meaning*. I shall confine my discussion of these notions to those aspects which are essential to my main purposes in this paper, but, even so, what I wish to say concerning each of these notions, if it were to be at all complete, would require a paper for each; however, sometimes it may be worth sacrificing thoroughness for the sake of scope and I shall therefore be very brief.

II. RULES

In recent years there has been in the philosophy of language considerable discussion involving the notion of rules for the use of expressions. Some philosophers have even said that knowing the meaning of a word is simply a matter of knowing the rules for its use or employment. One disquieting feature of such discussions is that no philosopher, to my knowledge at least, has ever given anything like an adequate formulation of the rules for the use of even one expression. If meaning is a matter of rules of use, surely we ought to be able to state the rules for the use of expressions in a way which would explicate the meaning of those expressions. Certain other philosophers, dismayed perhaps by the failure of their colleagues to produce any rules, have denied the fashionable view that meaning is a matter of rules and have asserted that there are no semantical rules of the proposed kind at all. I am inclined to think that this scepticism is premature and stems from a failure to distinguish different sorts of rules, in a way which I shall now attempt to explain.

I distinguish between two sorts of rules: Some regulate antecedently existing forms of behaviour; for example, the rules of etiquette regulate interpersonal relationships, but these relationships exist independently of the rules of etiquette. Some rules on the other hand do not merely regulate but create or define new forms of behaviour. The rules of football, for example, do not merely regulate the game of football but as it were create the possibility of or define that activity. The activity of playing football is constituted by acting in accordance with these rules; football has no existence apart from these rules. I call the latter kind of rules constitutive rules and the former kind regulative rules. Regulative rules regulate a pre-existing activity, an activity whose existence is logically independent of the existence of the rules. Constitutive rules constitute (and also regulate) an activity the existence of which is logically dependent on the rules.[1]

Regulative rules characteristically take the form of or can be paraphrased as imperatives, e.g. 'When cutting food hold the knife in the right hand', or 'Officers are to wear ties at dinner'. Some constitutive rules take quite a different form, e.g. a checkmate is made if the king is attacked in such a way that no move will leave it unattacked; a touchdown is scored when a player crosses the opponents' goal line in possession of the ball while a play is in progress. If our paradigms of rules are imperative regulative rules, such non-imperative constitutive rules are likely to strike us as extremely curious and hardly even as rules at all. Notice that they are almost tautological in character, for what the 'rule' seems to offer is a partial definition of 'checkmate' or 'touchdown'. But, of course, this quasi-tautological character is a necessary consequence of their being constitutive rules: the rules concerning touchdowns must define the notion of 'touchdown' in the same way that the rules concerning football define 'football'. That, for example, a touchdown can be scored in such and such ways and counts six points can appear sometimes as a rule, sometimes as an analytic truth; and that it can be construed as a tautology is a clue to the fact that the rule in question is a constitutive one. Regulative rules generally have the form 'Do *X*' or 'If *Y* do *X*'. Some members of the set of constitutive rules have this form but some also have the form '*X* counts as *Y*'.[2]

The failure to perceive this is of some importance in philosophy. Thus, e.g., some philosophers ask 'How can a promise create an obligation?' A similar question would be 'How can a touchdown create six points?' And as they stand both questions can only be answered by stating a rule of the form '*X* counts as *Y*'.

I am inclined to think that both the failure of some philosophers to state rules for the use of expressions and the scepticism of other philosophers concerning the existence of any such rules stem at

[1] This distinction occurs in J. Rawls, "Two Concepts of Rules', *Philosophical Review*, 1955, and J. R. Searle, 'How to Derive "Ought" from "Is" ', *Philosophical Review*, 1964.

[2] The formulation '*X* counts as *Y*' was originally suggested to me by Max Black.

least in part from a failure to recognize the distinctions between constitutive and regulative rules. The model or paradigm of a rule which most philosophers have is that of a regulative rule, and if one looks in semantics for purely regulative rules one is not likely to find anything interesting from the point of view of logical analysis. There are no doubt social rules of the form 'One ought not to utter obscenities at formal gatherings', but that hardly seems a rule of the sort that is crucial in explicating the semantics of a language. The hypothesis that lies behind the present paper is that the semantics of a language can be regarded as a series of systems of constitutive rules and that illocutionary acts are acts performed in accordance with these sets of constitutive rules. One of the aims of this paper is to formulate a set of constitutive rules for a certain kind of speech act. And if what I have said concerning constitutive rules is correct, we should not be surprised if not all these rules take the form of imperative rules. Indeed we shall see that the rules fall into several different categories, none of which is quite like the rules of etiquette. The effort to state the rules for an illocutionary act can also be regarded as a kind of test of the hypothesis that there are constitutive rules underlying speech acts. If we are unable to give any satisfactory rule formulations, our failure could be construed as partially disconfirming evidence against the hypothesis.

III. PROPOSITIONS

Different illocutionary acts often have features in common with each other. Consider utterances of the following sentences:

(1) Will John leave the room?
(2) John will leave the room.
(3) John, leave the room!
(4) Would that John left the room.
(5) If John will leave the room, I will leave also.

Utterances of each of these on a given occasion would characteristically be performances of different illocutionary acts. The first would, characteristically, be a question, the second an assertion about the future, that is, a prediction, the third a request or order, the fourth an expression of a wish, and the fifth a hypothetical expression of intention. Yet in the performance of each the speaker would characteristically perform some subsidiary acts which are common to all five illocutionary acts. In the utterance of each the speaker *refers* to a particular person John and *predicates* the act of leaving the room of that person. In no case is that all he does, but in every case it is a part of what he does. I shall say, therefore, that in each of these cases, although the illocutionary acts are different, at least some of the non-illocutionary acts of reference and predication are the same.

The reference to some person John and predication of the same thing of him in each of these illocutionary acts inclines me to say that there is a common *content* in each of them. Something expressible by the clause 'that John will leave the room' seems to be a common feature of all. We could, with not too much distortion, write each of these sentences in a way which would isolate this common feature: 'I assert that John will leave the room', 'I ask whether John will leave the room', etc.

For lack of a better word I propose to call this common content a proposition, and I shall describe this feature of these illocutionary acts by saying that in the utterance of each of (1)–(5) the speaker expresses the proposition that John will leave the room. Notice that I do not say that the sentence expresses the proposition; I do not know how sentences could perform acts of that kind. But I shall say that in the utterance of the sentence the speaker expresses a proposition. Notice also that I am distinguishing between a proposition and an assertion or statement of that proposition. The proposition that John will leave the room is expressed in the utterance of all of (1)–(5) but only in (2) is that proposition asserted. An assertion is an illocutionary act, but a proposition is not an act at all, although the act of expressing a proposition is a part of performing certain illocutionary acts.

I might summarise this by saying that I am distinguishing between the illocutionary act and the propositional content of an illocutionary act. Of course, not all illocutionary acts have a posititional content, for example, an utterance of 'Hurrah!' or 'Ouch!' does not. In one version or another this distinction is an old one and has been marked in different ways by authors as diverse as Frege, Sheffer, Lewis, Reichenbach and Hare, to mention only a few.

From a semantical point of view we can distinguish between the propositional indicator in the sentence and the indicator of illocutionary force. That is, for a large class of sentences used to perform illocutionary acts, we can say for the purpose of our analysis that the sentence has two (not necessarily separate) parts, the proposition indicating element and the function indicating device.[1] The function indicating device shows how the proposition is to be taken, or, to put it in another way, what illocutionary force the utterance is to have, that is, what illocutionary act the speaker is performing in the utterance of the sentence. Function indicating devices in English include word order, stress, intonation contour, punctuation, the mood of the verb, and finally a set of so-called performative verbs: I may indicate the kind of illocutionary act I am performing by beginning the sentence with 'I apologize', 'I warn', 'I state', etc. Often in actual speech situations the context will make it clear what the illocutionary force of the utterance is, without its being necessary to invoke the appropriate function indicating device.

If this semantical distinction is of any real importance, it seems likely that it should have some syntactical analogue, and certain recent developments in transformational grammar tend to support the view that it does. In the underlying phrase marker of a sentence there is a distinction between those elements which correspond to the function indicating device and those which correspond to the propositional content.

The distinction between the function indicating device and the proposition indicating device will prove very useful to us in giving an analysis of an illocutionary act. Since the same proposition can be common to all sorts of illocutionary acts, we can separate our analysis of the proposition from our analysis of kinds of illocutionary acts. I think there are rules for expressing propositions, rules for such things as reference and predication, but those rules can be discussed independently of the rules for function indicating. In this paper I shall not attempt to discuss propositional rules but shall concentrate on rules for using certain kinds of function indicating devices.

[1] In the sentence 'I promise that I will come' the function indicating device and the propositional element are separate. In the sentence 'I promise to come', which means the same as the first and is derived from it by certain transformations, the two elements are not separate.

IV. MEANING

Speech acts are characteristically performed in the utterance of sounds or the making or marks. What is the difference between *just* uttering sounds or making marks and performing a speech act? One difference is that the sounds or marks one makes in the performance of a speech act are characteristically said to *have meaning*, and a second related difference is that one is characteristically said to *mean something* by those sounds or marks. Characteristically when one speaks one means something by what one says, and what one says, the string of morphemes that one emits, is characteristically said to have a meaning. Here, incidentally, is another point at which our analogy between performing speech acts and playing games breaks down. The pieces in a game like chess are not characteristically said to have a meaning, and furthermore when one makes a move one is not characteristically said to mean anything by that move.

But what is it for one to mean something by what one says, and what is it for something to have a meaning? To answer the first of these questions I propose to borrow and revise some ideas of Paul Grice. In an article entitled 'Meaning',[1] Grice gives the following analysis of one sense of the notion of 'meaning'. To say that *A* meant something by *x* is to say that '*A* intended the utterance of *x* to produce some effect in an audience by means of the recognition of this intention'. This seems to me a useful start on an analysis of meaning, first because it shows the close relationship between the notion of meaning and the notion of intention, and secondly because it captures something which is, I think, essential to speaking a language: In speaking a language I attempt to communicate things to my hearer by means of getting him to recognize my intention to communicate just those things. For example, characteristically, when I make an assertion, I attempt to communicate to and convince my hearer of the truth of a certain proposition; and the means I employ to do this are to utter certain sounds, which utterance I intend to produce in him the desired effect by means of his recognition of my intention to produce just that effect. I shall illustrate this with an example. I might on the one hand attempt to get you to believe that I am French by speaking French all the time, dressing in the French manner, showing wild

[1] *Philosophical Review*, 1957.

enthusiasm for de Gaulle, and cultivating French acquaintances. But I might on the other hand attempt to get you to believe that I am French by simply telling you that I am French. Now, what is the difference between these two ways of my attempting to get you to believe that I am French? One crucial difference is that in the second case I attempt to get you to believe that I am French by getting you to recognize that it is my purported intention to get you to believe just that. That is one of the things involved in telling you that I am French. But of course if I try to get you to believe that I am French by putting on the act I described, then your recognition of my intention to produce in you the belief that I am French is not the means I am employing. Indeed in this case you would, I think, become rather suspicious if you recognized my intention.

However valuable this analysis of meaning is, it seems to me to be in certain respects defective. First of all, it fails to distinguish the different kinds of effects—perlocutionary versus illocutionary—that one may intend to produce in one's hearers, and it further fails to show the way in which these different kinds of effects are related to the notion of meaning. A second defect is that it fails to account for the extent to which meaning is a matter of rules or conventions. That is, this account of meaning does not show the connection between one's meaning something by what one says and what that which one says actually means in the language. In order to illustrate this point I now wish to present a counter-example to this analysis of meaning. The point of the counter-example will be to illustrate the connection between what a speaker means and what the words he utters mean.

Suppose that I am an American soldier in the Second World War and that I am captured by Italian troops. And suppose also that I wish to get these troops to believe that I am a German officer in order to get them to release me. What I would like to do is to tell them in German or Italian that I am a German officer. But let us suppose I don't know enough German or Italian to do that. So I, as it were, attempt to put on a show of telling them that I am a German officer by reciting those few bits of German that I know, trusting that they don't know enough German to see through my plan. Let us suppose I know only one line of German, which I remember from a poem I had to memorize in a high school German course. Therefore I, a captured American, address my

Italian captors with the following sentence: 'Kennst du das Land, wo die Zitronen blühen?' Now, let us describe the situation in Gricean terms. I intend to produce a certain effect in them, namely, the effect of believing that I am a German officer; and I intend to produce this effect by means of their recognition of my intention. I intend that they should think that I am trying to tell them is that I am a German officer. But does it follow from this account that when I say 'Kennst du das Land . . .' etc., what I mean is, 'I am a German officer'? Not only does it not follow, but in this case it seems plainly false that when I utter the German sentence what I mean is 'I am a German officer', or even 'Ich bin ein deutscher Offizier', because what the words mean is, 'Knowest thou the land where the lemon trees bloom?' Of course, I want my captors to be deceived into thinking that what I mean is 'I am a German officer', but part of what is involved in the deception is getting them to think that that is what the words which I utter mean in German. At one point in the *Philosophical Investigations* Wittgenstein says 'Say "it's cold here" and mean "it's warm here" '.[1] The reason we are unable to do this is that what we can mean is a function of what we are saying. Meaning is more than a matter of intention, it is also a matter of convention.

Grice's account can be amended to deal with counter-examples of this kind. We have here a case where I am trying to produce a certain effect by means of the recognition of my intention to produce that effect, but the device I use to produce this effect is one which is conventionally, by the rules governing the use of that device, used as a means of producing quite different illocutionary effects. We must therefore reformulate the Gricean account of meaning in such a way as to make it clear that one's meaning something when one says something is more than just contingently related to what the sentence means in the language one is speaking. In our analysis of illocutionary acts, we must capture both the intentional and the conventional aspects and especially the relationship between them. In the performance of an illocutionary act the speaker intends to produce a certain effect by means of getting the hearer to recognize his intention to produce that effect, and furthermore, if he is using words literally, he intends this recognition to be achieved in virtue of the fact that the rules for using the expressions he utters associate the expressions with the production of that

[1] *Philosophical Investigations*, Oxford 1953, para. 510.

effect. It is this *combination* of elements which we shall need to express in our analysis of the illocutionary act.

V. HOW TO PROMISE

I shall now attempt to give an analysis of the illocutionary act of promising. In order to do this I shall ask what conditions are necessary and sufficient for the act of promising to have been performed in the utterance of a given sentence. I shall attempt to answer this question by stating these conditions as a set of propositions such that the conjunction of the members of the set entails the proposition that a speaker made a promise, and the proposition that the speaker made a promise entails this conjunction. Thus each condition will be a necessary condition for the performance of the act of promising, and taken collectively the set of conditions will be a sufficient condition for the act to have been performed.

If we get such a set of conditions we can extract from them a set of rules for the use of the function indicating device. The method here is analogous to discovering the rules of chess by asking oneself what are the necessary and sufficient conditions under which one can be said to have correctly moved a knight or castled or checkmated a player, etc. We are in the position of someone who has learned to play chess without ever having the rules formulated and who wants such a formulation. We learned how to play the game of illocutionary acts, but in general it was done without an explicit formulation of the rules, and the first step in getting such a formulation is to set out the conditions for the performance of a particular illocutionary act. Our inquiry will therefore serve a double philosophical purpose. By stating a set of conditions for the performance of a particular illocutionary act we shall have offered a partial explication of that notion and shall also have paved the way for the second step, the formulation of the rules.

I find the statement of the conditions very difficult to do, and I am not entirely satisfied with the list I am about to present. One reason for the difficulty is that the notion of a promise, like most notions in ordinary language, does not have absolutely strict rules. There are all sorts of odd, deviant, and borderline promises; and counter-examples, more or less bizarre, can be produced against my analysis. I am inclined to think we shall not be able to get a set of knock down necessary and sufficient conditions that will exactly mirror the ordinary use of the word 'promise'. I am confining my discussion, therefore, to the centre of the concept of promising and ignoring the fringe, borderline, and partially defective cases. I also confine my discussion to full-blown explicit promises and ignore promises made by elliptical turns of phrase, hints, metaphors, etc.

Another difficulty arises from my desire to state the conditions without certain forms of circularity. I want to give a list of conditions for the performance of a certain illocutionary act, which do not themselves mention the performance of any illocutionary acts. I need to satisfy this condition in order to offer an explication of the notion of an illocutionary act in general, otherwise I should simply be showing the relation between different illocutionary acts. However, although there will be no reference to illocutionary *acts*, certain illocutionary *concepts* will appear in the analysans as well as in the analysandum; and I think this form of circularity is unavoidable because of the nature of constitutive rules.

In the presentation of the conditions I shall first consider the case of a sincere promise and then show how to modify the conditions to allow for insincere promises. As our inquiry is semantical rather than syntactical, I shall simply assume the existence of grammatically well-formed sentences.

Given that a speaker *S* utters a sentence *T* in the presence of a hearer *H*, then, in the utterance of *T*, *S* sincerely (and non-defectively) promises that *p* to *H* if and only if:

(1) *Normal Input and Output Conditions obtain.*

I use the terms 'input' and 'output' to cover the large and indefinite range of conditions under which any kind of serious linguistic communication is possible. 'Output' covers the conditions for intelligible speaking and 'input' covers the conditions for understanding. Together they include such things as that the speaker and hearer both know how to speak the language; both are conscious of what they are doing; the speaker is not acting under duress or threats; they have no physical impediments to communication, such as deafness, aphasia, or laryngitis; they are not acting in a play or telling jokes, etc.

(2) *S expresses that p in the utterance of T.*

This condition isolates the propositional content from the rest of the speech act and enables us to concentrate on the peculiarities of promising in the rest of the analysis.

(3) *In expressing that p, S predicates a future act A of S.*

In the case of promising the function indicating device is an expression whose scope includes certain features of the proposition. In a promise an act must be predicated of the speaker and it cannot be a past act. I cannot promise to have done something, and I cannot promise that someone else will do something. (Although I can promise to see that he will do it.) The notion of an act, as I am construing it for present purposes, includes refraining from acts, performing series of acts, and may also include states and conditions: I may promise not to do something, I may promise to do something repeatedly, and I may promise to be or remain in a certain state or condition. I call conditions (2) and (3) the *propositional content conditions.*

(4) *H would prefer S's doing A to his not doing A, and S believes H would prefer his doing A to his not doing A.*

One crucial distinction between promises on the one hand and threats on the other is that a promise is a pledge to do something for you, not to you, but a threat is a pledge to do something to you, not for you. A promise is defective if the thing promised is something the promisee does not want done; and it is further defective if the promisor does not believe the promisee wants it done, since a non-defective promise must be intended as a promise and not as a threat or warning. I think both halves of this double condition are necessary in order to avoid fairly obvious counter-examples.

One can, however, think of apparent counter-examples to this condition as stated. Suppose I say to a lazy student 'If you don't hand in your paper on time I promise you I will give you a failing grade in the course'. Is this utterance a promise? I am inclined to think not; we would more naturally describe it as a warning or possibly even a threat. But why then is it possible to use the locution 'I promise' in such a case? I think we use it here because 'I promise' and 'I hereby promise' are among the strongest function indicating devices for *commitment* provided by the English language. For that reason we often use these expressions in the performance of speech acts which are not strictly speaking promises but in which we wish to emphasize our commitment. To illustrate this, consider another apparent counter-example to the analysis along different lines. Sometimes, more commonly I think in the United States than in England, one hears people say 'I promise' when making an emphatic assertion. Suppose, for example, I accuse you of having stolen the money. I say, 'You stole that money, didn't you?' You reply 'No, I didn't, I promise you I didn't'. Did you make a promise in this case? I find it very unnatural to describe your utterance as a promise. This utterance would be more aptly described as an emphatic denial, and we can explain the occurrence of the function indicating device 'I promise' as derivative from genuine promises and serving here as an expression adding emphasis to your denial.

In general the point stated in condition (4) is that if a purported promise is to be non-defective the thing promised must be something the hearer wants done, or considers to be in his interest, or would prefer being done to not being done, etc.; and the speaker must be aware of or believe or know, etc. that this is the case. I think a more elegant and exact formulation of this condition would require the introduction of technical terminology.

(5) *It is not obvious to both S and H that S will do A in the normal course of events.*

This condition is an instance of a general condition on many different kinds of illocutionary acts to the effect that the act must have a point. For example, if I make a request to someone to do something which it is obvious that he is already doing or is about to do, then my request is pointless and to that extent defective. In an actual speech situation, listeners, knowing the rules for performing illocutionary acts, will assume that this condition is satisfied. Suppose, for example, that in the course of a public speech I say to a member of my audience 'Look here, Smith, pay attention to what I am saying'. In order to make sense of this utterance the audience will have to assume that Smith has not been paying attention or at any rate that it is not obvious that he has been paying attention, that the question of his paying attention has arisen in some way; because a condition for making a request is that it is not obvious that the hearer is doing or about to do the thing requested.

Similarly with promises. It is out of order for me to promise to do something that it is obvious I am going to do anyhow. If I do seem to be making such a promise, the only way my audience can make sense of my utterance is to assume that I believe that it is not obvious that I am going to do the thing promised. A happily married man who promises his wife he will not desert her in the next week is likely to provide more anxiety than comfort.

Parenthetically I think this condition is an instance of the sort of phenomenon stated in Zipf's law. I think there is operating in our language, as in most forms of human behaviour, a principle of least effort, in this case a principle of maximum illocutionary ends with minimum phonetic effort; and I think condition (5) is an instance of it.

I call conditions such as (4) and (5) *preparatory conditions*. They are *sine quibus non* of happy promising, but they do not yet state the essential feature.

(6) *S intends to do A.*

The most important distinction between sincere and insincere promises is that in the case of the insincere promise the speaker intends to do the act promised, in the case of the insincere promise he does not intend to do the act. Also in sincere promises the speaker believes it is possible for him to do the act (or to refrain from doing it), but I think the proposition that he intends to do it entails that he thinks it is possible to do (or refrain from doing) it, so I am not stating that as an extra condition. I call this condition the *sincerity condition*.

(7) *S intends that the utterance of T will place him under an obligation to do A.*

The essential feature of a promise is that it is the undertaking of an obligation to perform a certain act. I think that this condition distinguishes promises (and other members of the same family such as vows) from other kinds of speech acts. Notice that in the statement of the condition we only specify the speaker's intention; further conditions will make clear how that intention is realized. It is clear, however, that having this intention is a necessary condition of making a promise; for if a speaker can demonstrate that he did not have this intention in a given utterance, he can prove that the utterance was not a promise. We know, for example, that Mr Pickwick did not promise to marry the woman because we know he did not have the appropriate intention.

I call this the *essential condition.*

(8) *S intends that the utterance of T will produce in H a belief that conditions* (6) *and* (7) *obtain by means of the recognition of the intention to produce that belief, and he intends this recognition to be achieved by means of the recognition of the sentence as one conventionally used to produce such beliefs.*

This captures our amended Gricean analysis of what it is for the speaker to mean to make a promise. The speaker intends to produce a certain illocutionary effect by means of getting the hearer to recognize his intention to produce that effect, and he also intends this recognition to be achieved in virtue of the fact that the lexical and syntactical character of the item he utters conventionally associates it with producing that effect.

Strictly speaking this condition could be formulated as part of condition (1), but it is of enough philosophical interest to be worth stating separately. I find it troublesome for the following reason. If my original objection to Grice is really valid, then surely, one might say, all these iterated intentions are superfluous; all that is necessary is that the speaker should seriously utter a sentence. The production of all these effects is simply a consequence of the hearer's knowledge of what the sentence means, which in turn is a consequence of his knowledge of the language, which is assumed by the speaker at the outset. I think the correct reply to this objection is that condition (8) explicates what it is for the speaker to 'seriously' utter the sentence, i.e. to utter it and mean it, but I am not completely confident about either the force of the objection or of the reply.

(9) *The semantical rules of the dialect spoken by S and H are such that T is correctly and sincerely uttered if and only if conditions* (1)–(8) *obtain.*

This condition is intended to make clear that the sentence uttered is one which by the semantical rules of the language is used to make a promise. Taken together with condition (8), it eliminates counter-examples like the captured soldier example considered earlier. Exactly what the formulation of the rules is, we shall soon see.

So far we have considered only the case of a sincere promise. But insincere promises are promises nonetheless, and we now need to show how to modify the conditions to allow for them. In making an insincere promise the speaker does not have all the intentions and beliefs he has when making a sincere promise. However, he purports to have them. Indeed it is because he purports to have intentions and beliefs which he does not have that we describe his act as insincere. So to allow for insincere promises we need only to revise our conditions to state that the speaker takes responsibility for having the beliefs and intentions rather than stating that he actually has them. A clue that the speaker does take such responsibility is the fact that he could not say without absurdity, e.g. 'I promise to do *A* but I do not intend to do *A*'. To say 'I promise to do *A*' is to take responsibility for intending to do *A*, and this condition holds whether the utterance was sincere or insincere. To allow for the possibility of an insincere promise then we have only to revise condition (6) so that it states not that the speaker intends to do *A*, but that he takes responsibility for intending to do *A*, and to avoid the charge of circularity I shall phrase this as follows:

(6*) *S intends that the utterance of T will make him responsible for intending to do A.*

Thus amended (and with 'sincerely' dropped from our analysandum and from condition (9)), our analysis is neutral on the question whether the promise was sincere or insincere.

VI. RULES FOR THE USE OF THE FUNCTION INDICATING DEVICE

Our next task is to extract from our set of conditions a set of rules for the use of the function indicating device. Obviously not all of our conditions are equally relevant to this task. Condition (1) and conditions of the forms (8) and (9) apply generally to all kinds of normal illocutionary acts and are not peculiar to promising. Rules for the function indicating device for promising are to be found corresponding to conditions (2)–(7).

The semantical rules for the use of any function indicating device *P* for promising are:

Rule 1. *P* is to be uttered only in the context of a sentence (or larger stretch of discourse) the utterance of which predicates some future act *A* of the speaker *S*.
I call this the *propositional content rule*. It is derived from the propositional content conditions (2) and (3).

Rule 2. *P* is to be uttered only if the hearer *H* would prefer *S*'s doing *A* to his not doing *A*, and *S* believes *H* would prefer *S*'s doing *A* to his not doing *A*.

Rule 3. *P* is to be uttered only if it is not obvious to both *S* and *H* that *S* will do *A* in the normal course of events.
I call rules (2) and (3) *preparatory rules*. They are derived from the preparatory conditions (4) and (5).

Rule 4. *P* is to be uttered only if *S* intends to do *A*.
I call this the *sincerity rule*. It is derived from the sincerity condition (6).

Rule 5. The utterance of *P* counts as the undertaking of an obligation to do *A*.
I call this the *essential rule*.

These rules are ordered: Rules 2–5 apply only if Rule 1 is satisfied, and Rule 5 applies only if Rules 2 and 3 are satisfied as well.

Notice that whereas rules 1–4 take the form of quasi-imperatives, i.e. they are of the form: utter *P* only if *x*, rule 5 is of the form: the utterance of *P* counts as *Y*. Thus rule 5 is of the kind peculiar to systems of constitutive rules which I discussed in section II.

Notice also that the rather tiresome analogy with games is holding up remarkably well. If we ask ourselves under what conditions a player could be said to move a knight correctly, we would find preparatory conditions, such as that it must be his turn to move, as well as the essential condition stating the actual positions the knight can move to. I think that there is even a sincerity rule for competitive games, the rule that each side tries to win. I suggest that the team which 'throws' the game is behaving in a way closely analogous to the speaker who lies or makes false promises. Of course, there usually are no propositional content rules for games, because games do not, by and large, represent states of affairs.

If this analysis is of any general interest beyond the case of promising then it would seem that these distinctions should carry over into other types of speech act, and I think a little reflection will show that they do. Consider, e.g., giving an order. The preparatory conditions include that the speaker should be in a position of authority over the hearer, the sincerity condition is that the speaker wants the ordered act done, and the essential condition has to do with the fact that the utterance is an attempt to get the hearer to do it. For assertions, the preparatory conditions include the fact that the hearer must have some basis for supposing the asserted proposition is true, the sincerity condition is that he must believe it to be true, and the essential condition has to do with the fact that the utterance is an attempt to inform the hearer and convince him of its truth. Greetings are a much simpler kind of speech act, but even here some of the distinctions apply. In the utterance of 'Hello' there is no propositional content and no sincerity condition. The preparatory condition is that the speaker must have just encountered the hearer, and the essential rule is that the utterance indicates courteous recognition of the hearer.

A proposal for further research then is to carry out a similar analysis of other types of speech acts. Not only would this give us an analysis of concepts interesting in themselves, but the comparison of different analyses would deepen our understanding of the whole subject and incidentally provide a basis for a more serious taxonomy than any of the usual facile categories such as evaluative versus descriptive, or cognitive versus emotive.

XII

QUANTUM PHYSICS AND THE PHILOSOPHY OF WHITEHEAD

by ABNER SHIMONY

Associate Professor of the Philosophy of Science
Massachusetts Institute of Technology

I. INTRODUCTION

One of the virtues which Whitehead claims for his philosophy of organism is that it provides a conceptual framework for quantum theory (*SMW* chapter 8, *PR* 121–2 and 145).[1] The theory which he has in mind is the 'old' quantum theory, consisting of the hypotheses of Planck (1901) and of Einstein (1905) that electromagnetic energy is emitted and absorbed in quanta, together with Bohr's model of the atom (1913) in which discontinuous transitions were supposed to occur between discrete electronic orbits. The philosophy of organism was presented in a preliminary form in the Lowell Lectures of 1925 (published in the same year as *SMW*) and in its most systematic form in the Gifford Lectures of 1927–8 (published as *PR* in 1929). It was during the years 1924–28 that De Broglie, Schrödinger, Heisenberg, Born, Jordan, Bohr, Dirac, and others developed the 'new' quantum theory, which was more systematic than the old, much more successful in its predictions, and more revolutionary in its departures from classical physics. Whitehead never refers to the new quantum theory,[2] and it would be unreasonable to expect that even so imaginative a philosopher and scientist could have anticipated it except in the most general terms. Nevertheless, it is important in evaluating the philosophy of organism to determine how well its physical implications agree with quantum theory and with contemporary microphysical theory

[1] The abbreviations of the titles of Whitehead's works and the editions to which the page numbers refer are as follows:

SMW *Science and the Modern World* (New York: Macmillan 1925).
PR *Process and Reality* (New York: Macmillan 1929).
AI *Adventures of Ideas* (New York: Macmillan 1933).

[2] Hereafter the qualification 'new' will be omitted.

in general. To do this is the primary purpose of the present essay. It will appear that the agreement is only partial and that there are several crucial discrepancies both in detailed predictions and in general spirit.

The second purpose of this essay is to suggest the possibility of a modified philosophy of organism, which would preserve Whitehead's essential ideas while according with the discoveries of modern physics. This is a very ambitious programme, and only a few tentative speculations on how one might proceed will be presented. It is, furthermore, a somewhat hazardous programme, for one can cite many examples in the history of thought of philosophical schemes which attempted to conform to current science but succeeded only in amplifying scientific error. One can but hope that the comparison of quantum theory with a philosophical system of such great scope as Whitehead's will not only improve the philosophical system, but will throw light upon some of the conceptual difficulties in modern physics.

II. IMPLICATIONS OF THE PHILOSOPHY OF ORGANISM FOR MICROPHYSICS

In *SMW* Whitehead criticizes classical physics for supposing that there exist material entities without any intrinsic mental characteristics, and for supposing that these entities are simply located, i.e. '*here* in space and *here* in time, or *here* in space-time, in a perfectly definite sense which does not require for its explanation any reference to other regions of space-time' (*SMW* 72). Both of these suppositions, he claims, are instances of the 'fallacy of misplaced concreteness', which consists in regarding abstract characteristics of things as their complete and concrete natures. The philosophy of organism, which is an attempt to avoid misplaced concreteness, requires a radically different conception of physical reality from that of classical materialism. In this Section some propositions of 'Whiteheadian physics' (omitting relativity theory) will be listed, partly on the basis of Whitehead's explicit remarks and partly by inference. For this purpose, the following theses of the philosophy of organism are relevant.[1]

[1] Except for thesis (5), for which a special reference is given, these theses are selected from the 'categories of explanation' and 'categoreal obligations' (PR 33–41) with much condensation, rearrangement, and simplification.

(1) The ultimate concrete objects in the universe[1] are the 'actual occasions', each of which has proto-mental characteristics and can be characterized as a unit of experience. The word 'experience' is obscure, and various of Whitehead's statements have the effect of postulating that the word may be applied to entities usually considered to be inorganic, without entirely vitiating its ordinary intension.

(2) Every actual occasion is distinguishable from every other in virtue of its intrinsic character and not merely because of its external relations to the rest of the world.

(3) An actual occasion 'prehends' each occasion antecedent to it, i.e. it recognizes the experience of the antecedent occasions in qualitative detail, though with loss of immediacy and shift of emphasis. It is the relation of prehension which prevents actual occasions from being simply located (cf. *PR* 208).

(4) The temporal duration of an actual occasion is finite, and even though phases of the becoming of an occasion can be distinguished, each phase is only derivatively real and is incomplete without reference to the entire occasion.

(5) Each actual occasion occupies a definite spatial region and is indefinitely divisible, but the parts have only derivative reality relative to the whole occasion (*PR* 434–5).

(6) The total set of prehensions of antecedent occasions by an occasion in process of becoming does not suffice to determine that process in all its details. There is, thus, an element of freedom in the process, negligible in low-order occasions but permitting radical novelty in those of higher order.

The foregoing fragment of Whitehead's philosophy not only contains implicitly most of his views on physics, but also contains his explanation of the existence of the subject-matter for special sciences such as physics. Most occasions are almost entirely constituted by their prehensions of antecedent occasions, since spontaneity and originality are usually negligible. As a result, the world, or at least that part of it contained in our 'cosmic epoch', is populated largely by 'enduring objects'. An enduring object is a temporally ordered chain of actual occasions, all sharing a common defining characteristic and sharing it because it is the dominant element in the prehensions of each successive occasion in the chain. Thus the

[1] The one exception to this statement is the actual entity God, who shares some but not all of the characteristics of the actual occasions.

enduring object is, in a sense, self-sustaining. Even in a heterogeneous society of occasions there may be characteristics common to all or nearly all members, so that the prehensions of new occasions will be virtually uniform in certain respects and the common characteristics will tend to persist. Conformity to a basic law of physics is an outstanding example of a persistent set of characteristics in a heterogeneous society. Special laws, such as those of biology, may hold in sub-societies of the vast society governed by the basic physical laws. The special laws may not be derivable from the more basic laws, and yet they may presuppose the order established by the latter. Similarly, the basic laws governing a heterogeneous society determine its tolerance for various kinds of simple enduring objects, with the result that the number of species of elementary particles may be small, although the number of exemplars of each may be enormous. (Cf. *AI* 257 and 264, *PR* 138–140.)

It follows from Whitehead's view of the nature of physical laws that they cannot be derived from his philosophical first principles. In fact, since he supposes that the propagation of dominant characteristics in a society is subject to lapses, he infers that the type of order expressed by physical laws may decay or change. Nevertheless, Whitehead's philosophical principles do seem to have at least the following physical consequences, which would presumably be valid in any cosmic epoch.

(i) Even though physics abstracts from the detailed content of an actual occasion, it cannot overlook the spatial and temporal extendedness of occasions. *Hence, the most direct microphysical consequence of Whitehead's scheme is atomicity.* Thus, the physical fact that energy is transferred in quanta follows from the supposition that 'physical energy . . . must then be conceived as an abstraction from the complex energy, emotional and purposeful, inherent in the subjective form of the final synthesis in which each occasion completes itself' (*AI* 239), in conjunction with the thesis that the actual occasion is an extended atom of experience. Furthermore, there must be a temporal atomicity in physical processes, since the individual actual occasion is not divisible into concrete events, one of which is earlier than the other (*PR* 107). Whitehead seems to believe that from the fundamental atomicity of actual occasions there follow other types of physical atomicity—e.g. the integral character of elementary particles and the indivisibility of electric charge into units smaller than the charge of the electron—but he is vague on this point.[1] One would also expect him to claim that the elementary particles of physics exhibit spatial extendedness in spite of their integral character, since each occasion constituting a link in the career of a particle has an internal spatial structure. Whitehead does not make such a claim explicitly, but perhaps it is implicit in his discussion of 'vibratory organic deformations' of a proton (*SMW* 195).

(ii) *Elementary particles should be capable of creation and destruction.* According to Whitehead an elementary particle is an especially simple kind of enduring object, and the continuation of any enduring object depends upon the degree to which each new occasion in the appropriate neighbourhood will re-enact the experience of earlier occasions. Since the experience of a new occasion is partially coloured by prehensions of other occasions than those constituting the enduring object, as well as by exercise of its intrinsic spontaneity, the elementary particle will almost certainly end after a finite number of links. An inverse argument explains how an elementary particle can be initiated.

(iii) *A consequence of atomicity, according to Whitehead, is the association of some sort of vibratory motion with all elementary particles.* An elementary particle is a chain of occasions, all having nearly the same internal development, so that the particle has a definite periodic structure with a definite frequency. It is clear, however, that Whitehead conceives of waves as more generic than particles, for particles always exhibit some characteristics of waves but not conversely. Thus:

the doctrine, here explained, conciliates Newton's corpuscular theory of light with the wave theory. For both a corpuscle, and an advancing element of wave front, are merely a permanent form propagated from atomic creature to atomic creature. A corpuscle is in fact an 'enduring object'. The notion of an 'enduring object' is, however, capable of more or less completeness of realization. Thus, in different stages of its career, a wave of light may be more or less corpuscular. A train of such waves at all stages of its career involves social order; but in the earlier stages this social order takes the more special form of loosely related strands of personal

[1] He is also careless, for example in saying that 'Electrons and protons and *photons* are unit charges of electricity' (AI 238, italics not in the original text).

order. This dominant personal order gradually vanishes as the time advances. Its defining characteristics become less and less important, as their various features peter out. The waves then become a nexus with important social order, but with no strands of personal order. Thus the train of waves starts as a corpuscular society, and ends as a society which is not corpuscular. (*PR* 53–4)

(iv) *As a result of thesis* (6) *strict determinism cannot hold in physics.* However exhaustively the antecedents of a physical event are specified, the character of the event cannot, in principle, be predicted with certainty.

(v) *The specification of the state of a composite system containing several elementary particles is equivalent to the specification of the states of the individual particles.* This follows from the natural identification of the state of an elementary particle at a given time as an actual occasion, together with Whitehead's theses that actual occasions are pre-eminently real and that all groupings of occasions have derivative status.

Several further physical consequences of Whitehead's philosophy appear plausible, except for doubts regarding the extent to which physics abstracts from concreteness.

(vi) If concrete reality is considered, there is clear asymmetry between past and future, since the occasions of the past are fully determinate while those of the future are not. *It is reasonable, consequently, to expect the asymmetry between the past and the future to be exhibited in the laws of microphysics,* and not merely in macroscopic laws such as those of thermodynamics.

(vii) An occasion prehends, with suitable gradations of relevance, all previous actual occasions. *Consequently, the physical properties of an elementary particle* (*e.g. its charge or its magnetic moment*) *should be slightly modified by the inclusion of the particle in a highly organized society such as an animal body.*

(viii) If the occasions of an enduring object are considered in full concreteness, they will exhibit 'aging' from earlier to later parts of the chain, simply in virtue of the accumulation of prehensions. *Consequently, one expects a systematic development of physically observable characteristics of elementary particles*—perhaps a drift towards instability, indicative of primitive feelings of satiation, or perhaps a drift towards greater stability, indicative of the entrenchment of a habit.

III. COMPARISONS WITH CURRENT PHYSICS

Propositions (i)–(viii) will now be examined in the light of current physics. Whenever possible, these propositions will be confronted with direct experimental evidence. In most cases, however, one can do no more than compare them with their counterparts in quantum theory, so that experimental evidence can be invoked only to the extent that quantum theory as a whole is experimentally confirmed.[1]

(i) Part of Whitehead's conception of atomicity is in excellent agreement with current physics. Specifically, energy is transferred in quanta, and matter has a granular structure in the small which prevents indefinite divisibility. There is also evidence, although it is not decisive, that the integral character of an elementary particle is compatible with spatial extendedness and internal structure. Thus, experiments in which protons are scattered by protons indicate that these particles have a definite charge and current distribution, even though it is not possible to subdivide their charge into discrete parts.[2] Furthermore, it is difficult to envisage how a particle which is localized at a mathematical point could exhibit spin angular momentum; but one should be cautious in advancing this argument, since in actual calculations theoretical physicists are able to treat the spin simply as a 'quantum number' without any commitments to the extendedness or non-extendedness of the particles. With regard to temporal atomicity, which is the most radical of Whitehead's assertions concerning atomism, the

[1] Individual references will not be given for each of the propositions of quantum theory mentioned in the following discussion. Although these propositions are explained in every standard exposition of quantum theory, several books are particularly worth noting for their treatment of topics that are philosophically significant: D. Bohm, *Quantum Theory* (New York 1951), J. von Neumann, *Mathematical Foundations of Quantum Mechanics* (Princeton 1955), F. London and E. Bauer, *La Théorie de l'Observation en Mécanique Quantique* (Paris 1939), P. A. M. Dirac, *The Principles of Quantum Mechanics*, 3rd edition (Oxford 1947).

[2] Cf. R. Hofstadter, F. Bumiller, and M. R. Yearian, *Reviews of Modern Physics*, vol. 30 (1958), p. 482. The standard model for interpreting these experimental results pictures the observed proton as a 'cloud' of virtual particles, fluctuating in and out of existence. Although the cloud exhibits a statistically describable structure, the virtual particles are supposed to be 'bare' and perhaps without structure. Cf. E. M. Henley and W. Thirring, *Elementary Quantum Field Theory* (New York 1962), pp. 77–78, 219–231. This model is so different from Whitehead's conception of a spatially extended actual occasion that one must hesitate to say that the scattering experiments really support his conception.

testimony of current physics is unfavourable, but not decisively so. One of Heisenberg's uncertainty relations is $\Delta E \Delta t \sim h$, i.e. the uncertainty of the duration of a physical process can be reduced only at the price of increasing the uncertainty of the energy of the system during the process. The limitation which Heisenberg's relation places upon the sharpness of temporal specification is reminiscent of Whitehead's proposition, yet it is not the same. Whitehead is not attributing an *indeterminate* stretch of time to the actual occasion, but rather a *determinate finite* stretch; he denies temporal definiteness only to the phases within the occasion, for 'this genetic passage from phase to phase is not in physical time' (*PR* 434). Moreover, there is no hint in Whitehead's work that an occasion of short duration has a less definite energy than one of longer duration. On the contrary, he says that every actual occasion, when it has completed its process of becoming, is completely definite with respect to every family of attributes (*PR* 38, Category of Explanation xxv). It should be noted, incidentally, that although the duration of each actual occasion is indivisible, Whitehead does not assume a lower limit to the set of all durations (*SMW* 198). Nevertheless, his proposal of temporal atomicity would be supported if the postulation by March, Darling, *et al.* of a minimum length or minimum space-time region proved successful in removing the troublesome 'divergences' of quantum field theory.[1] So far their postulates have not led to outstanding successes, but in view of the great mathematical difficulties and the large number of variants to be examined their failure is not decisive.

(ii) The Whiteheadian proposition that elementary particles can be created and destroyed has been strikingly confirmed by experiments, with regard to the 'stable' as well as to the 'unstable' particles. For example, physicists have not only observed ordinary beta-decay, in which the unstable neutron decays into three stable particles, the proton, the electron, and the anti-neutrino, but they have also detected inverse beta-decay, in which a proton and an anti-neutrino are annihilated and a neutron and positron are

[1] B. T. Darling, *Physical Review*, vol. 80 (1950), p. 460, A. March, *Quantum Mechanics of Particles and Wave Fields* (New York 1951). Their postulates are motivated by the desire to eliminate the 'divergences' of quantum field theory. Because of the quantum mechanical proportionality of energy to frequency and the fact that a minimum length would imply a maximum frequency, their postulates would cut off the high range of frequencies responsible for the theoretically computed infinite energies.

created. Thus, the integral character of elementary particles is not associated with permanence, contrary to Democritean atomism but in accordance with Whiteheadian physics.

(iii) Whitehead's account of the association of waves with particles is only superficially in accord with quantum theory. The passage from pp. 53–4 of *PR*, quoted in (iii) of the preceding Section, shows that he conceives of a wave front as a set of actual occasions (a 'nexus') with each occasion occupying a small region of the front. The mutual relations among contiguous occasions, whereby they begin and end in unison, ensure that all parts of the wave front are in phase with each other. Whitehead's picture is reminiscent of Schrödinger's attempt to interpret the wave function of a particle as a description of an ordinary physical field, which manifests particle-like properties whenever the region of high field intensity is very small. This interpretation was abandoned because Schrödinger's own equation for the time dependence of the wave function implies that in the absence of confining forces an initially concentrated wave packet will disperse.[1] In order to account for the experimental fact that particles do not disperse, Born proposed that the physical content of the wave function was to determine the probabilities of experimental outcomes (e.g., $|\psi(x, y, z)|^2 dxdydz$ is the probability of finding the particle in a small volume $dxdydz$). In the Born interpretation, the wave function characterizes the state of the particle in its entirety and does not describe the physically real parts of a field. There is a sharp discrepancy between this point of view, which at present is accepted by most physicists, and Whitehead's attribution of primary reality to the occasions of a wave front.

Deeper insight into this discrepancy can be achieved by considering the following fundamental principle of quantum theory, called 'the superposition principle': if u_1, u_2, u_3, . . . represent physically possible states, then the combination $\Sigma c_i u_i$, where the c_i are arbitrary complex numbers, represents a superposition of the original states which 'overlaps' each of them in a certain sense and which, moreover, is itself a physically possible state. The nature of the 'overlap' is mostly clearly exhibited if there is an observable

[1] Cf. M. Born, *Atomic Physics* (Fifth edition, New York 1951), p. 93 and pp. 142–4, for discussion of reasons for abandoning Schrödinger's interpretation in favour of Born's and for a general discussion of attempts to rationalize wave-particle dualism.

property A of the system having definite values a_i in the states represented by the u_i, such that all the a_i are different. If the u_i are then specified as being of a standard length ('normalized' to 1), then according to quantum theory the probability of finding that $A = a_i$ when a measurement of A is performed is $|c_i|^2/|c_1|^2 + |c_2|^2 + \ldots$. It must be insisted that $\psi = \Sigma c_i u_i$ is a maximum specification of the system; it is not a statistical description of a system which really is in a state represented by a definite, but unknown, one of the u_i. The superposition therefore has the counter-intuitive characteristic of being a state in which the observable A is objectively indefinite and not merely unknown. It follows that the uncertainty principle of Heisenberg, which limits the simultaneous determination of complementary quantities such as position and momentum, refers to the objective properties of the particle and not simply to human knowledge about these properties. The wave function $\psi(x,y,z)$ can now be understood in terms of the superposition principle: roughly, $\psi(x,y,z)$ represents a superposition of states in each of which the particle has a position localized within a small region $dxdydz$, with the numbers $\psi(x,y,z)dxdydz$ serving as the expansion coefficients in the superposition (i.e., they are the c_i in $\Sigma c_i u_i$). It should now be obvious that the quantum mechanical account of the waves associated with particles is entirely alien to the spirit of Whitehead's philosophy. In particular, the postulation of indefinite values of observable quantities, as required by the quantum mechanical account, would be repugnant to Whitehead. He might admit that indefiniteness is characteristic of the spatial or temporal parts of actual occasions, but surely not of the complete occasions, for the twenty-fifth Category of Explanation, on p. 38 of *PR*, asserts:

> The final phase in the process of concrescence, constituting an actual entity, is one complex, fully determinate feeling. . . . It is fully determinate (*a*) as to its genesis, (*b*) as to its objective character for the transcendent creativity, and (*c*) as to its prehension—positive or negative—of every item in its universe.

An important technical disagreement follows from the fundamental conceptual difference between Whitehead's analysis of wave-particle dualism and that of quantum theory. According to Whitehead, a sharp frequency may be characteristic of a well-localized particle, since the periodicity is essentially due to the reiteration of a basic pattern in successive actual occasions. In quantum theory, on the other hand, a sharp frequency is characteristic of a particle which has a definite momentum, and therefore, by the uncertainty principle, a completely indefinite position; and conversely, the wave function of a well-localized particle has a very broad spectrum of frequencies.

A final note on Whitehead's account of waves and particles is to point out a striking disconfirmation by experiment. He explicitly states, in the passage quoted above from p. 53 of *PR*, that the corpuscular character of light is gradually lost as the light is propagated—a reasonable remark given his general analysis of particles. However, the phenomenon which most vividly illustrates the particle aspect of electromagnetic radiation, the photo-electric effect, is entirely independent of the age of the radiation. In fact, photo-electric cells are attached to telescopes in order to study starlight which has travelled for millions of years.

(iv) Quantum theory and Whiteheadian physics are both indeterministic, but in quite different ways. According to quantum theory, the state of a physical system evolves in a continuous and fully deterministic manner as long as the system is isolated. Probability enters only when a measurement is made of an observable which does not have a sharp value in the state of the system prior to the measurement. The interruption of the deterministic evolution of the state does not contradict the Schrödinger equation, since a measurement requires the interaction of the system with another system—a macroscopic piece of apparatus and perhaps a conscious observer. According to Whitehead, the evolution of an isolated system (the concept of which is an idealization, since an actual occasion prehends all occasions in its past) cannot be entirely deterministic, because of the element of freedom in each occasion. If one attempts to adjudicate between these two different accounts of indeterminism by considering the success of statistical predictions, one must certainly prefer quantum theory, for its statistical predictions are remarkably good, while Whitehead's proposals are too vague to yield any quantitative statistics. Nevertheless, there may be strong reasons for exploring the hypothesis that chance events occur in isolated systems, since, as will be discussed in Section IV, the quantum theoretical account of indeterministic transitions leads to conceptual difficulties.

(v) The Whiteheadian treatment of the state of a composite system is at odds with a quantum mechanical principle which has attracted little attention in spite of its revolutionary philosophical implications: *that a several-particle system may be in a definite state, i.e. may have as definite properties as quantum theory permits, without the individual particles being in definite states.* To illustrate this principle consider two systems I and II and let $\phi_1(\mathrm{I})$ and $\phi_2(\mathrm{I})$ represent states of I in which observable A has values a_1 and a_2 respectively ($a_1 \neq a_2$), and $\psi_1(\mathrm{II})$ and $\psi_2(\mathrm{II})$ represent states of II in which observable B has values b_1 and b_2 respectively ($b_1 \neq b_2$). Let $\phi_1(\mathrm{I}) \otimes \psi_1(\mathrm{II})$ represent that state of the composite system I plus II in which system I is described by $\phi_1(\mathrm{I})$ and system II by $\psi_1(\mathrm{II})$; and let $\phi_2(\mathrm{I}) \otimes \psi_2(\mathrm{II})$ be similar. The superposition principle can now be invoked to affirm the physical possibility of a remarkable state, namely, the one represented by

$$\psi = \frac{1}{\sqrt{2}} (\phi_1(\mathrm{I}) \otimes \psi_1(\mathrm{II})) + \frac{1}{\sqrt{\ }} (\phi_2(\mathrm{I}) \otimes \Psi_2(\mathrm{II})) \ .$$

Neither I nor II is in a definite state when ψ represents the state of I plus II. A rigorous proof will be omitted, but the following rough argument indicates the essential reason: if one tries to claim that I is to some extent described by ϕ_1, and to some extent by ϕ_2, the claim is vague unless the expansion coefficients of ϕ_1 and ϕ_2 are specified, but in the above expression for ψ it is clear that the expansion coefficients refer to states of II. One might try to reconcile the existence of such states of several-particle systems with Whitehead's consequence (v) by identifying the state of a several-particle system with a single actual occasion, and identifying the individual particles at a given moment with subdivisions of the occasion. Divisions of an occasion could be reasonably expected to lack the specificity implied in saying that an entity is in a definite state, for 'in dividing the region we are ignoring the subjective unity which is inconsistent with such divisions' (*PR* 435). This attempt at reconciliation fails, however, because quantum mechanics permits the parts of a system described by ψ to be indefinitely far apart spatially.[1] An actual occasion which not only is macroscopically extended, but even broken into non-contiguous parts, is evidently contrary to Whitehead. To be sure, he is reticent about the exact extent of an occasion, but he seems to fear that the

[1] Cf. D. Bohm and Y. Aharonov, *Physical Review*, vol. 108 (1957), p. 1070.

identification of a large scale process as a single occasion will remove the barriers to Spinozistic monism (cf. *PR* 10–11).

It is appropriate at this point to interpolate a discussion of another quantum mechanical principle concerning several-particle systems, even though it has no clear counterpart in Whiteheadian physics: *that if a system contains several elementary particles of the same species, they must all play the same role in the system as a whole.* Consider, for example, a system composed of two pi-mesons, and suppose ϕ_1 and ϕ_2 each represents a possible state of a single pi-meson. Then the principle forbids the composite system to be in the state represented by $\phi_1 \otimes \phi_2$, for in this state pi-mesons I and II have different roles; but the principle permits the state represented by

$$\frac{1}{\sqrt{2}} (\phi_1(\mathrm{I}) \otimes \phi_2(\mathrm{II})) + \frac{1}{\sqrt{2}} (\phi_2(\mathrm{I}) \otimes \phi_1(\mathrm{II})),$$

for this state is 'symmetrized' with respect to the two particles.[1]

To fit symmetrization into the framework of Whiteheadian physics is a delicate matter, since it implies a kind of loss of identity of the individual particles. In particular, the simple model of particle I as a chain of occasions $O_1, O_1', O_1'', \ldots$ and of particle II as a chain $O_2, O_2', O_2'', \ldots$ will not work, because individual occasions are always distinguishable in virtue of intrinsic characteristics (thesis 2 of Sect. II) and hence the two chains are distinguishable. A possible reply is that physics does not treat actual occasions *in concreto* and hence can fail to take cognizance of the respect in which the chains $O_1, O_1', O_1'', \ldots$ and $O_2, O_2', O_2'', \ldots$ are different; but the symmetrization obtained in this manner would appear to be a coincidence rather than a general law.

A more promising explanation is that the chains O_1, O_1', O_1'', $\ldots$ and $O_2, O_2', O_2'', \ldots$ intersect and the occasions which are shared by several chains have a quite different character—the physical manifestation of which is symmetrization—from the character of the occasions prior to the merger of the chains or after their separation. This explanation conforms to Whitehead's

[1] Symmetrization is actually a property of states of systems composed of particles with 'integral spin'. When the particles have 'half-integer spin', as do electrons, neutrinos, neutrons, and protons, the state of the composite system must be 'anti-symmetrized'. However, the difference between symmetrization and anti-symmetrization is irrelevant for the present purpose, which is to insist upon the identity of roles of all particles of the same species.

general view that the corpuscular nature of a variety of occasions is highly special and easily dissipated. However, the explanation encounters the same difficulty that was noticed in the preceding paragraph. Composite systems containing particles of the same species can have indefinitely large spatial extent, as in the case of the conduction electrons in a bar of metal. Since all the particles play the same role, it becomes necessary to identify the state of a macroscopically extended system with a single actual occasion, contrary to Whitehead's conception of the actual occasion as a microscopic entity.

(vi) In contemporary physics the only laws which involve a definite direction of time are macroscopic, the outstanding one being the thermodynamic law of entropy increase. No microphysical law has yet been discovered which is not invariant under reversal of the direction of time. If this peculiarity remains a permanent feature of physics, it would constitute evidence detrimental to Whitehead's scheme, in which the asymmetry of past and future is essential.The only defence of a Whiteheadian physics would then be the desperate one that the asymmetry of past and future is one of the features of concrete reality neglected by physics. However, since the discovery of parity non-conservation by Yang and Lee *et al.*, the confidence of physicists in some of the physical symmetry principles has been shaken, and many suspect that a violation of time-reversal invariance will also be detected.[1]

(viii) The Whiteheadian expectation that the physical properties of an elementary particle are slightly modified when the particle enters a structural society is counter to the reductionist spirit of physics, chemistry, and biophysics. Many of the predictions of these sciences rest upon the assumption that such properties of elementary particles as charge, mass, and magnetic moment are unchanged by the incorporation of the particles into highly structured macroscopic objects. Of course, the same predictions would be made if the changes due to incorporation are extremely small. Since Whitehead gives no indication of the amount of modification to be expected there can be no crucial experiment.

(viii) The 'aging' of elementary particles implied by Whitehead's philosophy is contrary to current physical theory and is not confirmed by experiment. The intrinsic properties of newly

[1] Cf. P. Morrison, *American Journal of Physics*, vol. 26 (1958), p. 358.

created elementary particles seem to be no different, at least statistically, from those of particles which have endured a long while. Particularly significant is the decay rate in a population of unstable particles. The number of neutrons, for example, decaying per unit time is proportional to the number of neutrons in the population (with allowance, of course, for statistical fluctuations), and is independent of the 'age' of the population. It is reasonable to infer that the probability that a given neutron will decay during an interval of time is independent of the age of the neutron, thus suggesting that no physically significant changes occur in the neutron due to aging. Again, however, Whitehead's statements permit no quantitative estimate of the change to be anticipated in the decay rate, and therefore no crucial experiment is possible.

IV. PROPOSALS FOR RECONSTRUCTION

The discrepancies noted in Sect. III between Whiteheadian physics and current microphysics constitute strong disconfirmation of Whitehead's philosophy as a whole. The possibility remains, however, of constructing a philosophical system, Whiteheadian in its general conceptions though not in details, and according with the fundamental discoveries of science. A few tentative suggestions will be given here concerning the initiation of such a large philosophical undertaking.

A useful first step is to distinguish both in the philosophy of organism and in quantum theory those elements which are radical by the standards of classical physics from those which are conservative. Most radical in Whitehead's philosophy are the attribution of proto-mental properties to entities normally considered to be physical, and the postulation of prehension as the fundamental relation between occasions. The assumption of the complete definiteness of the occasion in its final stage is conservative, although the correlative assumption of indefiniteness in the early stages of concrescence is not. Also conservative is his reductionist assumption that the characteristics of a nexus are entirely determined by the characteristics of its constituent occasions. Quantum theory is conservative in supposing that certain quantities initially introduced in the study of macroscopic physical objects—especially spatio-temporal position, energy, momentum, angular momentum, charge, and magnetic moment—can be used meaningfully in characterizing microscopic entities. On the other hand, the superposition principle is radical, for it has the consequence that a physical quantity can have an indefinite value in a maximally specific state of a microscopic system and has a sharp value only in exceptional states (the 'eigenstates' of that quantity). Quantum theory is also radical in its treatment of the relation between the state of a several-particle system and the states of its constituent particles.

The foregoing juxtaposition suggests a programme of reconstruction: *to graft the radical elements of quantum theory onto the radical elements of the philosophy of organism, by assuming that elementary entities have proto-mental characteristics while treating the states of these entities in accordance with the combinatory principles of quantum theory.* The synthesis contemplated here does not seem forced from a Whiteheadian point of view. Whitehead often engages in a dialectical analysis which is reminiscent of the quantum mechanical treatment of complementary quantities,[1] but he never achieves what is most remarkable in quantum theory—a set of systematic rules for predicting statistically what will appear when a shift is made from one description to a complementary one. A modification of Whitehead's philosophy in accordance with the combinatory principles of quantum theory would perhaps make explicit and precise certain tendencies that are implicit and haphazard in his work.

Such a modification of Whitehead's system would surely change the conception of an actual occasion. For example, it would be impossible to maintain that an actual occasion, in its final phase, is definite with respect to every family of attributes (*PR* 38, Category of Explanation xxv). Instead, in accordance with the uncertainty principle, the specificity of any attribute is always attained at the price of indefiniteness of other attributes. In particular, an occasion may have a quite sharp location in time and an arbitrarily short duration, provided that properties complementary to duration are

[1] This is most striking in Whitehead's theology: 'It is as true to say that God is permanent and the World fluent, as that the World is permanent and God is fluent. . . .' (PR 528). Whitehead explains that 'In each antithesis there is a shift of meaning which converts the opposition into a contrast' (*ibid.*). Dialectical analysis is also exhibited in the more mundane parts of his philosophy, for example in his statements that an actual occasion is prehended in its concreteness and yet with loss of immediacy.

sufficiently indefinite.[1] It is also possible that the actual occasions may lose their status of being (along with God) the only ultimate real entities, and they may appear instead only as special cases of ultimate reality. Elementary particle theory and quantum electrodynamics may provide a hint as to the more general form of ultimate reality: i.e., it might be some kind of 'field' of diffused primitive feeling, of which the actual occasions are 'quanta' existing whenever there are individual loci of feeling. The hypothesis of diffused feelings is no more of an extrapolation from psychological data than is Whitehead's attribution of proto-mental characteristics to elementary particles, and indeed our everyday experience of sensitivity pervading the whole human body may possibly be construed as confirmation of the hypothesis.

The physical evidence concerning composite systems, discussed in (v) of Sect. III, suggests a quantum-theoretical refinement of Whitehead's treatment of the relation between the nexus and its constituent occasions. Whitehead conceives of the nexus in a reductionist manner, as the totality of its constituent occasions, and he supposes the internal relations exhibited in a nexus to be completely explicable in terms of the prehensions of earlier occasions of the nexus by each new occasion. Quantum theory, on the other hand, treats a composite system in a subtle manner, which at first seems paradoxical: it allows the state of the composite system to be described, in a certain sense, in terms of its components, and yet it permits the composite system to be in a definite state even when its components are not. This treatment, of course, is intimately bound up with the superposition principle. Thus, in the example cited in the previous Section, the composite system I plus II is in the state represented by

$$\Psi = \frac{1}{\sqrt{2}}(\phi_1(\mathrm{I}) \otimes \psi_1(\mathrm{II})) + \frac{1}{\sqrt{2}}(\phi_2(\mathrm{I}) \otimes \psi_2(\mathrm{II})),$$

which is clearly describable in terms of the states ϕ_1 and ϕ_2 of component I and ψ_1 and ψ_2 of component II; yet, because of the character of the superposition, neither I nor II is in a definite state. If this quantum theoretical treatment of the whole-part relationship is introduced into the philosophy of organism, it

[1] According to the Heisenberg relation $\Delta E \Delta t \sim h$, the property complementary to duration is energy. But if Whitehead's thesis is maintained that physical energy is an abstraction from emotional and purposive energy (AI 239), then Heisenberg's relation may require supplementation.

opens a number of possible lines of exploration. For example, the 'field of feeling', the existence of which was hypothesized in the preceding paragraph, might be characterized holistically as being in a definite state. This state could always be described as a superposition of field states, in each of which there is a definite set of actual occasions, just as in quantum electrodynamics the state of the entire electromagnetic field can be described as a superposition of field states in each of which there is a definite set of photons. Moreover, special states of the 'field of feeling' can exist in which the superposition is in part reduced, so that definite actual occasions exist. Consequently, the existence of many independent loci of feeling, which is an essential aspect of the experienced plurality of the world, is permitted—though not required—in this modified Whiteheadian scheme. A nexus of the type described by Whitehead is also permitted but is a rather special case: it occurs when there is a network of occasions sharing some common characteristic, each in a definite single-quantum state. What the modified scheme permits which Whitehead's does not is the existence of a composite system more complex than a nexus: an 'n-quanta system' in which each of the n occasions is so correlated with the others, *via* the superposition principle, that none is in a definite single-quantum state.

An evident advantage of the quantum-theoretical modification of the philosophy of organism is that it removes some of the discrepancies with modern physics noted in Sect. III—a virtue which is not surprising, since the modification was inspired by these discrepancies. A further advantage is a possible improvement in treating the question of 'simple location'. Whitehead's rejection of simple location in *SMW* is a dramatic criticism of classical physics, but his sketch of an alternative in *PR* is somewhat disappointing. His alternative is essentially to postulate the relation of prehension, whereby an actual occasion is felt in complete detail in the initial phase of each later occasion. Even if the ambiguities inherent in the conception of prehension can be dispelled, the relation of prehension can at best provide a kind of multiple location in time, i.e. the occasion as 'subject' and the same occasion as 'ingredient' in later subjects. By contrast, the quantum-theoretical modification exhibits a breakdown in simple location in space in two respects: first, the quantum state of an individual occasion may be such that its position is indefinite; and, secondly, a composite system can have spatially separated components which are not in definite states, but which are so correlated with each other that the composite system is in a definite state. Finally, there is an advantage which was briefly mentioned earlier but which deserves amplification: the possibility that the modification of Whitehead's philosophy will greatly improve the account of high-order mental phenomena—which, after all, are the only mental phenomena we know about without resorting to radical hypotheses and extrapolations. Because Whitehead conceives actual occasions to be microscopic in size, and because the human personality at any moment has a unity which entitles it to the status of an actual occasion, he is led to the strange doctrine of a microscopic locus of high-order experience wandering through the society of occasions that compose the brain:

Thus in an animal body the presiding occasion, if there be one, is the final node, or intersection, of a complex structure of many enduring objects. . . . There is also an enduring object formed by the inheritance from presiding occasion to presiding occasion. This endurance of the mind is only one more example of the general principle on which the body is constructed. This route of presiding occasions probably wanders from part to part of the brain, dissociated from the physical material atoms. (*PR* 166–7)

The question of the location of mentality is extremely complicated, but introspection seems to indicate that it is diffused throughout the body, and neuro-physiology has not yielded evidence of extreme localization. Various of the concepts of the modified Whiteheadian scheme seem relevant in describing high-order mentality: the concept of an indefinitely located actual occasion, the concept of a field of feeling which is generally diffused but occasionally quantized, and the concept of quantum correlations among the components of a composite system. Which one of these, or which combination of them, will be most fruitful is a matter of speculation, but all of them seem preferable to Whitehead's microscopic localization of high-order mentality.[1]

This list of advantages must be weighed against some strong reservations. The first concerns a particular proposal made above

[1] Some speculations on the application of quantum theoretical concepts to mentality are given in D. Bohm, *Quantum Theory*, pp. 168–172.

rather than the general programme of a quantum-theoretical modification of the philosophy of organism. The proposal was to consider the entire 'field of feeling' as being in a definite state and to consider actual occasions as quanta of this field. One may wonder, in view of the notorious difficulties of quantum field theories, whether they are suitable models for a metaphysical scheme describing all of reality, and one may wonder whether a single field suffices for this purpose. Setting aside these doubts, however, one may still be sceptical about the adequacy of this proposal to account for the experienced plurality of the world. It was noted that the existence of a definite state of the entire field is permissive of individual loci of feeling, but is permissiveness sufficient? Is it a mere contingency, characteristic perhaps of our cosmic epoch, that there are definite actual occasions, or are there deep-lying reasons why this should always be so? Merely raising these questions exhibits the vagueness of the proposal and its need for supplementation.

A second reservation arises from the apparent absence of any clear psychological manifestations of the superposition principle, which one would expect if the combinatory principles of quantum theory apply to actual occasions. There are, to be sure, psychological phenomena which at first sight could be construed as evidence of the superposing of mental states—e.g., perceptual vagueness, emotional ambiguity, conflict of loyalties, and the symbolism of dreams. Yet in all these cases the quantitative characteristics of the superposition principle, as it is exhibited in physics, are missing.[1] This reservation, however, is not decisive, for one can optimistically reply that the absence of confirming evidence is not equivalent to the presence of disconfirming evidence. It is possible that the psychological manifestations of the superposition principle are too delicate to be detected by the introspective, behaviouristic, and physiological techniques in current use.[2] It is also possible that these techniques are sufficient, but that no one has yet been sufficiently serious about using the superposition principle in psychology to design a good experiment.

[1] This point is discussed in A. Shimony, *American Journal of Physics*, vol. 31 (1963), p. 755.

[2] Dr Karl Kornacker pointed out in a private communication that the interference effects characteristic of superpositions are no more to be expected in gross emotional and perceptual phenomena than in macroscopic physical phenomena.

A third reservation is that quantum theory, in spite of its striking successes in physics, is beset by a serious conceptual difficulty, which should perhaps be resolved before the theory is incorporated into a philosophical system. This conceptual difficulty concerns the 'reduction of a superposition', which occurs if an observable A, having sharp and distinct values in the states represented by u_i, is measured when the state is represented by $\Sigma c_i u_i$. As a result of the measurement there is a non-deterministic transition from the initial state to a final state represented by a definite one of the u_i. Although many textbooks and popular accounts say that the transition occurs when a microscopic system interacts with the macroscopic measuring apparatus, this explanation is inadequate, since the Schrödinger equation, which is the equation governing the evolution of the state, implies that the final state of the apparatus plus microscopic system will also be a superposition with respect to the observable A. Some theoreticians have concluded that the reduction of the superposition does not take place until the result of the measurement is registered in the consciousness of an observer. This desperate conclusion is unsatisfactory for several reasons.[1] It suffices to say here that if observation is a natural process, it is difficult to understand why a non-deterministic transition should occur when an observation is made, while all other natural processes are deterministic. One possible solution to the problem of the reduction of superpositions is to suppose that the evolution of the quantum state is to some extent stochastic and hence only approximately governed by the Schrödinger equation. The non-deterministic reduction of a superposition could then occur in a system remote from anything ordinarily called 'an observer'. In this way the superposition principle could be maintained in microphysics, but at the price of changing the dynamics of quantum theory. The success of a solution along this line would remove the third reservation about a quantum-theoretical modification of Whitehead's philosophy, for the modification depends primarily upon extending the application of the superposition principle. The proposal of a chance element in the evolution of the state does not disrupt the programme envisaged here, for in fact this proposal is closer to Whitehead's version of indeterminism than is the indeterminism of current quantum theory. One could

[1] E. Wigner, article in *The Scientist Speculates*, ed. I. J. Good (London 1962); also the paper by A. Shimony cited on the previous page.

even speculate that Whitehead's account of the concrescence of an actual occasion provides some insight into the way in which the reduction of the superposition occurs. Such speculations, however, are rather empty until stochastic generalizations of the Schrödinger equation are proposed and their physical consequences are studied.

A methodological remark is appropriate in conclusion. It has been tacitly assumed throughout this paper that the hypothetico-deductive method is an appropriate instrument in philosophical inquiry. This assumption is in the spirit of Whitehead's philosophy, for he deliberately formulated a categoreal scheme which could be confirmed or disconfirmed only by examining its remote consequences (*PR* 7–8). Regrettably, the difficulties of employing the hypothetico-deductive method in philosophy are illustrated only too clearly in this paper. The conclusions which can be drawn from philosophical first principles are generally qualitative, and therefore their confrontation with experience lacks sharpness. When they are confirmed, it is gross rather than fine confirmation, and when they are disconfirmed there is often a plausible way of saving the appearances. The moral, however, is not that the hypothetico-deductive method should be abandoned. Rather, it is to seek refinements of philosophical first principles and liaisons of these principles with scientific hypotheses, in such a way that sharp predictions and fine confirmations may result.[1]

[1] I am deeply indebted to Dr Howard Stein for his criticism of an early draft of this paper and, more important, for stimulating and suggestive conversations over many years concerning the topics which it treats. I am grateful for a careful reading of the manuscript by Prof. J. M. Burgers.

Added in proof: An experiment by J. W. Christenson *et al.*, described in *Physical Review Letters*, vol. 13 (1964), p. 138 (and reported in *The New York Times*, Aug. 5, 1964), indicates a violation of 'time-reversal invariance' (see p. 253 above).

XIII
PREDICABILITY

by FRED SOMMERS

Associate Professor of Philosophy, Brandeis University

I

In the *Metaphysics* Aristotle says that 'Being' has at least as many senses as there are categories. Thus, if we suppose chairs and questions to belong to different categories, we cannot say that chairs exist and that questions exist and mean the same thing by 'exist' in both statements. Apparently Plato would not have agreed with this. For in the *Sophist* Plato stresses that a single form of existence 'blends' with things at Rest and things in Motion. Thus, for Plato, justice, as something 'at rest', and chairs, as something 'in motion', both exist, since both blend with existence. And, presumably, we can predicate existence univocally of both.

The question whether 'exists' can be univocally predicated of such different things as questions and chairs, gods and men, received much attention in the middle ages. It is still not settled. In our own day, Quine, on this question, is a disciple of Plato and Ryle has followed Aristotle.

The only progress we can record is one of formulation. The topic has been generalized beyond a concern with 'exists'. In its present form the question is whether any predicate *P* can be univocal when predicated of things of different types.

Now it seems obvious that a type difference between subjects of predication does have a logical bearing on the ambiguity of certain predicates. Thus in the statements 'Some chairs are hard' and 'Some questions are hard' most of us are prepared to argue for the ambiguity of 'hard' from the type difference between chairs and questions. I say *most* of us. Quine, who is the latter-day Platonist on the univocity of existence, is concerned to preserve its univocity. For, if the type difference between chairs and questions is sufficient to ensure the ambiguity of 'hard', then why not the ambiguity of 'exists' as well? For this reason, Quine says that 'hard' too is univocal, when predicated of chairs and of questions.[1] When

[1] W. V. O. Quine. *Word and Object* (Cambridge, Mass. 1960), pp. 130–131.

Quine turns Platonist, he does so with a vengeance. But he is surely wrong about hard questions and hard chairs. If he were right, and 'hard' could mean the same thing in both, then we could perfectly well say that this question is harder than that chair. Quine's concern for the univocity of existence must also lead him to consider the possibility of predicating 'tall' of stories and buildings univocally. And then we could say, 'That building is taller than the story he is now telling me'. And so on.

On the other hand, those philosophers who maintain the strong Aristotelian thesis and assume that all heterotypical predication is necessarily equivocal are also wrong. I can say of a lecture that it lasted an hour and I can say this also of a headache. I can also say 'My headache lasted as long as the lecture'. In such statements, lasting must be univocally predicated; otherwise they would make as little sense as the statements which attempt to make 'hard' do univocal work with questions and chairs.

Evidently, heterotypical predication is sometimes univocal and sometimes equivocal. Our problem is: When does a type difference enforce ambiguity on a predicate? Why, for example, is 'hard' equivocal over questions and chairs, while 'lasts an hour' is univocal over headaches and lectures?

This question is straightforward enough and can be given a straightforward answer. One wonders why it has not been asked before. Even more strangely: Why has it been assumed by philosophers that heterotypical predication is necessarily equivocal when there are so many counter-examples to this? I have mentioned 'lasts an hour' as applied to headaches and lectures. I could have used 'interests Mary' as applied to mathematics and men. For the statement that Mary is more interested in men than in mathematics makes good sense; Mary's 'interest' in both is univocal. What could have led philosophers to ignore the obviously univocal predicates that are predicable of things of different types?

The answer, I believe, is this: Once we generalize from cases like hard questions and hard chairs to the principle that a type difference between *a* and *b* enforces ambiguity in a predicate expression, *P*, that is applicable to *a* and to *b*, then the converse doctrine must also hold true: Given the fact that *P* is univocally predicable of *a* and of *b*, it follows that *a* and *b* must be of the same type. This being so, as soon as someone points out that 'lasts' is univocally predicable of headaches and lectures, he is told that headaches and lectures are really of the same type, both being events and so on. I think that this is one reason why the logical evidence against the strong Aristotelian thesis has been ignored. Russell, for example, has sometimes agreed with Aristotle that 'exists' is necessarily equivocal. And Russell offers just this criterion for being of the same type:[1] Two things are of the same type if and only if some predicate *P* is significantly applicable to both. The procedure is viciously circular, for now, if we begin by assuming the univocity of *P* over the two things in question, then they are of the same type; on the other hand, if we assume independently that the things in question are of different types the predicate will be considered equivocal. Nor is this procedure confined to the adherents of the Aristotelian thesis on existence. Quine, who maintains that predications over things like chairs and questions is univocal, is led to the view that there is no difference that deserves the special name of type difference. Since for Quine 'exists' applies univocally to anything we can talk about, this results in the view that any two things are of the same type. That is only an extreme application of the formula: Two things are of the same type if there is some predicate *P* that applies to both univocally. And, of course, this amounts to denying type difference altogether.[2] What is fundamentally wrong with Quine's typeless world is that he gets it by applying the contrapositive of the Aristotelian formula: Assuming two things to be of different types, 'exists' would be equivocally predicated of them; assuming that 'exists' is univocally predicated of them, then the two things are of the same type. But the Aristotelian formula is originally applicable to a type-partitioned universe. It cannot be used to destroy distinctions of type.[3]

It is in any case evident that in order to formulate the problem of the relation of type difference to ambiguity we need a definition of type difference that does not depend on the question whether covering predicates are ambiguous or not. Thus, it must at least be possible for two things to be of different types, even though some predicate *P* applies univocally to both. We want to be able to accept Plato's view on existence without being forced to give up type differences. Similarly, we want to be able to predicate 'lasts an hour' over headaches and lectures without being forced to say

[1] *Contemporary British Philosophy* I (London 1924), p. 371.
[2] Cf. Quine, *op. cit.*, p. 229. [3] Cf. *ibid.*, p. 275.

that they are of the same type. The criterion[1] for type difference is this:

Two things are of different types if and only if there are two predicates *P* and *Q* such that it makes sense to predicate *P* of the first thing but not of the second, and it makes sense to predicate *Q* of the second thing but not of the first.

By this criterion, lectures and headaches are of different types since it makes sense to say of a lecture that it was delivered by a speaker, while it makes no sense to say this of a headache—and, on the other hand, it makes sense to say of a headache that it was cured while it makes no sense to say this of a lecture. Similarly, questions and chairs are of different types; we can ask a question and we can sit on a chair but we cannot ask a chair or sit on a question.

Using this criterion, we find that lectures and headaches, chairs and questions, statements and men, are pairs of things of different types and we still want to know why 'lasts an hour' can be univocally said of the first pair, while 'hard' cannot be univocally said of the second pair and 'rational' cannot be univocally said of the third pair. More generally, our problem is this: Given that *a* and *b* are of different types and given that *P* is some term that can be predicated of *a* and of *b*, what are the logical conditions that will force us to judge that *P* is ambiguous?

It is part of the job of a theory of predication to provide answers to questions like this. However, before I show how the answer is part of a theory of predication, or even explain what I mean by such a theory, I think it would be well to state the answer dogmatically and to give some illustrations of its philosophical consequences. The rule for enforcing ambiguity is this:

If *a*, *b*, and *c* are any three things and *P* and *Q* are predicates such

[1] A similar criterion of type difference may be found in Max Black's article, 'Russell's Philosophy of Language' in *The Philosophy of Bertrand Russell*, ed. by P. A. Schilpp (Evanston, Ill. 1944), p. 238. Unfortunately, Black adopts the strong Aristotelian thesis and concludes that a formal theory of types applicable to natural language will require too much ambiguity. He believes the application of formal type theory to natural language to be a '*reductio ad absurdum* of a point of view which seeks to apply to ordinary language segregatory criteria appropriate to an artificially constructed calculus', *ibid.*, p. 239. For discussion of Black's criticism of Russell see my 'Types and Ontology', *Philosophical Review*, vol. 72 (1963), pp. 327–363.

that it makes sense to predicate P of a and of b but not of c and it makes sense to predicate Q of b and of c but not of a, then P must be equivocal over a and b or Q must be equivocal over b and c. Conversely, if P and Q are univocal predicates, then there can be no three things, a, b, and c such that P applies to a and to b but not to c while Q applies to b and to c but not to a.

We saw earlier that the strong Aristotelian thesis is wrong and that we cannot argue from a type difference between a and b to the ambiguity of a single predicate P that applies to both. Thus we cannot argue from the type difference between men and statements to the ambiguity of 'thoughtful' as it applies to both. Yet 'thoughtful' is obviously ambiguous. And, just as obviously, this ambiguity has something to do with the type difference between men and statements. Applying our rule, we can see why.

We take a third thing, e.g. a fence. The term 'five feet tall' applies to fences and to men but not to statements, while the term 'thoughtful' applies to men and to statements but not to fences. Thus, by the rule, either 'tall' is ambiguous when applied to fences and men, or 'thoughtful' is ambiguous when applied to men and to statements.

Note that the rule for ambiguity does not tell us *which* of two predicates is ambiguous, but tells us only that one of them must be. This is important; we apply such rules to check the coherence of philosophical positions and we find that any one of a number of different positions is consistent with a rule. For example, I shall show that Ryle's doctrine of persons and Descartes' doctrine are both consistent with the rule just stated. Nevertheless, despite the fact that the rule, being logical, states only a consistency condition that may be satisfied in more than one way, it is—especially in its converse form—quite a strong rule. It is, anyhow, strong enough to rule out as incoherent even so plausible a doctrine as that of Strawson's.[1]

On Strawson's view, it is essential to persons that they sustain significantly such 'P-predicates' as *thinks* and such 'M-predicates' as *weighs a hundred pounds*. This doctrine, like Ryle's, is calculated to eliminate the ghost in the machine. On the other hand, Strawson does admit into his ontology ghosts outside of machines, bodiless

[1] Cf. P. F. Strawson, *Individuals* (London 1959), ch. 3.

spirits. Of such ghosts it is essential that they should once have been persons, that they should be *dis*embodied. But they are no longer persons and many *M*-predicates do not apply to them. We cannot, for example, say of the immortal spirit of Socrates that it is purple. Nor can we say of it that it weighs a hundred pounds. Thus, in Strawson's ontology, we have three things, spirits, persons, and rocks, such that the predicate *weighs a hundred pounds* applies to rocks and to persons but not to spirits, while the predicate *thinks* applies to persons and to spirits but not to rocks. But if these predicates are univocally predicated, there can be no such three things. Yet if we are to make sense of any belief in immortality, we must predicate *some* predicates univocally of persons and immortal spirits. If Strawson does not believe 'thinks' is the predicate he can choose any other *P*-predicate. And surely we do not find ambiguity in 'weighs a hundred pounds' as this is said of a person and a stone. Thus Strawson's ontology of persons, spirits, and bodies is logically incoherent because it violates the rule. I shall make one suggestion here; if Strawson wants immortal spirits in his ontology, he must allow them full personal status, i.e. it must be essential to spirits that they permit significant predication of all of the *M*-predicates applicable to a living man. Categorially at least, spirits must have bodies. Thus it must make sense to say of the immortal spirit of Socrates *now* that it weighs a hundred pounds. But then how much does it weigh?

I have said that Descartes' ontology is coherent. I believe something much stronger can be said for it. Once we choose to speak of immortal spirits in the usual sense, we become committed to a dualism of the living person. Descartes' doctrine is inevitable even if we wish to deny the existence of such spirits. Calling it an error, Strawson has correctly pointed out the fundamental move made by Descartes:

The Cartesian error is a special case of the general error . . . of thinking of the designations, or apparent designations, of persons as not denoting precisely the same thing or entity for all kinds of predicates ascribed to the entity designated. That is, if we are to avoid the general form of this error, we must not think of 'I' or 'Smith' as suffering from type ambiguity.[1]

[1] P. F. Strawson, *Individuals*, p. 105.

Strawson is right in saying that for Descartes I do not and cannot mean the same thing by 'Smith' in the statements 'Smith thinks' and 'Smith is fat'. But for anyone who chooses to speak of disembodied spirits this is no error. For now it is no longer possible to consider 'Smith' univocal in statements predicating weight and consciousness of him. Neither Descartes nor Strawson is prepared to find ambiguity in either 'thinks' or 'weighs' as these are said of spirits and men and men and stones respectively. If we are to save this piece of ontology, we have no choice left but to find the ambiguity in 'Smith'. What Strawson calls an error is just what results from talk about thinking spirits, heavy stones, and fat conscious persons. Strawson's avoidance of this 'error' is precisely what is responsible for the incoherence of his own doctrine. For as we have seen it applied, the rule here requires that we lay all the ghosts in the language or else let them inside the machine as well. Letting them inside Smith's machine causes 'Smith' to suffer from type ambiguity. Keeping them out and asserting Strawson's doctrine that persons are 'primitive' individuals, requires that we give up talk of spirits altogether. It means keeping them out of the language. This radical solution, which Ryle proposed in *The Concept of Mind*, is the only one consistent with Strawson's doctrine of the primitiveness of persons. My suggestion that we may talk of how much spirits weigh, what colour they are, and so on, is consistent with this. That amounts to getting rid of them as a special type of thing; for now spirits are not what they used to be, they are not disembodied; they are primitive persons.

Strawson does hint that he might be prepared to avoid dualism by finding ambiguity in the *M*-predicates common to persons and to physical objects:

If we want to find type ambiguity somewhere, we would do better to locate it in certain predicates like 'is in the drawing room', 'was hit by a stone' and say they mean one thing when applied to material objects and another when applied to persons.[1]

As we have seen, it is not a question of wanting to find ambiguity somewhere; it is a question of having to find it somewhere. It is either in 'Smith', or in the *M*-predicates, or in the *P*-predicates.

[1] Strawson, *ibid.*, p. 105. Strawson is here tempted by the strong Aristotelian thesis.

Formally speaking, we could find it in the *M*-predicates and avoid violation of type rules. But then we could not get by with finding ambiguity in a few *M*-predicates common to persons and to physical objects; all *M*-predicates must be found ambiguous. If we take this way of avoiding the Cartesian 'error', then 'weighs a hundred pounds' could not be applied in the same sense to Smith and to his excess baggage, even though both are weighed on the same scale. But this way of saving the doctrine of primitive persons is useless anyway. For what would be the point of defining persons by their type characteristic of entertaining both *M*- and *P*-predicates essentially when all of the *M*-predicates mean one thing when applied to persons and another when applied to physical objects? Exactly the same considerations apply if all *P*-predicates become systematically ambiguous when predicated of persons and disembodied spirits respectively.

It is clear that the type rule leaves us only two reasonable alternatives: either to adopt a *spiritless language* or to accept Cartesian dualism. Should a non-Cartesian now wish to deny the existence of immortal spirits, he must be understood in one of two ways. Either he is saying that talk of immortal spirits is like talk of red earaches; that is, he is denying that such things can logically exist—and that is different from an ordinary denial of existence. Or he understands by 'spirits' a peculiar type of conscious body, perhaps colourless and weightless and extensionless, in which case he may deny their existence in the way he ordinarily denies that unicorns exist. But if, for some reason, he wishes to speak of a special type of thing called a spirit, of which it makes no sense to predicate certain *M*-predicates that apply to living persons, but of which it does make sense to predicate some of the *P*-predicates, then he is a Cartesian, and if so he is committed to the type-ambiguity of proper names for living persons.

Of course Strawson has another alternative. He may choose to deny the validity of the fundamental type rule I have been applying to check the coherence of his position. If he does so, he will have to reject the proofs for its validity I shall presently offer.

Before leaving Strawson, I wish to comment on his general preference for locating ambiguity in universals rather than in particulars whenever we are faced with the choice of locating it in one or the other. We do in general prefer this. For example, given the statements, 'This apple is circular', 'This argument is circular', 'This argument is memorized', 'This phone number is memorized', we can show that either 'circular' is ambiguous over apple and argument or 'memorized' is ambiguous over argument and number. But now, remembering Descartes' move, we can keep both of these terms univocal and find the ambiguity in 'argument'. 'Argument' would then be ambiguous in 'memorized argument' and 'circular argument'. Of course we prefer to locate the ambiguity in either 'circular' or 'memorized'. The reason is this: If 'argument' were chosen for type ambiguity, it would be difficult to see how we could speak of having memorized a circular argument. For example, it seems we could not say 'This argument was circular but I memorized it'. For it would be like saying 'This period is smudged but I enjoyed every minute of it'. The latter sentence is nonsensical because we do need two senses of 'period' for smudged periods and vacation periods; equally, if we needed two senses of argument for circular and memorized arguments, the first sentence should be nonsensical. One of the most persuasive reasons for avoiding Cartesianism, with its splitting of the meaning of 'Smith' in the fat Smith and the thinking Smith, is that we can and do want to say significantly that the fat Smith thinks. If we take the Cartesian way, it seems we ought not to be able to say this. It is like saying 'This cape which is very stormy in the wintertime is loose at the shoulders'. Of course this argument against Descartes is an ordinary language argument. Descartes is recommending that we reconstrue all statements about fat thoughtful people. He would say that such statements—if they are taken to be about individuals—have as little meaning as the one about the young lady who came home in a sedan chair and a flood of tears.

Splitting particulars is a favourite pastime of empiricist philosophers. And sometimes it is done quite unintentionally. For example, I have heard it said that Austin maintained the predicate 'seen' to be univocal when applied to a colour and a material object. Thus in the statements, 'I saw a colour' and 'I saw a skunk', Austin considers 'saw' univocal. Similarly I suppose he would say that 'was smelled' is univocal in 'The skunk was smelled' and 'The odour was smelled'. But now if Austin did indeed maintain this, he would have found himself in an extreme Humian position. It is of course nonsense to speak of seeing an odour or of smelling a colour. And our little ontology of skunks, odours, and colours becomes incoherent unless we are prepared to do what Hume did and split up the skunk. For Hume makes the Cartesian move; the skunk that we see is not the one that we smell. What we see is a skunk-sight, what we smell is a skunk-odour. This ontology, like that of Descartes, is logically coherent. Indeed it is logically necessary once we have committed ourselves to the univocity of perceptual verbs like 'is seen', 'is heard', over skunks and colours and over skunks and sounds. What seems to count against it is that we can and do say of a single skunk that we saw it, heard it, smelled it. Putting the skunk together again by means of some principle of association does not affect the fundamental logical issue. I do not know what Austin would say to this; I understand he did not find the Humian way congenial. I merely cite this as an example of the dangers involved in fixing certain predicates as univocal without bothering to check what happens to the rest of the language. For my part, I here prefer to take the Strawsonian injunction against splitting particulars seriously and to use different meanings of 'see' for colours and skunks, different meanings of 'smell' for odours and skunks, different meanings of 'hear' for sounds and skunks.

In general, anyone who uses univocal meanings of perceptual verbs for phenomenal objects and material objects will be forced to split particulars in the way Hume did; he will have a different skunk for each perceptual operation. His decision to keep the perceptual verbs univocal amounts to a decision to reject the language of material objects in favour of a language of sights and sounds, colours and odours. If we are to keep the language of material objects and to allow that the same material object is heard, seen, smelled and touched, we must bear in mind that the perceptual verbs we use for material objects and for phenomenal data are necessarily equivocal. And if they are equivocal, we cannot argue the question 'Does one see material objects or does one only see colours?' In saying that we see a colour and that we see a house, we need different senses of 'see' to begin with and once we have them the argument cannot get started. For this reason, too, the language of material objects and the language of 'sense data' are separate parts of our language, using different perceptual meanings for their different sorts of objects. There can be no question of 'translation' or reduction of one to the other.

II

The rule I have been applying can be deduced from certain simple laws of predication. A theory of predication asserts these laws in the form of formal properties of the predicative relation, the basic notion being that of the predicability of a term. Thus on the traditional Aristotelian theory, which is correct in essentials, predication is transitive but not symmetrical.

We predicate a term of a thing by affirming or denying it of that thing, and a term is said to be predicable of a thing if and only if either the affirmation or denial is true. For example, the term *clean* is *im*predicable of the equator since neither the affirmation 'is clean' nor the denial 'is not clean' is true of the equator. A statement predicating the affirmation or the denial of the term *clean* of the equator is a category mistake. And in general, if *Pa* is a statement in which 'is *P*' is said of *a* and *P'a* is a statement in which 'is not *P*' is said of *a*, then the term *P* is said to be predicable of *a* only if either *Pa* or *P'a* is true[1]. When *Pa* and *P'a* are both false, we may call them vacuous statements. Category mistakes are one important species of vacuous statement: I shall presently show that the so-called syntactical and semantical paradoxes constitute another such species. Category mistakes and the paradoxes embody 'impredicable' predicates in the sense defined, and both have been called type mistakes.

Category mistakes are false statements whose denials are also false. Strictly speaking 'denial' applies to predicates and not to statements but we can speak derivatively of statements as denials of other statements. The denial of a subject-predicate statement *S* is another subject predicate statement *S'* that is similar to *S*

[1] 'Is not P' which is the logical denial of the term P is not true of *whatever* is outside of the extension of 'is P' but only of those subjects of predication that fail somehow to be P. For example if P is *a married citizen*, then P' is true of all and only those things that are unmarried citizens, married non-citizens, or unmarried non-citizens, and not true of the only even prime number. In the sense that the denial is true of only those things that are of the sort or type that fail to be P, we may say that it is not subject-free. It is, however, context-free. Thus if my house is on a hill we do not—unless special explanations are given—either affirm or deny that the house is taller than the hill; nevertheless *taller than the hill* is predicable of my house. Similarly, since Socrates never heard of Moses we should not say that he was or was not in awe of Moses. But this does not mean that being in awe of Moses (unlike being in awe of Parmenides) is impredicable of Socrates. The point is that special explanations could be given to free the context for predication in these cases and such explanation would not involve tampering with the sort or type of thing the house is or Socrates is.

except that where S affirms the predicate term, S' denies it. In saying that category mistakes are statements, I wish to emphasize that they are not exceptions to the law of the excluded middle. That law governs the assertion and negation of whole statements; it does not apply to the affirmation and denial of predicate terms within statements. Thus it is either the case that the equator is clean or it is not the case that the equator is clean. But it is neither the case that the equator is clean, nor is it the case that the equator is unclean (or not clean). When the distinction between denial and negation is respected, it becomes unnecessary to introduce special 'type' restrictions to account for impredicability and thereby to rule out certain utterances as non-statements. Any false statement (even one whose denial is false) can be negated and its negation is a true statement.

If S' is the denial of S, then S is the denial of S'. The analogue to the law of double negation thus holds for two denials. But negation does not cancel a denial; S is not equivalent to $-S'$. For any statement S, the following are analytically true:

1. $S \vee - S$
2. $S' \vee - S'$
3. $-(S \,.\, S')$

The third law is the denial analogue to the law of contradiction for negation. But none of the formulas prohibits $- S \,.\, - S'$. There is therefore no denial analogue to the law of the excluded middle. I call (3) the law of incompatibility. It is probably this law to which Aristotle referred as the law of contradiction. For Aristotle calls a statement false only if its denial is true.[1] He therefore considers certain statements to be neither true nor false. The most notable instance occurs in his discussion of contingent statements about the future. But category mistakes are also 'vacuous'. It is in this Aristotelian sense of 'false' that category mistakes are said to be neither true nor false.

Without the denial-negation distinction, type theory degenerates into a series of *ad hoc* restrictions on what counts as a statement. For when denial is identified with negation, category mistakes violate the law of excluded middle. But there is no reason to

[1] Aristotle, *Met.*, 1011b 26–9. Cf. also 1005b 17–20.

absorb denial into negation and every reason to distinguish these two ways of gainsaying a statement. I shall illustrate this fundamental point by showing how the distinction permits a simple formal resolution of the predication paradoxes.

Let I' be the statement 'The class of all classes that do not contain themselves as members is not a class that contains itself as a member'. If I' is true,it follows that I is true and if I is true it follows that I' is true. We therefore have

$$I \equiv I'$$

or $$I . I' \vee -I . -I'$$

Since the first disjunct is false by the law of incompatibility, it follows that $-I . -I'$ is true and hence that being a class that does not contain itself is impredicable of the class of all classes that do not contain themselves. Note that nothing is here said about 'illegitimate totalities' or self-reference. This saves possible embarrassment elsewhere.

A similar treatment can be given any of the so-called 'semantical' paradoxes. Thus let H be the statement ' "Heterological" is heterological'. Then $H \equiv H'$ will resolve itself as $-H . -H'$ from which it follows that being heterological is impredicable of 'heterological'. Note that the paradoxes are not generated as contradictory equivalences. We have in fact no warrant for deriving $H \equiv -H$ since the implication $-H \supset H'$ is unsupported. The negation of H is equivalent to $-H . H' \vee -H . -H'$. And from $-H . -H'$ we cannot infer H. It is because logicians identify denial with negation that they are forced to say that H is logically antinomous. And once they get a formal contradiction, they are further forced to rule out H as a non-statement.

Like category mistakes, the paradoxes of predication are vacuous. But they differ from category mistakes in two ways. (i) Their vacuous character can be formally proved. We can, for example, formally show that if a hypochondriac is a man who says he has a disease that he has not got, then 'I am a hypochondriac' is vacuous. Similarly, if L is the liar's statement, we can formally show that both L and its denial are false. (ii) Unlike any category mistake, a paradox is not vacuous *because* the subject of predication is not the 'sort' or 'type' of thing that is or is not P. I am the *sort* of thing that is or is not now lying. Nevertheless 'I am now lying' is a false statement whose denial is false. In what follows I shall confine myself to the consideration of category mistakes, that is to those statements whose vacuousness results from the fact that the subject is not the sort of thing that is or fails to be P[1].

The relation 'is predicable of' has so far been defined for statements of the form Pa in which a term is predicated of an individual. What of two terms? The theory of predication requires that terms like *men* and *white thing* be related by predicability. Thus Aristotle says that 'Some white things are men' does not predicate being a man except in an accidental way. In any predicative tie between *men* and *white thing*, the term that is the 'natural subject' is *men*. To account for this and other such examples on logical grounds, we need a definition of predicability as holding between any two general terms P and Q. Using the notion of predicability already defined, this is quite easily obtained: *P is predicable of Q if and only if P is predicable of whatever Q is predicable.* I shall use a reverse arrow to stand for the predicability relation between two terms. The following formula then defines the relation:

$$P \leftarrow Q \equiv (x)[(Qx \vee Q'x) \supset (Px \vee P'x)]$$

Thus *white things* is predicable of *men* since all things that are either men or not men are either white or not white. On the other hand, *men* is impredicable of *white things* since there are things (e.g. skies) that are either white or not white and these things are neither men nor not men. The statement 'This sky is not a man' is a category mistake. Similarly if (*theorem*, *interesting*) is a predicative tie, then *theorem* is the natural subject. For we have many things that are either interesting or not interesting of which neither 'is a theorem' nor 'is not a theorem' is true. Thus 'My desk is not a theorem' is false and so is its denial 'My desk is a theorem'. Both are category mistakes.

So defined, the predicative tie between terms is non-symmetrical. We have terms P and Q such that $(P \leftarrow Q)$ but—$(Q \leftarrow P)$. It is

[1] Certain definite descriptions are also vacuous but they are not 'type mistakes' since they are vacuous for the reason that the subject fails to refer. A statement like 'The present king of France is valid' is vacuous on two counts; we should probably classify it as a type mistake since its vacuousness is not the result of the failure to refer. Clearly the statement is vacuous even if it does succeed in referring. Conditionals whose consequents are vacuous are vacuous statements. And a conditional is vacuous when its antecedent is false. For a discussion of these and other sorts of vacuous statements, see my 'Truth Functional Counterfactuals', *Analysis Supplement* (Oxford 1964). See also, 'Meaning Relations and the Analytic', *The Journal of Philosophy*, vol. 60 (1963).

however entirely possible to have terms predicable both ways. Whatever is or is not a Quaker is or is not a painter and *vice versa.* Neither way of predicating the terms *Quaker* and *painter* is unnatural. Predication is non-symmetrical, not asymmetrical.

It is also evident that predication is reflexive and that $P \leftarrow P$ holds for any term P. And finally, predication is transitive. For if P is predicable of Q and Q is predicable of R, then P is predicable of R.

The statement 'Some even prime numbers are English Prime Ministers' is a category mistake. And we can now define the class of category mistakes that tie two general terms in a predicative tie. A statement 'Some P is Q' is a category mistake if P is impredicable of Q and Q is impredicable of P. Nothing that is or fails to be an even prime number is or fails to be an English Prime minister; any statement predicatively tying the terms in question is therefore a category mistake. We see that an unnatural predication contains terms that are predicable in only one direction, a category mistake contains terms predicable in *neither* direction.

To avoid confusion over different uses of the term 'predicable' I shall list several equivalent ways of rendering '$P \leftarrow Q$'.

Being P is predicable of (what is) Q.
It can be said of (what is) Q that it is P
The term P is predicable of the term Q
That it is P can be said of (what is) Q

All or any of these express what is meant by saying that a term P is predicable of another term Q.

We have just seen that a category mistake contains terms that are mutually impredicable. Let us call such terms 'N-related' to indicate that statements predicatively tying them are often called nonsensical. Thus *square* and *argument* are N-related terms but *circular* and *argument* are 'U-related'. I use the symbol 'U' for a pair of terms predicable of one another in at least one direction; it indicates that these terms can be *used* together to form significant subject-predicate statements. This thesis that category correct statements contain U-related terms may be stated as a theorem of the theory of predication:

$$U(P,Q) \equiv P \leftarrow Q \vee Q \leftarrow P.$$

The thesis states that any category-correct predication tying two terms must have at least one of the two terms predicable of the other. For example, any statement of the form 'Some P is Q' will be significant (although not necessarily 'natural') only if either it is the case that whatever can be said to be P can be said to be Q, or it is the case that whatever can be said to be Q can be said to be P. U-related terms are also called 'co-significant' or 'co-predicable'. If 'Some P is Q' is *true*, then there is at least one *individual* of which 'is P' is true and of which 'is Q' is true. It follows that if the statement is category-correct, then there is at least one individual of which 'is P' or 'is not P' is true and 'is Q' or 'is not Q' is true. This gives us another important equivalence:

$$U(P,Q) \equiv (\exists x)(Px \vee P'x)\,(Qx \vee Q'x))$$

Another principle is worth stating explicitly. If P is a predicable term, there must be something that is either P or P'. That is,

$$(\exists x)\,(Px \vee P'x)$$

If we formulate the theory of predication for predicable terms, then this formula will be a theorem. The theorem rules that such terms as *virtuous prime numbers* are impredicable terms.

I said earlier that talk of bodiless spirits forces upon us Descartes' dualistic doctrine of persons. For Descartes, the statement 'Some individuals that think of Vienna are individuals that weigh a hundred pounds' is a category mistake: it is *logically* impossible that there be any such individuals. Of course I do not mean to say that no Cartesian can speak of a man who weighs a hundred pounds and who happens also to think of Vienna. What the Cartesian denies is that the man in question is an *individual*. And the reason he denies it must now be clear. Spirits neither weigh nor fail to weigh one hundred pounds. (They are not that sort of thing.) Rocks neither think nor fail to think about Vienna. (Rocks are not that sort of thing.) On the other hand, spirits either think or fail to think of Vienna and rocks either weigh or fail to weigh one hundred pounds. It follows that being a thing that weighs one hundred pounds is impredicable of what thinks of Vienna and being a thing that thinks of Vienna is impredicable of what weighs one hundred pounds. Thus the original statement conjoins terms neither of which is predicable of the other. It is therefore a category mistake.

This distinction between individuals and non-individuals may be puzzling. For it seems that 'is thinking of Vienna' and 'weighs one hundred pounds' are co-predicable of an individual, since we do say they are both true of Smith. Moreover, 'Smith is thinking of Vienna and he weighs one hundred pounds' is not a zeugma like 'This cape is stormy in the winter and is loose at the shoulders'. And this must be because 'Smith' has one meaning in that statement. This argument, implicit in many recent attempts to reject the Cartesian conclusion, is a bad one. We certainly can define entities that are non-individuals and the fact that such entities entertain two predicates of different types in single statements of ordinary discourse cannot be used to argue for their individuality. To clarify the distinction between individuals and non-individuals, and incidently to expose this ordinary language argument as a bad one, I shall consider three examples.

Suppose someone defines a red earache to be what a man has when he has a red ear and a pain in that ear. By this definition, a red earache is an entity. But clearly, the entity so defined is not an individual. Moreover the statement 'Some aches are red' is still a category mistake, since there is no individual that instantiates the statement, nor could there be any such individual. It is nevertheless true that the (artificially composite) entity we have defined is literally red and literally an ache. For it is a pain *cum* red ear. But nothing about the category status of pains and ears has changed merely because we now have a new 'entity'.

Take a more natural and less obvious case. *A* maintains there can be no such thing as a blue event. But *B* points out that anything that can be said to occur at midnight is an event. We can speak of the blue lightning that occurred at midnight. It follows that there are blue events. *A* must deny that the blue lightning is an individual if he is to avoid this conclusion and this he can very plausibly do. When we say the lightning is blue, we mean something different by 'the lightning' than what we mean in 'The lightning occurred at midnight'. That which is blue is no more an event which occurs than is the brown murderer an event in a (brown) murder. The murderer cannot be said to occur; it is the murder that occurs or fails to occur. Similarly the lightning that is blue cannot be said to occur although it is something that participates in the lightning that does occur. So the fact that 'we can say' the blue lightning occurred is no proof that we are referring to an individual.

One further illustration of the dangers of relying on linguistic arguments to determine the individuality of what is referred to by a singular term: We do not literally wish to speak of bankrupt islands, and yet we can speak of Iceland as bankrupt and we can say that Iceland is an island. So characterized 'Iceland' does not name an individual, yet the statement 'Iceland is a bankrupt island' is hardly an obvious zeugma.

These examples must give pause to anyone who would argue against Descartes that Smith is an individual, from the usage that permits us to say that Smith is fat and thinks. Similarly Hume's phenomenalist position that material objects are non-individuals remains unaffected by the circumstance that 'we can say' of a material object that it was both seen and heard. What is or is not an individual can only be determined on *logical* grounds. As the 'red earache' shows, there is no theoretical reason why we could not *make* sense of any category mish-mash. But the criterion for individuality grounded in the theory of predication places the crucial *logical* restriction on the procedure. And that criterion—by now familiar—is this:

An entity x is an individual if and only if every pair of predicates P and Q that is true of x is such that either P is predicable of Q or Q is predicable of P.

By this criterion, the blue lightning that occurs at midnight is not an individual since there are things (e.g. accidents) that occur but are neither blue nor not blue and other things (chairs, for instance) that are blue but neither occur nor fail to occur at midnight. Thus being blue is impredicable of what occurs and occurring is impredicable of what is blue. Similarly the red earache is a non-individual; there are things that are mild or not mild but neither red nor not red (winters for example) and other things that are either red or not red but neither mild nor not mild (ears, chairs, and so forth) but the 'red earache' we have defined is something that is mild or intense and is also red. And finally, Iceland (*qua* bankrupt frozen island) is not an individual, since corporations are either bankrupt or not bankrupt but neither cold nor not cold, while twigs are either cold or not cold but neither bankrupt nor not bankrupt.

As for Hume and Descartes, the proper way to criticize them is in their assumptions. The existence of a categorially distinct thing called an ego is Descartes' dogma. The univocity of perceptual terms as applied to material objects and to phenomenal data is Hume's dogma. We cannot accept these assumptions and still hope to attempt to deny the Cartesian and Humian positions on the non-individuality of persons and material objects.

Two distinct sorts of sets of individuals are defined by predicability. Given any term *P* there is the set of individuals of which *P* is predicable. Let us call such a set a *category*. Categories are always relative to some given term. Thus Socrates and his philosophy belong to the same category with respect to the term *interesting* but not with respect to the term *white*. I shall use the symbol '*Cp*' to stand for the category of things that are defined by the term *P*. The word 'type' is reserved for another sort of set. Two individuals, *a* and *b*, belong to the same type if and only if whatever is predicable of *a* is predicable of *b* and whatever is predicable of *b* is predicable of *a*. Thus the members of a type have all of the same predicates predicable of them. Socrates and his philosophy do not belong to the same type since there are many predicates predicable of Socrates but not of his philosophy.

Using the language of 'categories', the relation of predication between any two terms is seen to be that of category inclusion. To say that *P* is predicable of *Q* is equivalent to saying that *Cq* is contained in *Cp*. It follows also that a 'category straddler' is never an individual. If *b* is some entity belonging to two different categories *Cp* and *Cq* such that it is neither the case that *Cp* is contained in *Cq* nor the case that *Cq* is contained in *Cp* then *b* is not an individual. Thus if Iceland is in *C*-bankrupt and also in *C*-cold, then Iceland is not an individual since *C*-bankrupt and *C*-cold then overlap and neither includes the other. It is more accurate to say that overlapping categories are really impossible, since categories are sets of *individuals* of which the defining terms are predicable. Strictly speaking, there are no category straddlers.

To summarize: A theory of predication determines the logical restriction on the applicability of predicates to the things we talk about. It answers the following question: Given a number of individuals *a*, *b*, *c*, etc. and a number of predicates *P*, *Q*, *R*, etc. how are these predicates applicable and inapplicable to the individuals? Philosophers have either ignored this problem or they have adopted a rule that is incorrect, e.g. we saw that many philosophers have adopted a rule for any two individuals and any three predicates that reads in the following way: Given any two individuals *a* and *b*, there can be no three predicates *P*, *Q*, and *R* such that *P* applies to *a* but not to *b*, whereas *Q* applies to *b*, but not to *a*, and *R* applies (without equivocation) to both *a* and *b*. This rule is incorrect, and indeed, it has led some philosophers who have attempted to apply it to despair of any theory of predication for a natural language. The correct rule is a rule for any three things and any two predicates. I have tried to show how this rule is a critical instrument, and how any piece of metaphysics may be checked through it, or ruled out by it.

I wish to add a final irreverent note. There is a critical technique that is much older than Kant's; it legislates for metaphysics from the theory of assertion, not from the theory of knowledge. Plato's *Parmenides*, Aristotle's *Analytics*, and parts of his *Metaphysics* are the representatives of a critique which uses philosophical logic, not epistemology, to correct metaphysics and to set its bounds. This classical style of critique has witnessed a refreshing revival in the twentieth century at the hands of Husserl, Russell, and Ryle. I cannot help thinking that it would be most unfortunate if the programme implicit in the best work of the above philosophers were sacrificed for still one more return to Kant. For it may turn out that once we solve the right problems in philosophical logic we shall discover that Kant belongs to his century and not to ours.

XIV

REASONS AND REASONING

by JUDITH JARVIS THOMSON

Associate Professor, Massachusetts Institute of Technology

When is *p* a reason for *q*? I am not asking when is *p* a good reason for *q*, but rather, when is *p* any reason at all for *q*? The fact that there is now a bit of lint on my carpet might be taken by someone as a reason for thinking that Eisenhower is dead, perhaps because he thinks there was a plot and that the bit of lint was to be left as a signal. But there is no plot, and the bit of lint is not a signal. The bit of lint is not even a poor reason for thinking Eisenhower dead; it is no reason at all.

This question is broader than the question when one thing is evidence for another. Smith's saying that Napoleon was bald may be a reason for thinking that he was, but it is not evidence that he was. And while you can have a reason for thinking that it will rain, I do not think you can have evidence that it will. 'Evidence' refers to traces and effects (what 'shows out' from a thing), so evidence must be contemporaneous with or later than what it is evidence for. And lastly, to have conclusive evidence for something is not, I think, to have a logically conclusive reason for it.

Nor am I asking when one thing can be taken as causally connected with another. That something is a short-haired beige cat with brown-tipped ears and paws and a brown tail is a reason for thinking it is a Siamese cat, although it neither implies nor is implied by that; yet it could hardly be thought that a thing's having that conjunctive property causally accounts for its being a Siamese cat, or conversely, or that the presence of the two properties always has a common cause.

I am not even going to try to give a set of logically necessary conditions for one thing to be a reason for another—I want only to discuss some conditions which have been said to be logically necessary.

Finally, no doubt we should say, The truth of '*p*' is, or would be, a reason for thinking that *q*. But I shall in general abbreviate this as: *p* is a reason for *q*.

1. It is sometimes said that *p* is not a reason for *q* if *p* implies *q*. 'What's your reason for thinking he's a bachelor?' 'He's an unmarried male.' The Duke of Wellington asks 'What's your reason for thinking I'm mortal?' and is told 'All men are, and you are a man'. As Mill said, in order to know that the premisses are true one has already to know that the conclusion is true—so if I am in doubt about the conclusion, and want to be given a reason for accepting it, it will do no good to offer me what I must regard as at least as doubtful as the conclusion. Logically conclusive 'reasons' are too good to be reasons.

This may be put in a different way. To say '*p*, so *q*', where *p* implies *q*, is not to *reason* (infer, draw a conclusion). For to be reasoning one should surely be arriving at a new bit of information, rather than just re-casting or re-stating what is already contained in the premisses.

Now this puzzle appears to me to be fairly easily dealt with—one begins by asking why the giving of reasons should always be helpful in just that way in which it is here denied that the giving of logically conclusive reasons is helpful. But what appears to me to be more difficult to deal with, and in proportion more important, is what one might call the preference for the deductive model, that is, the view that *p* is not really a reason for *q* *unless p* implies *q*. This latter is not, I think, in head-on collision with the former, for when you bring out what unfortunate consequences are supposed to ensue if *p* does not imply *q*, you see that these are not what, for example, Mill would say must be true of *p* and *q* if *p* is to be a reason for *q*. But I shall not try to show this, and will in fact concern myself only with the preference for the deductive model.

'*p* isn't a reason for *q* unless *p* implies *q*.' Well, perhaps nobody would actually say this: it is too obviously either false or a verbal recommendation. 'Strictly speaking, *p* is no reason for *q* unless *p* implies *q*.' Too strong still. 'It is perfectly all right to say that *p* is a reason for *q* even where *p* does not imply *q*; even to say that *p* is strictly speaking a reason for *q*. But *p* is not by itself a reason for *q* unless *p* implies *q*'. Still too strong, for surely Smith might be a man (and it be a topic) such that it would be true to say 'Smith says it is so, and that is by itself reason for thinking it is so'. Even

'Strictly speaking Smith's saying so is by itself reason for thinking it is so'.

In the course of the following I am going to set out some very familiar facts about the use of the expression 'reason for'; each one is important only in that some philosopher or other has at any rate appeared to be denying it. The first is this: we so use the expression 'reason for' that it is sometimes true to say *p* is a reason for, strictly speaking a reason for, by itself a reason for, strictly speaking by itself a reason for *q*, even though *p* does not imply *q*. (Henceforth I shall omit these qualifiers, for they change nothing.)

Now if a philosopher means to be denying this, he is simply mistaken. But if what he means to be doing is to propose that, for this or that reason, we ought not so to use this expression, then what he says may well be true—only now we need to see the reason. And the reason must not amount to nothing more than a proposal that we revise the use of some related term.

In fact, I think that the source of the inclination to narrow down the use of 'reason for' is this: 'If *p* does not imply *q*, then if a man says "*p*, so *q*" he cannot be supposed to be *reasoning* unless he is supposed to be suppressing a premiss *r*, where *r* is contingent, and such that the conjunction of *p* and *r* does imply *q*'. And then one who said this might go on 'so we ought not use "reason for" in the manner you describe', or he might go on 'for my part you can have "reason for"; all I'm interested in is "reasoning" '.

The first point to make about this is that one cannot call it either a denial of some fact about the use of 'reasoning' or a proposal to narrow down the use of this word. We do indeed say of some people who say '*p*, so *q*', where *p* does not imply *q*, that they are reasoning; but this is not being denied. What is being denied is that such people can be said to be reasoning and not suppressing a premiss of the required kind.

All the same, we may well ask why this should be said, for a man who said '*p*, so *q*' might deny that he had been assuming an *r* strong enough, together with *p*, to imply *q*. He might refuse to commit himself to anything quite so strong. Of course a man may be assuming a thing even when he believes he is not, but the question is, why *must* he be assuming such an *r*? 'Well, if *p* doesn't imply *q*, then *p* can be true and *q* false.' This is only to say that if *p* does not imply *q*, then it does not imply *q*. 'Well, if *p* does not imply *q*, then in knowing that *p* you do not yet know that *q*.' The same again. Is there nothing more to this than a stammer? 'If *p* does not imply *q*, then for all you know in knowing that *p*, *q* may well be false. If you are lucky, *q* is true. But this would be a matter of luck. An accident. A grace of fate. Now reasoning should surely involve drawing a conclusion from a set of premisses. But you can't be said to draw the conclusion that *q* from *p* if for all you know in knowing that *p* it would at best be a matter of luck if *q* as well. So to "reason" from *p* by itself to *q* isn't really to be reasoning; it's like saying one thing, and then taking a chance on it that something else is also true—like taking a leap in the dark, or more prosaically, like guessing.' (From here on I shall refer to this as the '*formula*'.) So there is only one kind of reasoning, namely deductive reasoning.

People often write as if it were quite clear what the problem of induction is, and only unclear how it is to be solved or shown to be insoluble. That is, many start straight off to discuss the nature of justification, and then try to show that in this or that sense induction is or is not justified. Or again, they say 'There was this old problem of induction that was clearly insoluble, but now there is this new one, which is soluble, but just very difficult.' Whereas, it seems to me exceedingly difficult to see even what the 'old' problem of induction was, much less how the new one is supposed to differ from it.

One form which the problem of induction took was this: What is the suppressed major premiss in a bit of inductive reasoning—namely an argument from some to all, or from all past ones to the next one, thus an argument in which the premisses do not imply the conclusion—and how do we know it to be true? What is of special interest, however, is that this problem can only arise for one to whom it seems that if *p* does not imply *q*, then '*p*, so *q*' is at best an argument with a suppressed premiss. (It is of interest to find that Mill is among those who were in search of the suppressed major, thereby *here* showing a preference for the deductive model.) But that a man who says '*p*, so *q*' (where *p* and *q* are as indicated) must be suppressing a premiss if he is really to be reasoning was not simply *assumed*—we can take Hume to have set the stage for the search for the suppressed premiss by having raised the question whether or not to 'reason' from *p* alone to *q* is to be reasoning, and having argued that it is not. So we can say that there was a prior form taken by the problem of induction, namely: Can a man be said to be reasoning who 'reasons' from p alone to q? Or, in other words, if a man says 'p, so q' must he be understood to be suppressing a premiss if he is to be understood to be reasoning?

What I called the 'formula' above is what it seems to me a man would have in mind who answered 'yes'—in fact what Hume had in mind. But then *if* I am right in this, it is astonishing that there should appear in the discussions of the problem of induction so many remarks to the effect that Hume showed conclusively that there can be no such thing as a justification (in a certain sense of justification?) of induction. For although the formula is not a mere stammer, it is certainly not wholly correct.

But first I shall discuss two currently fashionable attempts to reply to it which seem to me to be, the one inadequate, the other mistaken.

2. Inductive reasoning is not the only place at which it has been said 'Here it must be supposed that a premiss is suppressed'. Or rather we may take Lewis Carroll's tortoise to have said this for the case of what you might have thought to be, as they stand, deductively valid arguments. Thus (as it might be) 'This is red' does not imply 'This is coloured'—or does not imply it by itself. Only together with a further premiss 'If this is red it is coloured' (or something at least as strong as this) could it be said that 'This is red' implies 'This is coloured'. For suppose 'If this is red it is coloured' is not among the premisses of an argument from 'This is red' to 'This is coloured'; then, if it were false, the premiss of this argument (there is only one) could be, in fact would be, true and the conclusion false. But then if a man says 'This is red, so it is coloured' he must be understood to suppress this further premiss if he is to be understood to be deriving this conclusion from his premisses—for if he did not 'accept' this as a further premiss he could perfectly well think his premiss true, and just be taking a stab at it, a guess at it, that his conclusion was also true.

But if this is a reason for saying that such a man suppresses this one further premiss, there is equally good reason for saying that he suppresses yet another, namely the further premiss 'If this is red and if this is red it is coloured, then this is coloured'. And so on and on. So we never have enough premisses for us to be able to say that this set of premisses implies the conclusion; our man cannot be understood to be drawing his conclusion from his set of premisses, for it would be impossible for him even to set out all the premisses from which it is supposed he draws it.

The point to be made is of course this: there is no such possibility as the possibility 'if "If this is red it is coloured" were not true', for 'If this is red it is coloured' is not merely true, but necessarily true. And therefore 'This is red' could not be true and 'This is coloured' false. And therefore 'This is red' does, does by itself, imply 'This is coloured'. And therefore there is in this no reason for saying that a man who so argues suppresses a further premiss. Even if we grant that such a man is not reasoning unless he believes that if the thing is red it is coloured, there is in this no reason for saying that what he must believe if he is to *be* reasoning must be called a suppressed premiss *of* his reasoning.

Now it seems to me that this quite settles the issue, and that the point is adequately summarized in the following way: if 'If p then q' is a necessary truth, then p by itself implies q. But in fact many people have been inclined to summarize it in a different way. It is said that what Lewis Carroll brought home to us is that not everything can be a premiss; inference requires *rules*, too. So in particular, 'This is red' implies 'This is coloured' in virtue of a certain rule of inference, namely 'From a statement of the form "x is red" you are entitled to infer a statement of the form "x is coloured" '. But why it should be supposed that this way of putting the point is especially illuminating, I cannot understand. In the first place, what I set down in setting down the rule is a statement; and so the question might be raised: And what if this statement were not true? And so should it not appear as a premiss? To say 'But it is a rule!' ('an inference-ticket!') is just to shout. For there is, plainly enough, a statement—and here is a man who asks what if that statement were not true; and what has to be done with him is bring home that it is not merely true, but true of necessity.

Nor is there, so far as I can see, any other plausible way of setting out this 'rule'. To put it in the form of an imperative (about which, then, it could not be asked, what if it were not true?) would unfortunately be mad. Must I really be inferring statements from each other all the time? So also for attempts to set it out as a conditional imperative. Infer this from that, whenever—whenever what? whenever I want to infer something from that? whenever I want to infer this from something? Moreover, to put the rule in the form of an imperative brings out more sharply a difficulty which was concealed when, although it was called a rule, what we were given was a declarative statement. For we may well ask now just what *action* such an imperative enjoins us to perform? (Just what action did the rule in the first form say we are entitled to perform?) 'Infer this from that!' One would have no idea what was expected in response to such an imperative.

The same difficulty confronts the attempt to set these rules out as permission slips (licences to do this or that)—thus as 'You are hereby permitted to. . . .' *What* am I hereby permitted to do? And in this form yet another difficulty arises—for what would one make of 'You are hereby permitted to infer "This is coloured" from "This is red" '? Wasn't I permitted to do this before? (This difficulty is of particular interest, because a consideration of it would bring out how the rules of inference are *not* like the rules of a game.)

In the second place, this way of talking encourages one to think that certain difficulties can be eliminated if we allow for the possibility of non-necessary or non-analytic rules of inference. In particular, that the problem about the suppressed inductive premiss can be eliminated in this way.

'Well, for there to be inference at all there has to be a rule justifying the inference. Every inference proceeds from a set of premisses to a conclusion by or in accordance with a rule. And now why should there not be non-necessary rules of inference? But then we have solved the problem. For it may be that p does not imply q, and yet that a man who says "p, so q" is reasoning and not suppressing a premiss r (where r is contingent and the conjunction of p and r implies q). For it may be that he reasons in accordance with a non-necessary rule of inference. So for example, a man who says "This is a lion, so it is carnivorous" may well be reasoning, but this in accordance with the non-necessary rule of inference "Infer a statement of the form 'x is carnivorous' from a statement of the form 'x is a lion' ". Or again, a man who says "Half of the balls we examined are red, so half of the balls are red" may well be reasoning, but this in accordance with the non-necessary rule of inference "Posit that the limit of the relative frequency in a collection is the relative frequency in so far examined cases". Or again, a man who says "He killed his father, so he committed a sin" may well be reasoning, but this in accordance with the non-necessary rule of inference "Conclude that a man has committed a sin when it is given that he killed his father". Or again, a man who says "He looks green and he's groaning, so he's feeling sick" may well be reasoning, but this in accordance with the non-necessary rule of inference "Take it that a man who looks green and is groaning is feeling sick".'

Stating the rules in this form has seemed to some to simplify things (at least in the first three sorts of cases)—for what is in question is a kind of action, and now all that has to be done is to show that performing actions of this kind is reasonable (that is, we need only 'vindicate' the performing of actions of this kind). But these are in no clear sense actions, and so to call them this simplifies nothing. (What am I being told to do when I am told to *posit* thus and so? Presumably to think something, and not merely to say or write something. And what is one to make of: 'I'm not telling you it *is* this; I'm merely telling you to think it is'?)

So the rules have to be re-expressed as statements—the first, for instance, in the form 'From a statement of the form "x is a lion" you may infer a statement of the form "x is carnivorous" '.

And then we must ask if anything is gained by this move. The objection was this: 'If a man says "p, so q"—or in particular here, "This is a lion, so it is carnivorous", he must be suppressing a premiss if he is to be understood to be reasoning; for, for all he knows in knowing that the thing in front of him is a lion, it would at best be an accident, a stroke of luck, if the thing in front of him were also carnivorous. So to "reason" from "This is a lion" to "This is carnivorous" is not really to be reasoning; it is like saying one thing, and then taking a chance on it that something else is also true.' But if the argument is to the effect that passing from 'This is a lion' to This is carnivorous' is not reasoning, it is certainly an argument to the effect that passing from the former to the latter is not inferring anything. And so how are we helped when we are told 'Ah, but you might infer the latter from the former—via the non-necessary rule "You are entitled to infer the latter from the former" '? For the argument is to the effect that there is no such rule—that is, that it is not true to say that you are entitled to infer the latter from the former.

This point is quite independent of the question how strong this rule is supposed to be—that is, of the question whether or not its truth is supposed to be compatible or incompatible with there existing at some time a lion that is not carnivorous. Thus, with the question whether the rule is supposed always to give a true conclusion from a true premiss, or only usually. The argument is to the effect that there is no such thing as inferring 'This is carnivorous' from 'This is a lion', and thus that in neither of these interpretations is the statement of the rule true.

In sum, this proposed resolution of the problem is not that at all; it quite passes the problem by.

3. There is a modern form of 'solution' to the problem of induction that consists in saying that there are pairs of statements p and q such that p does not imply q, and yet such that, far from its being a matter of guessing to 'reason' from p to q, it is of the very essence of rationality to do so. For example, a pair of the form 'All present and past S's have been P' and 'The next S you meet will be P'. (To do this is just what we *mean* by 'being rational'—the rational man, by definition, does do this.) This is far from clear, but I am going to take it (I hope not without justification) to mean: by definition, or of necessity, the truth of a statement of the one form is reason for thinking the relevant statement of the second form is also true. Or: a statement of the one form implies that there is reason for thinking the relevant statement of the second form true. If this were correct, it looks as if our problem would be solved: there would after all be such a thing as inductive reasoning, and it would not need to be said that a man who so 'reasons' must be understood to be suppressing a premiss if he is to be understood to be reasoning.

It has been objected to this that it merely shifts the problem: if to reason so is, by definition, being 'reasonable', then all the same, what good reason is there for being reasonable? But the right objection is rather that the claim is false.

One way of defending it has been this: how could it be a mere matter of fact that one thing is a reason for another? Surely the question whether one thing is a reason for another is a question for reflection; and surely reflection alone shows you that 'All past and present S's have been P' is a reason for 'The next S will also be P'.[1]

But in fact the question whether one thing is a reason for another is often very obviously a question for investigation rather than

[1] Cf., e.g., N. R. Hanson, 'Good Inductive Reasons', *Philosophical Quarterly*, vol. 11 (1961), pp. 123–134.

reflection. Is 'Smith said it' a reason for thinking it true? You have to know something about Smith; if he is a habitual liar, or it is a subject on which he generally tells lies, it is not. Is 'This is a lion' a reason for thinking it carnivorous? We need to know something about lions.

These examples are worth considering for a moment. In section 1, I mentioned the following fact of usage: it is sometimes true to say that p is a reason for q even though p does not imply q. And I said that perhaps nobody means to be denying this; perhaps what is at stake is either the proposal that we narrow our usage in view of the 'formula', or rather just the 'formula' itself. We should now mention a second fact of usage—one which, once again, appears at first sight to have been denied—namely that we so use the words 'reason for' that it is sometimes true to say that *this* thing's being S is a reason for thinking it P, although it is not the case that, quite generally, just anything's being S is a reason for thinking it P. It might be, for example, that *Smith's* saying the thing is so is—given his character and the nature of the topic—a reason for thinking it is so; although Jones' saying it is so would be no reason at all for thinking it is so. Certain moral philosophers have at any rate appeared to deny this. Thus: 'Reasons are implicitly general—what is a reason for thinking one person acted wrongly must equally be reason for thinking any other person acted wrongly'. But as it stands, this is false—false even for the special case of reasons for thinking someone acted wrongly or rightly. For example, things being as they now are, the fact that a quite specific child, Jonathan, now looks uncomfortable is reason for thinking he has just done something wrong; but this would not be quite generally a reason for thinking this of anyone, or even a reason for thinking this of Jonathan at any time whatever. But of course it will be said: 'I never meant to deny this. What I meant was just this: it must equally be reason for thinking that any other person, in what are in all relevant respects the same circumstances as Jonathan, has acted wrongly'. And this, I think, is true, but the question is whether it comes to anything more than: must equally be reason for thinking that x acted wrongly for any x such that it would equally be reason for thinking that x acted wrongly.

By contrast, I would imagine that the fact that a thing (anything) is a lion is a reason for thinking it carnivorous.

At all events, the question whether one thing is a reason for another is very often quite obviously a question for investigation rather than reflection. One thing that seems plain is that if 'This is *S*' does not imply 'This is *P*' it will always be at best a matter of fact, to be established by investigation, that the first is a reason for the second.

'Suppose we know absolutely nothing else about blogs than just that all present and past blogs have been purple. Would it not be reasonable to expect that the next blog to come into existence will also be purple?' If it seems so to you, this is surely because you are supposing that 'blog' is an English name of a natural kind which you just have not run into as yet, and that, though you do not know of them, there are background facts in virtue of which being a blog has something to do with having this or that colour. Contrast this with: 'I am now going to introduce the word "blog" into English in such a way that as a matter of fact all present and past blogs are purple. Is it reasonable to expect that the next blog to come into existence will also be purple?' Here you would be mad to bet on it. In fact, the context being what it is, you would do well to bet that the next blog will not be purple.

The fact that all present and past blogs have been purple is no doubt a necessary condition for the truth of the hypothesis that all blogs are purple. But *p* can surely be a necessary condition for *q* without thereby being a reason for it, and so certainly without thereby being of necessity a reason for it. The fact that I see over the hedge something with the head and torso of a man is no reason whatever to think that what I see over the hedge is a centaur. Again, the fact that someone is coming to dinner is no reason whatever to think that someone is coming to dinner who once murdered a President, and who will one day own the State of California.

Reflection alone does not show that 'All present and past *S*'s have been *P*' is reason for 'The next *S* will be *P*'. In the first place, there are pairs of predicates *S* and *P* such that a present and past correlation between the *S*'s and *P*'s was, as we sometimes say, merely accidental. Thus, for example, the correlation between being chairman of the philosophy department of a certain university and having a last name beginning with B or M or L. Of course there might have been a world in which this was not an accidental correlation, but ours is not in fact such a world. And to regard a present and past correlation between *S* and *P* as accidental is to regard it as no reason for thinking the next *S* you meet will be *P*; for the correlation to *be* accidental is for it to be no reason for thinking this.

On the other hand, there are pairs of predicates such that one might be inclined to think that in no world could they be merely accidentally correlated. Could there be a world in which it was a mere accident that all past and present lions have been carnivorous? The second point is that we do not need to make this out in order to make out that a present and past correlation between *S* and *P* is not of necessity a reason for thinking the next *S* you meet will be *P*. Imagine there have existed exactly 100 lions, all now in process of being destroyed. Of all other non-omnivorous species, the following has (perhaps we do not as yet know why) always been true: the first 100 members of the species had a consistent dietary preference, but the 101st (and all the following so far) have had a contrary dietary preference. Thus the 101st horse would not touch oats; the 101st cow ate only meat; and so on and on. If a man knew that all this was so he would *ipso facto* be a fool to bet that the next lion he met would be carnivorous.

Things being as they are, if your new friend brings out a coin that comes up heads in the first four throws, you will bet on a head in the fifth throw, for it is likely that his is not a fair coin. But in a world in which all coins, however thrown, come up four heads, then four tails, then four heads . . . , you will certainly bet on a tail in the fifth throw.

'But suppose that *all* I knew was that there had been a correlation. Would it not be reasonable for me to expect it to continue?' Are you supposed to have no other relevant beliefs at all? None about the past behaviour of other coins? No information about how things in general have behaved which would make it antecedently implausible that coins should have behaved in this world in the way I described? If indeed you did have no other relevant beliefs, then in believing that this coin came up heads four times in a row when thrown in the normal way you would have no reason whatever for thinking anything at all about how it would come up on the fifth throw. The fact that background information is required if we are to do anything at all with the question, Is this correlation reason for thinking that thus and so? is normally

K*

concealed by the fact that the examples always point to background information, and that we always supply it.

It is just this point about background information which is overlooked by the view under consideration in this section, the reflection-view, and which makes it false.

I am not here saying that we shall always be able to decide whether *p* is or is not just as a matter of fact a reason for *q*, for there may well be cases in which we should not be able to decide whether or not to say that *p* implies *q*. Take, in particular, statements of the form 'This is *S*' and 'This is *P*'. 'This is a short-haired beige cat with brown-tipped ears and paws and a brown tail' does not imply 'This is a Siamese cat', for you could shave and dye a Persian. Does 'This is and was throughout its life a short-haired . . .' imply 'This is a Siamese cat'? I cannot offhand imagine a counter-case, but perhaps someone else could. And this case is, I think, the model for certain interesting non-causal cases of reasons: as the behavioural reports are filled in with greater and greater detail one becomes the more inclined to regard them as of necessity reason for 'He's in pain' ('He acted wrongly')—but what this reflects is an increasing inclination to say that the reports imply these things.

At all events, the problem of induction is not solved by saying that what entitles us to draw a conclusion about the future from a report of a past correlation is the fact that the report is of necessity reason for the statement about the future. Where 'This is *S*' does not imply 'This is *P*', 'All present and past *S*'s have been *P*' is never of necessity, but at best as a matter of fact, reason for 'The next *S* you meet will be *P*'.

4. The claim which the 'formula' of p. 285 above was to support was this: suppose *p* does not imply *q*, and suppose a man says '*p*, so *q*'; then he is not reasoning in saying this unless he believes that *r*, where the conjunction of *p* and *r* implies *q*, and *r* is a suppressed premiss of his reasoning.

But suppose such a man believes that *p* is reason for *q*; would this not be enough? 'It would if "*p* is reason for *q*" were construed as a suppressed premiss of his argument'. Then let us so construe it. The question is, must it be interpreted as strong enough, together with *p*, to imply *q*?[1] If *p* is 'This is *S*' and *q* is 'This is *P*',

[1] This is sometimes asked in the form: must the 'inductive rule', if it is to be 'correct', always, or only usually, yield true conclusions from true premisses?

then the minimum *r* such that *p. r* implies *q* is 'If this is *S* it is *P*'. Is ' "This is *S*" is reason for "This is *P*" ' compatible with the falsity of 'If this is *S* it is *P*'?

Yes—for I think we are entitled to set out a third fact about the use of 'reason for' (once again, it appears to have been denied[1]), namely that we so use this expression that it may very well have been true to say that the fact that this is *S* is reason for thinking it *P*, even though the thing turns out not to be *P*. (This is different from the first fact about usage I mentioned; there I said that 'If this is *S* it is *P*' need not be a necessary truth, while here I say that it need not even be true.) A mother, for instance, might well be speaking truly if she said 'Okay, he hasn't in fact done anything wrong. All the same, there was good reason for thinking he had—you saw that look on his face!'

In general, a claim to the effect that there is reason for thinking something so, or for thinking an event will take place, is not falsified by its not being so, its not taking place. And so also there can be reason for thinking that something is so, and equally good reason for thinking that it is not so.

It is a consequence of this that a quite general claim to the effect that a thing's being *S* is reason for thinking it *P* may be true even though there are or will be *S*'s which are not *P*. And surely this is so. Suppose Peterson has a policy of never allowing anyone else to see his secret manuscripts unless his last name begins with a 'P'; this being so, and Peterson being the man he is, and in fact keeping his secret manuscripts in a steel safe, and steel safes being what they are, and so on, the fact that a man (any man) is reading Peterson's secret manuscripts is reason for thinking his last name begins with a 'P'. And this even though a Jones at one time did or will break in and read them. True enough, too many exceptions may (but only *may*—cf. section 5 below) falsify the claim; all the same, our usage is not such that it is logically necessary for the truth of the general claim that there be no exceptions at all. And it is perhaps just worth noting that this holds of the causal sub-class of reasons. Cutting off a man's supply of oxygen for a prolonged period causes death—even though once a man to whom

Cf. e.g., Wesley C. Salmon's critique of Max Black in 'Should We Attempt to Justify Induction?', *Philosophical Studies*, vol. 8 (1957), pp. 33–48, and Black's reply in *Models and Metaphors*, Ithaca 1962, pp. 215 ff.

[1] E.g. by Salmon, *op. cit.*, p. 47.

this happens does not die, for example because he is sealed in a block of ice.

The other side of the same coin is, of course, that a thing's turning out to be *P* will not show that its having been *S* was reason for thinking it *P*. And that all *S*'s being *P* will not show that the fact that a thing is *S* is reason for thinking it *P*.

But then even if we do count a man's belief that 'This is *S*' is reason for 'This is *P*' as a suppressed premiss of his argument 'This is *S*, so it's *P*', his premisses still do not imply his conclusion.

This was no doubt the motive for insisting that ' "This is *S*' is' reason for "This is *P*" ' be interpreted as strong enough, together with 'This is *S*', to imply 'This is *P*'. If it were, then the matter would be settled; to construe it as a suppressed premiss would neatly turn the argument into a deductively valid argument.

But it is not strong enough for this. What then? One possible reaction is this. 'So a man who says "This is *S*, so it's *P*" must be construed as suppressing not only the premiss " 'This is *S*' is reason for 'This is *P*' ", but also the premiss " 'This is *S*' and ' "This is *S* " is reason for "This is *P*" ' are jointly reason for 'This is *P*' " '. And from here presumably on into the night, for at no point will the expanded set of premisses imply 'This is *P*'.[1]

We cannot show there is no regress here in precisely the way in which we showed it in the case of the argument from 'This is red' to 'This is coloured'. For while ' "This is *S*" is reason for "This is *P*" ' may well be true for some *S* and *P*, it is not a necessary truth for any *S* and *P* such that 'This is *S*' does not imply 'This is *P*'.

All the same, we can proceed in an analogous manner, for we can ask why this regress should even begin.

In the first place, it might be asked why a man who says '*p*, so *q*' must believe that *p* is a reason for *q*. The 'formula' is in part an answer to this. 'Surely he must believe that *p* is a reason for *q* or he can't mean his "so". "So" (and its cognates) rules out a guess. But if he does not believe this then he is at best guessing. For, for all he knows, it would be an accident if *q*, and a stroke of luck for him if he were right in saying that *q*. His "conclusion" is not a conclusion at all.' This seems to me to be correct. There is a perfectly good sense of 'accident' in which if you said 'The

[1] The possibility of a regress here as well as in the case of deductive arguments was noticed by W. E. Johnson; cf. his *Logic*, Part II, Chapter I, Cambridge 1922.

philosophy department has a new chairman, so his last name begins with a B or M or L', knowing full well how things stand—that is, knowing that your 'premiss' is not in fact reason for thinking your conclusion true—you would have to be joking, for it would be an accident, a stroke of luck, if you were right.

People do often reason without the use of an explicit 'so', often, indeed, without saying anything at all. In particular, a child might reason that *q* because someone said it was, and the question might be raised whether the child must be supposed to believe that *X*'s saying that *q* is reason for *q*. Does a child so much as 'have the concept' *reason for*? No doubt the child may not have the words 'reason for' in his vocabulary, but it seems to me to be wrong to take this as a reason for thinking he cannot have a belief which we might express by the use of these words. Surely the matter is like this: the more his behaviour (or the behaviour of a chimpanzee) makes it look as if he was reasoning—as opposed to guessing, or to its being a mere reaction to a stimulus or a conditioned reflex—the more we can say he does have beliefs of this sort. But then of course when the matter is seen to come to this, it becomes plain that the point is analytic. No wonder it is right to say: you are not reasoning unless you believe your premiss to be a reason for your conclusion.

Moreover, to show that you must believe that *p* is a reason for *q* if you are to be reasoning in saying '*p*, so *q*' is not yet to show that '*p* is a reason for *q*' must be construed as a suppressed premiss of the argument. One might well say that a man must believe that 'This is red' is a reason for 'This is coloured' if he is to be reasoning when he says 'This is red, so it's coloured'; all the same, 'This is red' implies 'This is coloured', and it need not be said that a man who reasons from the former to the latter suppresses a premiss.

The argument goes like this. 'Suppose "This is *S*" does not imply "This is *P*", but that a man says "This is *S*, so it's *P*". Suppose he does believe that "This is *S*" is reason for "This is *P*", but that we do not construe it as a suppressed premiss of the argument. Then while perhaps given his beliefs as well as his premiss it won't be an accident or a stroke of luck for him if his conclusion is also true, for all his *premiss* says it will be. For, for all his premiss says, it might well be false that "This is *S*" is reason for "This is *P*"; and if so, it will be an accident if his conclusion is true. But reasoning should surely involve drawing a conclusion from a premiss—the premiss itself should at least rule out that it would at best be a lucky guess if you said the conclusion was also true.'

What is true in this is, it seems to me, that ' "This is *S*" is reason for "This is *P*" ' must be construed as a part of the reasoning, in a way in which ' "This is red" is reason for "This is coloured" ' need not be in the case of an argument from 'This is red' to 'This is coloured'. It is not merely that you are not reasoning in saying 'This is *S*, so it's *P*' unless you do believe this, for this is also true in the case of 'This is red, so it's coloured'. It is rather that if your belief that 'This is *S*' is reason for 'This is *P*' were false, then it would at best be an accident if your conclusion were true. Only together with ' "This is *S*" is reason for 'This is *P*" ' does your premiss (if they are jointly true) make it any better than at best an accident or a stroke of luck if your conclusion is true. So your conclusion has only been reasoned to from your premiss together with your supposition (true or false) that your stated premiss is reason for your conclusion. By contrast, your belief that 'This is red' is reason for 'This is coloured' cannot be false; and if 'This is red' is true, not merely will it be no accident, no stroke of luck, if your conclusion is true, but more, your conclusion must be true.

We need not mark this role which ' "This is *S*" is reason for "This is *P*" ' must play in the argument by using the words 'It is a suppressed premiss'. You could mark it by the words 'It is the rule of inference'. My objection to this is not that it is false, but rather that it is less clear than calling it a premiss. ' "This is *S*" is a reason for "This is *P*" ' is no more an imperative or a permission slip of any kind than was 'If this is *S* it is *P*' (cf. section 2 above); it is a statement of fact, which may or may not be true. And the speaker must believe it true. So why confuse things by calling it 'his rule'?

But then if we call it a suppressed premiss, it looks as if the regress is under way. 'For the conjunction of "This is *S* and 'This is *S*' is a reason for 'This is *P*' " does not imply "This is *P*". So for all these two premisses say it would at best be an accident, a stroke of luck, if you were right in saying "This is *P*". So you must be supposed to suppress still another premiss, namely that the conjunction of these two premisses is a reason for your conclusion'. But here the formula does go wrong; no further premisses are in fact required.

In the first place, it should be noticed that all the further premisses are very different in kind. ' "This is *S*" is reason for "This is *P*" ' is contingent for any *S* and *P* such that 'This is *S*' does not imply 'This is *P*'; but all the further premisses are, if true at all, necessarily true—the conjunction of 'This is *S*' and ' "This is *S*" is reason for "This is *P*" ' is of necessity reason for 'This is *P*'. Or, as we might have put it, the conjunction implies 'There is reason for thinking this is *P*'.

Secondly, we must look at the sense in which 'accident' is here being used.

Learning that a thing is *S*, and knowing that a thing's being *S* is reason for thinking it *P*, you might say 'so it's *P*', and yet in a perfectly good sense of 'accident' it might *be* an accident, a stroke of luck for you, if you were right. You are told that someone is now reading Peterson's secret manuscripts, and of course, things being as they are, this is reason for thinking his last name begins with a 'P'. I suggested above that this is compatible with its turning out that the man who now reads the manuscripts is a Jones, who broke in and stole them. But we could have imagined a Perkins or Parker to break in and steal them. In that case, your conclusion 'His last name begins with a "P" ' would be true, but, as we might well say, it was an accident, a stroke of luck for you that it was so. Peterson's policy and precautions did not bring it about that the manuscripts should now be read by a man whose last name begins with a 'P'.

And in general, where *p* does not imply *q*, the truth of the conjunction of *p* and '*p* is a reason for *q*' is compatible with its turning out all the same to be an accident that *q*. I said in section 3 above that to regard a present and past correlation between *S* and *P* as an accidental correlation is to regard it as no reason for thinking the next *S* will be *P*, and to regard 'This is *S*' as no reason for 'This is *P*'. It is worth stressing, however, that to regard the correlation as non-accidental, and these things as reasons, is compatible with one's allowing that there may be cases in which it is a mere accident that a given thing which is *S* is also *P*. The correlation between cancer and death is scarcely an accidental correlation, and the fact that a man has cancer is reason for thinking he will die; and this even though some man who has cancer, and does die, dies because he falls off a cliff.

So there surely is a good sense of 'accident' in which if you know that p and that p is reason for q, and therefore say 'so q', it may well be an accident if you are right. But this is equally surely no good ground for denying that you were reasoning. For your premisses do at least rule out that it *must* be an accident if q—they rule out that it would at best be a lucky guess if you were right.

Unless of course 'accident' here takes on another sense, and is so used that so long as X does not imply Y it must be an accident if, given X, it turns out that Y. But on this interpretation, the formula is no more than the mere stammer, If X does not imply Y, it does not imply Y. Or no more than a linguistic proposal. And we were to be given an argument for saying that only deductive reasoning is really reasoning which does not rest merely on a proposal to revise the use of some expression related to 'reason for' and 'reasoning'.

In sum, it seems to me that there is something in what I have called the 'formula' and therefore something in that which leads people to say that only deductive reasoning is really reasoning. But also that what there is in it is not enough to justify the conclusion in which it issues.

5. It may be said that none of this goes any way at all toward settling *the* problem of induction. No doubt one who says 'This is S and the fact that a thing is S is reason for thinking it P, so it's P' is reasoning; no doubt reasoning in accordance with this pattern is sound or reliable reasoning. But *the* problem of induction is, How does one know that the second premiss is true? Under what circumstances is one entitled to suppose that one knows a statement of this form to be true? Or, connected, How does one know when p is a better reason for q than r is for $-q$?

If this is *the* problem of induction, then it is very simply solved. We know that p is a reason for q, and that p is a better reason for q than r is for $-q$, when we do, by observations of the present and past. We are entitled to suppose we know such things when we have made sufficient numbers of the right kinds of observations of the present and past.

There are two familiar objections. (1) 'Observations of the present and past do not entitle you to suppose you know that the fact that a thing is S is reason for thinking it P. In order to know that a statement of this form is true you would have to know, not merely that most (if not all) observed S's have been P, but also that most (if not all) future S's will be P—and no amount of observation of the present and past can guarantee this. For however constant the correlation between *S* and *P* may have been in the past, it may yet turn out that it was a mere accident that there was any correlation between them at all.'

It has often been said that the problem of induction is not specifically a problem about the relation between statements about the present and past, and statements about the future, but rather a more general problem about the relation between statements about the observed and statements about the unobserved, which include statements about the present and past as well as statements about the future. But I think that this is misleading, and that the point to bring out is that the future has no direct bearing on the matter at all.

This is a consequence of (what I take to be) yet another fact about the use of 'reason for': we so use the expression that it is very often true to say that *X* is a reason for *Y* though it formerly was not, or that *X* was once a reason for *Y* but is so no longer—certain futures that you might not have expected sometimes make it true to say, not that we were mistaken, but rather that *X* was a reason and now is not, or was not a reason but now is. If Americans were, say, to take actively to ancestor-worship, and make their Presidents take the names of past favourites, then it would be true to say 'A man's being President was not, but now is, reason for thinking his name is Washington or Lincoln'. Or again, they may find an (as these things go) infallible cure for cancer, in which case it will be true to say, not 'We thought that the fact a man had cancer was reason for thinking he would die, but we were mistaken', but rather 'The fact that a man has cancer used to be a reason for thinking he would die (or cancer used to cause death), but is not so (does not do) any longer'.

And in general: we do *not* need to know even that most (much less all) future *S*'s will be *P* in order to know that the fact that a thing is *S* is a reason for thinking it *P*. The truth of this is compatible with its turning out, starting tomorrow, that *no* future *S* is ever a *P*. We do not need to know what will happen in order to know that, now, the fact that a thing is *S* is a reason for thinking it *P*.

The point can be made in another way. We want to consider in what way the future bears on the claim 'The fact that a thing is *S* is a reason for thinking it *P*'. So let us imagine that the only thing we are in ignorance of is what will happen in the future—we are to imagine that we know all there is to know about what is happening and did happen. (Let us suppose this makes sense.) What imaginable future would falsify the claim made now, on the basis of what we know, that the fact that a thing is *S* is a reason for thinking it *P*? What is required is a future that will show that if a thing is *S* now, it is at best an accident if it is also *P*. 'No future *S* is ever a *P*'. This is not enough; you would have to add that there is no new factor *F* such that it would be true to say that a thing's being *S* used to be reason for thinking it *P*, but now there is *F* and it is so no longer. Very well: there is no explanation of the fact that the *S*'s are not *P*. For no reason at all, men can now walk on water—not that men or water have changed in a manner which would explain this, but just: for no reason they do not sink. But surely this is to be described as 'Inexplicably they no longer sink', not as 'This shows that there never was reason for thinking they would'. For this latter you would need that all the other correlations and super-correlations which supported the view that there was reason for thinking a man would sink if he tried to walk on water were also merely accidental. Are we to imagine all of them to break down too? But in imagining this you are imagining just such changes in men or water or both as would explain why, though there used to be reason for thinking men would sink, there is so no longer.

So the bearing of the future is at most indirect. It is because and only because we do not know everything about the present and past that the future is relevant. If we did, we should not have to wait on the future for the establishment or disestablishment of claims to the effect that this is reason for that. We could put it this way: the question is not 'Will the future be like the past?' but rather 'Will the future show we were right about the present and past?'

All the same, we do not have unlimited knowledge about the present and the past. And the question might be raised: given that we have only limited knowledge of the present and the past, what entitles us to suppose that this is reason for that? That is, *when* have we made sufficient numbers of the right kinds of observations of the present and past? Or: what are the necessary and sufficient conditions for having done this?

One could try to show that this question is self-defeating—not that it is unanswerable, but that no correct answer will satisfy—by showing that nothing would be correct unless it essentially involved a member of the same family of terms as 'reason for' (such as 'non-accidental'), and that nothing that essentially involves a term in this family will satisfy. One could also try to show that the question does not matter, and that its not having been both correctly and satisfyingly answered (if this is possible) does not in the least show that we do not in some cases know that *p* is a reason for *q*, and that *p* is a better reason for *q* than *r* is for —*q*. I think that both these things are true, but also that it would be exceedingly difficult to prove them, and that no one has so far succeeded in doing so. On the other hand, no one has, so far as I know, shown that the question is answerable and must be answered. Fortunately, however, the job here was not to set out necessary and sufficient conditions for one thing to be a reason for another, and for us to know that it is, but only to make out that some things which have been thought to be necessary are not necessary. And therefore it can just be left open here that there may be other things which are necessary, and that there *may* even be good reason for thinking we do not know any of these things we think we do know, such as that a bit of lint on my carpet is a reason for thinking me no perfectionist about carpets but no reason whatever for thinking that Eisenhower is dead. But here, surely, the onus of proof is on the sceptic.

INDEX OF NAMES